IMAGES
of Rail

THE CHICAGO GREAT WESTERN RAILWAY

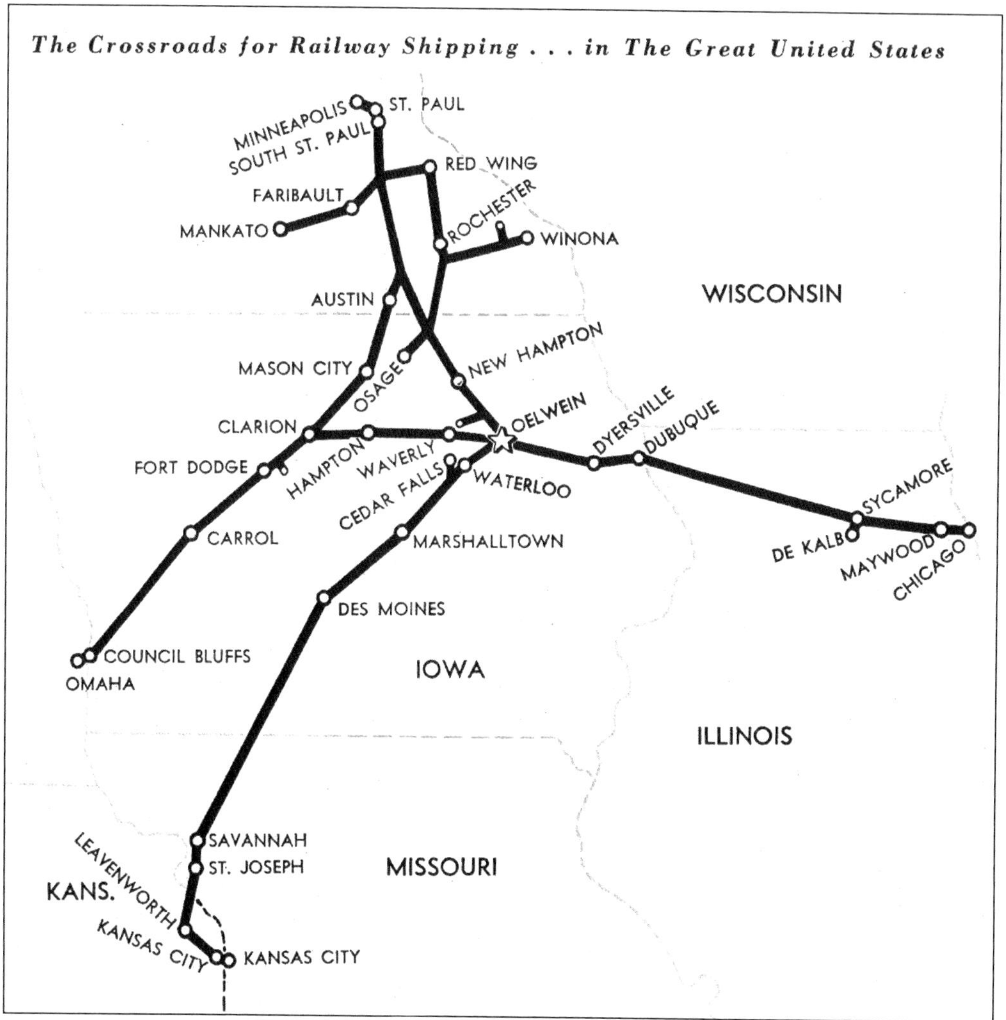

This stylized map of the Chicago Great Western (CGW) Railway system was published in the company's 1957 annual report. The main lines formed a misshapen letter *x* or plus sign, with one line between Minneapolis–St. Paul and Kansas City, and the other between Chicago and Omaha. The lines crossed at Oelwein, Iowa, the system hub, which included a classification yard and repair shops for rolling stock and locomotives. Although there were several branches, the system primarily consisted of main lines and connections with other railroads, which enabled the CGW to serve chiefly as a bridge carrier between railroads. The company operated 1,458 route miles of track divided into divisions and districts to facilitate managing operations. Illinois was located in the Eastern Division, which extended from Chicago to Oelwein. The division was renamed the Illinois Division in 1930 and renamed again as Eastern Division in the early 1950s. This complex organization moved 268,221 carloads of freight the same year the map was published.

On the cover: CGW steam locomotive No. 502 with passenger train was photographed crossing over the Des Plaines River Bridge west of Forest Park, Illinois, on March 16, 1919. (James L. Rueber.)

IMAGES
of Rail

THE CHICAGO GREAT WESTERN RAILWAY

David J. Fiore Sr.

ARCADIA
PUBLISHING

ISBN 978-0-7385-4048-1

Published by Arcadia Publishing
Charleston, South Carolina

Printed in the United States of America

Library of Congress Catalog Card Number: 2006926360

For all general information contact Arcadia Publishing at:
Telephone 843-853-2070
Fax 843-853-0044
E-mail sales@arcadiapublishing.com
For customer service and orders:
Toll-Free 1-888-313-2665

Visit us on the Internet at www.arcadiapublishing.com

This book is dedicated to my family for their support and patience while I spent time away from them researching and writing. And it is also dedicated to the former employees of the Chicago Great Western Railway.

CONTENTS

ACKNOWLEDGMENTS

I wish to acknowledge the following persons and institutions for their generous assistance: Sue Breese and the Joiner History Room, Sycamore, Illinois; James L. Rueber; Joseph Piersen and Fred Klinger with the Archives Sub-Committee of the Chicago and North Western Historical Society, Elmhurst, Illinois; Conrad "Pete" Pedersen; Donald Vaughn; Julie Bunke, St. Charles Heritage Center, St. Charles, Illinois; Dawn M. Johnson, Byron Museum of History; Carol Stream Historical Society, Carol Stream, Illinois; Elizabeth Historical Society, Elizabeth, Illinois; Villa Park Historical Society, Villa Park, Illinois; Lombard Historical Society, Lombard, Illinois; Jeff Ruetsche, editor, and John Pearson, publisher, Arcadia Publishing.

INTRODUCTION

On March 4, 1854, the Minnesota territorial legislature granted a charter to a group of Eastern capitalists to build the Minnesota and Northwestern Railroad (M&NW) between Lake Superior and Iowa. However, the M&NW was not completed due to a federal land grant scandal and the financial panic of 1857.

A. B. Stickney, a St. Paul railroad executive, acquired the charter in the early 1880s for the purpose of building a new rail line in the Midwest. Stickney's experience and managerial abilities combined with sufficient capital from local and foreign investors enabled the M&NW to start construction at St. Paul and Randolph, Minnesota, in September 1884. A year later, on September 20, 1885, the first train departed St. Paul for Chicago, which it reached through a convoluted route over three other railroads. By January 1, 1889, the M&NW was in operation with its own rails between Chicago, Minneapolis–St. Paul, and Kansas City. Further expansion occurred between July 1901 and November 1903, when the company increased its mileage in Minnesota and built an extension to Omaha.

Stickney achieved his goal through several methods, including incorporating companies that actually constructed railways, leasing property, and acquiring existing railroads. The Chicago, St. Paul and Kansas City Railway (CStP&KC), incorporated in Iowa on June 1, 1886, was one of the companies organized by Stickney. M&NW was subsequently deeded to CStP&KC on December 8, 1887, and, five years later, Stickney incorporated the first Chicago Great Western Railway (CGW) on January 16, 1892, to effect a financial reorganization of CStP&KC.

This first CGW relied upon debenture stock rather than bonds for capitalization, and Stickney proudly boasted in 1899 that the company was "a western trunk line railway without a mortgage." However, the CGW borrowed a substantial amount of money through promissory notes to finance improvements. In 1908, $8 million in notes came due, but CGW lacked the funds to pay its debt due to a decline in earnings in 1907. On January 8, 1908, CGW was placed into receivership.

On August 19, 1909, a syndicate organized by J. P. Morgan and Company incorporated a new company, Chicago Great Western *Railroad*, which purchased CGW *Railway* on August 21, 1909, for $12 million. Samuel M. Felton became president, and he began an extensive program of rehabilitation and improvements that totaled over $32 million by 1925.

Patrick H. Joyce, vice president of the Standard Steel Car Company, and a group of associates took an interest in the CGW during the late 1920s. They were aware that CGW had failed to pay dividends on its preferred stock at various times since 1909, and accumulations totaled $50 per share. They also knew that the company could pay the accumulation and resume regular dividends if earnings improved.

To provide the railroad with more business, transportation managers at various companies were solicited to purchase shares of stock in CGW and then route as much freight as possible over the line. The syndicate organized a holding company, Bremo Corporation, on January 5, 1929, and they eventually secured complete control of CGW through stock ownership by April 1930. Unfortunately, the new management conducted unethical business practices during the next two decades, which resulted in investigations by the Interstate Commerce Commission (ICC) and the federal Senate Committee on Interstate Commerce.

The combination of mismanagement and a business downturn due to the Great Depression forced CGW to file for bankruptcy on February 28, 1935. The reorganization process required six years to complete and included incorporation of the Chicago Great Western *Railway*, on April 22, 1940. CGW *Railway* took possession of CGW *Railroad* on February 19, 1941.

CGW experienced a significant decline in intercity freight and passenger business by the 1950s. The situation mirrored the predicament faced by the entire railroad industry at that time. Total mileage in service in the United States had reached an all-time high of 254,000 miles in 1916. At the same time, the trunk lines were transporting 77 percent of intercity freight traffic and 98 percent of intercity passenger traffic. These ratios declined to 46 percent and 31 percent, respectively, by 1957, as the industry lost business to other modes of transportation. There were simply too many railroads competing for limited business and, despite various efficiencies, the number of employees, locomotives, rolling stock, track, and facilities were in excess of what was required. Edward T. Reidy, CGW president, summed up the situation when he informed the ICC in 1965 that there was too much transportation service available between principal cities.

One solution was to consolidate railroads into fewer companies. CGW began to aggressively seek a partner during the early 1960s after management decided that a favorable merger was crucial to protect the interests of the company's shareholders. CGW and Chicago and North Western Railway (C&NW) began discussions in September 1964 on consolidating the two companies. They determined that a merger, with C&NW as the surviving company, would save $6 million per year through the elimination of duplicate track and facilities. It would also provide C&NW with access to Kansas City, a desire long held by that company. On November 13, 1964, the two railroads filed a petition with the ICC to approve their merger plans.

The regulatory process took three years to complete, and the ICC unanimously approved the merger on April 20, 1967. The decision, however, was appealed by the Soo Line, which sought protective conditions from traffic diversions caused by the consolidation. The ICC eventually imposed these conditions and issued a final reaffirmation of its decision on June 8, 1968.

On Monday, July 1, 1968, at 12:01 a.m., CGW ceased to exist as an independent company, and it became the C&NW Missouri Division. Both railroads had once served 44 points in common in four states, and much of the CGW was redundant. Most of the line was abandoned during the 1970s and 1980s, and only a few segments of former CGW right-of-way remain in operation. Elsewhere, it has been converted into other uses, including nature trails.

The objective of this book is to add more information to a limited historical record. Only a handful of books have been published about CGW and, on occasion, various historical journals or the railfan press will print an article about the railroad. The Chicago and North Western Historical Society has undertaken the task of preserving the history of CGW to a more extensive degree, including preservation of invaluable documents and maps, and there are a few railroad museums in the Midwest that maintain and display collections of CGW memorabilia.

The following chapters will take a look at CGW employees, locomotives, freight and passenger service, and the company's line in Illinois. Geographical coverage was limited to Illinois, although the company's history begins in Minnesota and most of its mileage was located in Iowa, because Illinois is the author's home state. He was partly raised near the CGW main line in Chicago and Bellwood, and a mix of memories and nostalgia has led to years of research about this interesting railroad and its operations in Illinois.

The chapter on locomotives covers the primary motive power operated, both steam and diesel-electric (called motors by CGW). Information on steam locomotives includes the Whyte system for wheel arrangement and name. The Whyte system shows the number of wheels starting at the front end with lead truck, drivers, and trailing truck. CGW engines were used throughout the Midwest, and most of the company's business consisted of interstate shipments and travel. Therefore, the chapters on motive power, freight service, and passenger service include coverage outside Illinois.

The chapter on the company's main line in Illinois begins in Chicago and heads west to Iowa. It was mainly a single-track route that passed through several counties, including Cook, DuPage, Kane, DeKalb, Ogle, a tip of Stephenson, and finally Jo Daviess. There were 49 CGW stations in Illinois by 1910, which included milk sheds and platforms at road crossings and are more than can be shown in the following pages. Instead, this book will look at the company's important terminals and a few smaller stations selected at random.

CGW published a directory of industries in January 1957 that listed businesses at its stations, including industries served by other railroads. Excerpts are included for the stations covered in this book. The directory included a yes or no column to show if the serving railroad switched cars for CGW. Also, some customers were shown as served by the local CGW team track. These companies picked up or delivered their shipments at CGW depot.

Chicago Great Western emblems

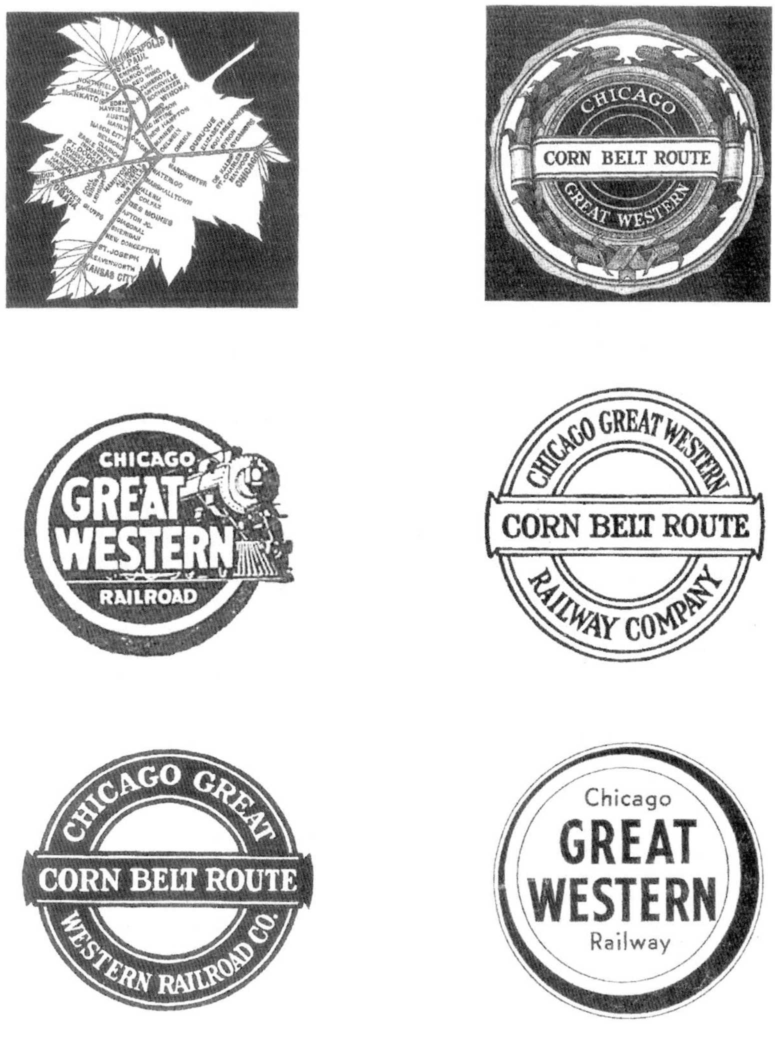

CGW used these various emblems over the years, which were printed on the covers of public timetables, advertisements, rolling stock, and locomotives. The maple leaf was in use from 1892 to 1910; the corn belt logo, in various formats, from 1910 to 1950; and the so-called "Lucky Strike" from 1950 to 1968. The emblem that features a steam locomotive was also used at various times during the 1920s and 1930s. (Author's collection.)

One

EMPLOYEES

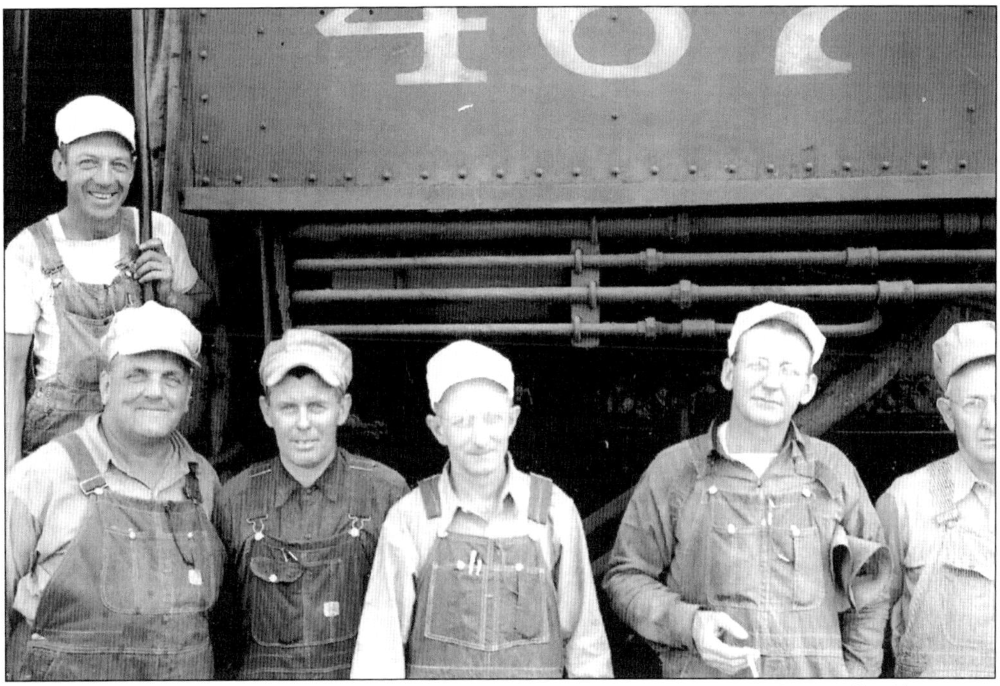

This is the train crew assigned to switching service between Sycamore and DeKalb, Illinois, on July 9, 1949. The occasion was the run of the last CGW steam locomotive in Illinois. The engine was No. 467, nicknamed "The Goat." (Joiner History Room, Sycamore, Illinois.)

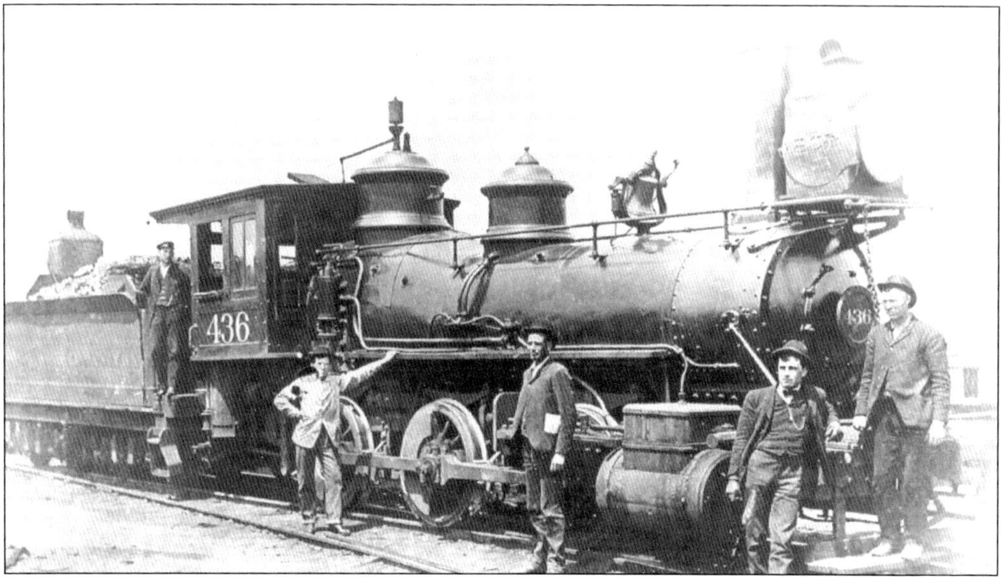

Famous people who worked for CGW included Walter P. Chrysler, the founder of Chrysler Corporation, and Frank B. Kellogg, secretary of state in the Coolidge administration. However, the majority were workers like the officials and crew of No. 436, who provided patrons with reliable and (usually) safe service. (Joiner History Room, Sycamore, Illinois.)

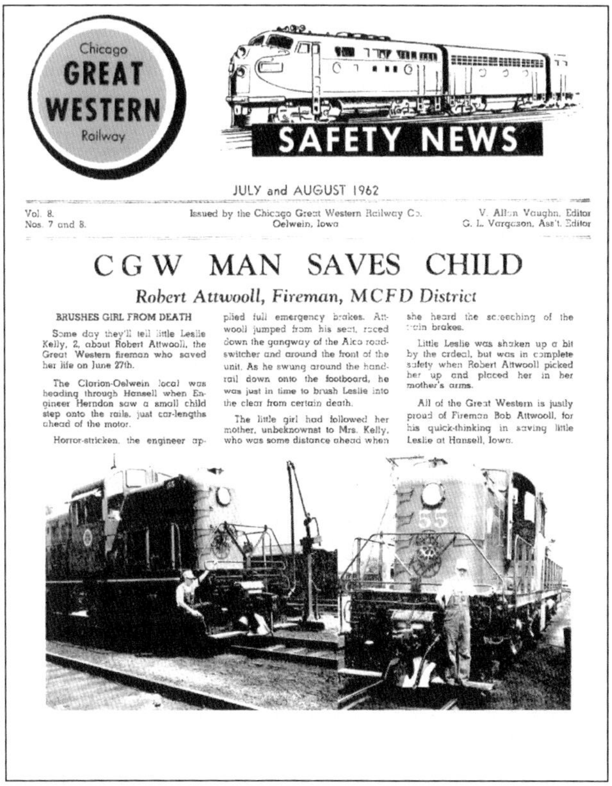

Chicago GREAT WESTERN Railway

SAFETY NEWS

JULY and AUGUST 1962

Vol. 8.
Nos. 7 and 8.

Issued by the Chicago Great Western Railway Co.
Oelwein, Iowa

V. Allan Vaughn, Editor
G. L. Vargason, Ass't. Editor

CGW MAN SAVES CHILD

Robert Attwooll, Fireman, MCFD District

BRUSHES GIRL FROM DEATH

Some day they'll tell little Leslie Kelly, 2, about Robert Attwooll, the Great Western fireman who saved her life on June 27th.

The Clarion-Oelwein local was heading through Hansell when Engineer Herndon saw a small child step onto the rails, just car-lengths ahead of the motor.

Horror-stricken, the engineer applied full emergency brakes. Attwooll jumped from his seat, raced down the gangway of the Alco road-switcher and around the front of the unit. As he swung around the hand-rail down onto the footboard, he was just in time to brush Leslie into the clear from certain death.

The little girl had followed her mother, unbeknownst to Mrs. Kelly, who was some distance ahead when she heard the screeching of the train brakes.

Little Leslie was shaken up a bit by the ordeal, but was in complete safety when Robert Attwooll picked her up and placed her in her mother's arms.

All of the Great Western is justly proud of Fireman Bob Attwooll, for his quick-thinking in saving little Leslie at Hansell, Iowa.

On June 27, 1962, fireman Robert Attwooll saved the life of a toddler at Hansell, Iowa. The child was standing too close to the track, and the engineer was unable to stop in time. Attwooll climbed onto the locomotive footboard and pushed the toddler clear. CGW published an article about Attwooll's heroism in the company newsletter, *Safety News*. (Author's collection.)

Two

LOCOMOTIVES

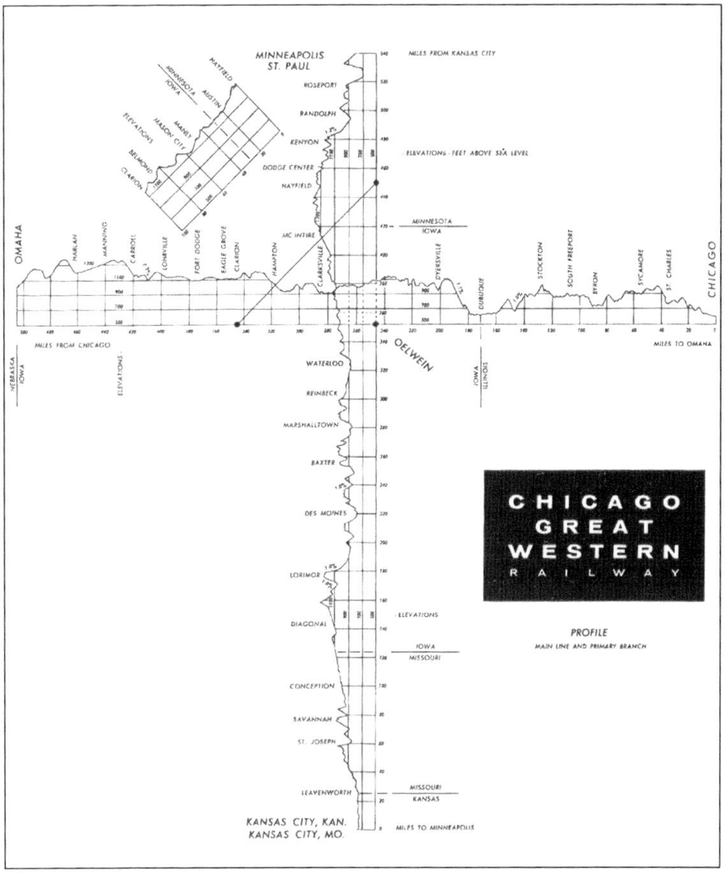

This track profile from the company's 1957 annual report displays ruling grades on CGW main lines. The choice of locomotive is partly based upon ruling grades, which is where the engine has to produce the most power to prevent a heavy train from stalling as it ascends upgrade. (Author's collection.)

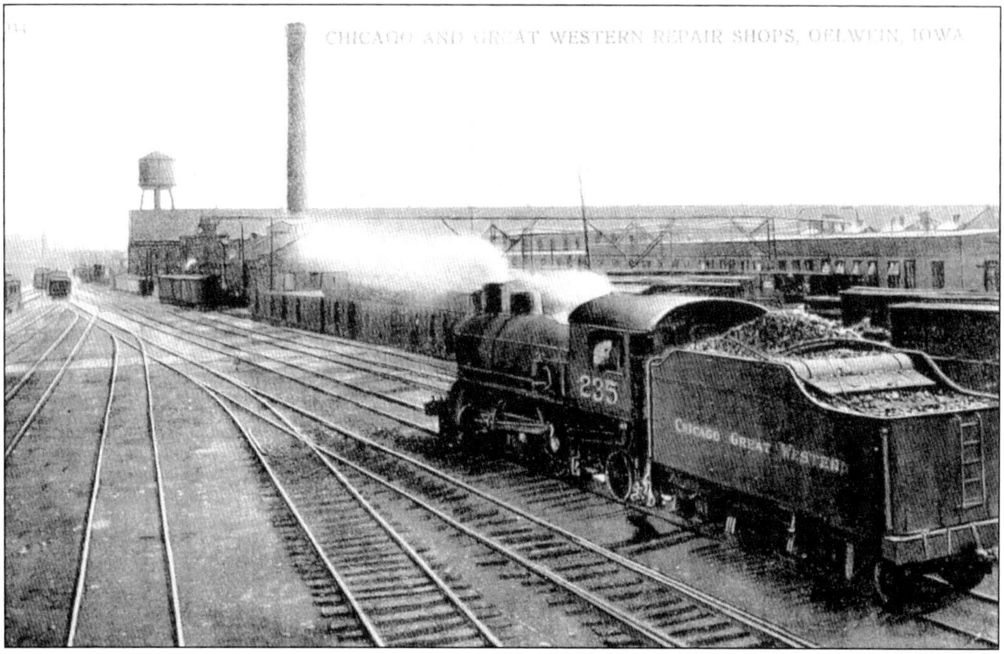

CGW located its locomotive repair shops at Oelwein, Iowa, because it was centrally located. Oelwein shops were placed in service on September 28, 1899, and replaced a smaller facility at South Park, Minnesota. (Author's collection.)

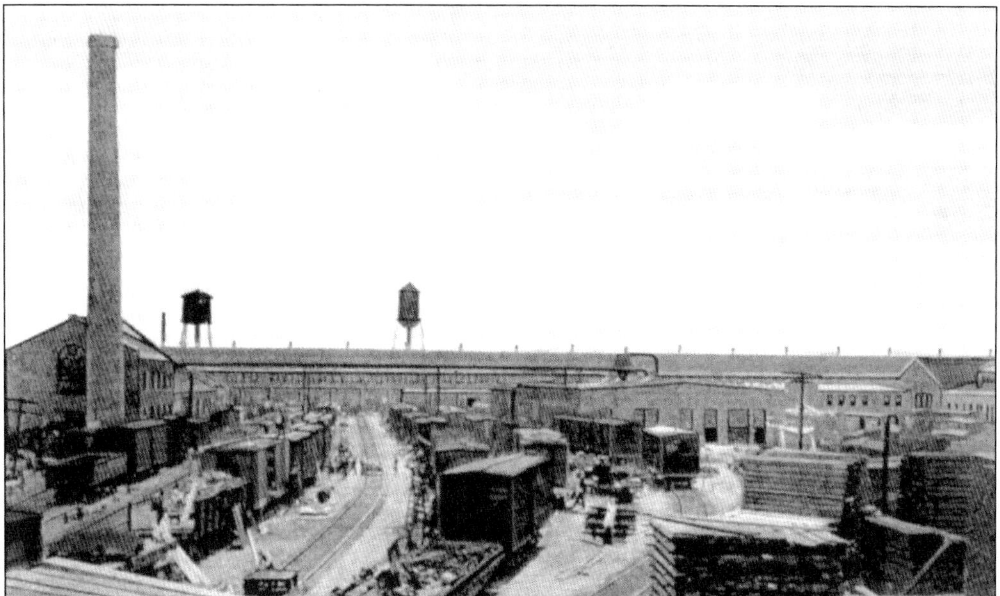

Oelwein consisted of a storehouse and shops for erecting locomotives, fabricating boilers, and repairing and painting equipment. Walter P. Chrysler was employed at Oelwein as master mechanic in 1906 and was promoted to superintendent of motive power the following year. He remained with the CGW until 1909. (Author's collection.)

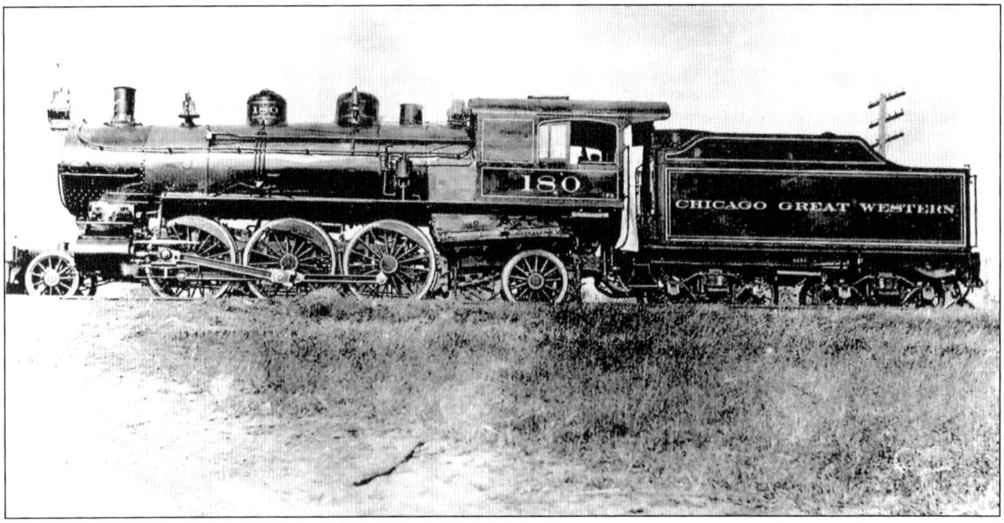

CGW operated a fleet of typical 19th-century motive power consisting of 4-4-0 American and 2-6-0 Mogul–type steam locomotives during the 1880s and 1890s. These engines were no longer suitable for requirements by 1901, and CGW began to acquire 2-6-2 Prairie and 2-8-0 Consolidation types as replacements. No. 180 was the first of 95 Prairies purchased from American Locomotive Company (ALCO) between 1902 and 1903. (Joiner History Room, Sycamore, Illinois.)

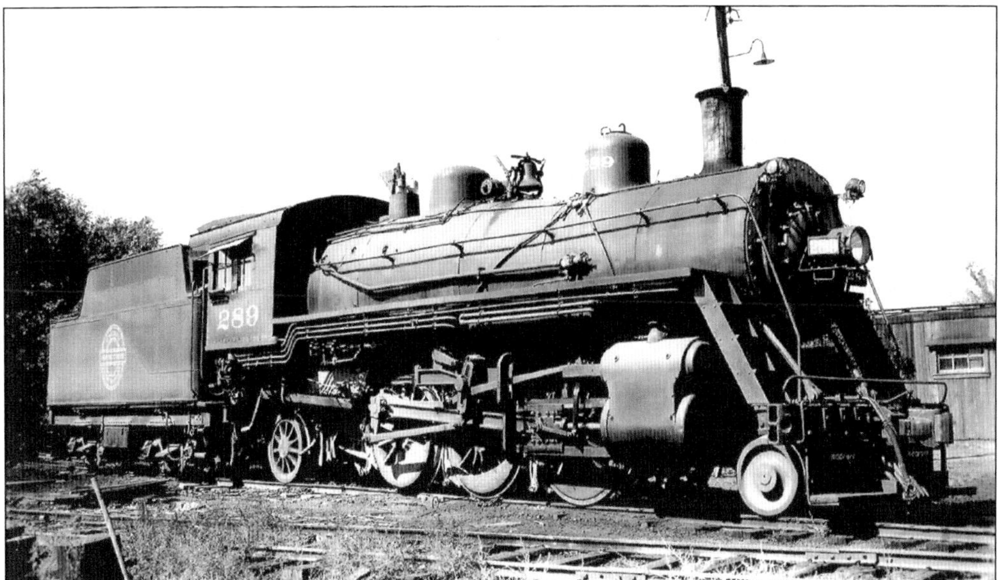

No. 289 was one of the Prairies purchased from ALCO in 1903. This photograph shows its appearance years later. Twenty-three Prairies were assigned to passenger service, and the remainder was used to power freight trains. CGW owned more Prairies than any other type of steam locomotive. (Joiner History Room, Sycamore, Illinois.)

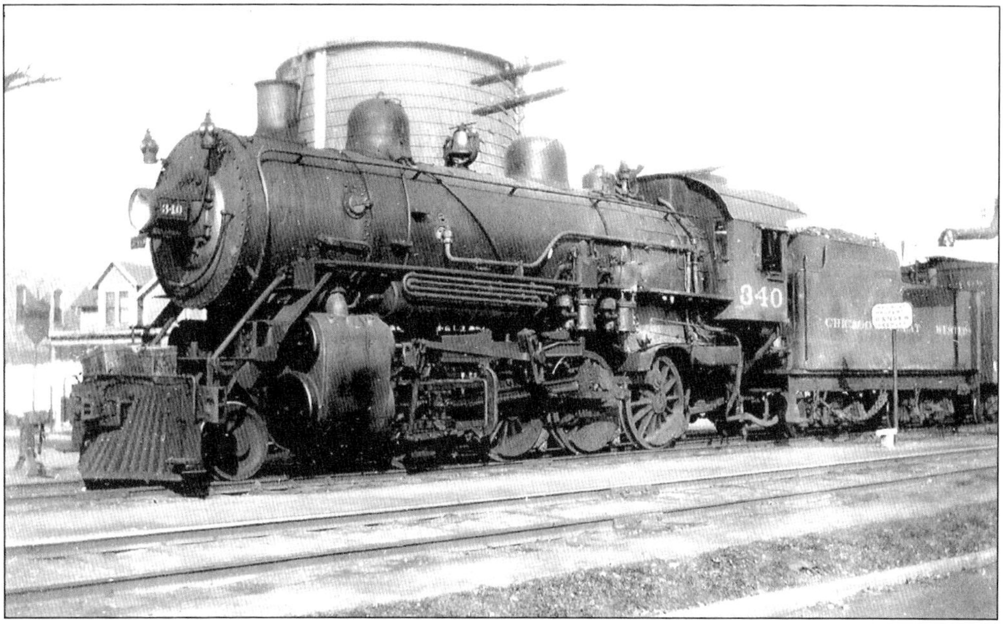

The 2-8-0 Consolidation type was the workhorse on almost all railroads in the United States between 1866 and 1916. CGW acquired a total of 60 from Baldwin Locomotive Works and Rhode Island Locomotive Works between 1900 and 1910. The Consolidations were used to power heavy freight trains, especially between Chicago and Oelwein. The main line west of Stockton, Illinois, consisted of steep grades, which necessitated the use of powerful locomotives. No. 340 was purchased from Baldwin in 1910. (Author's collection.)

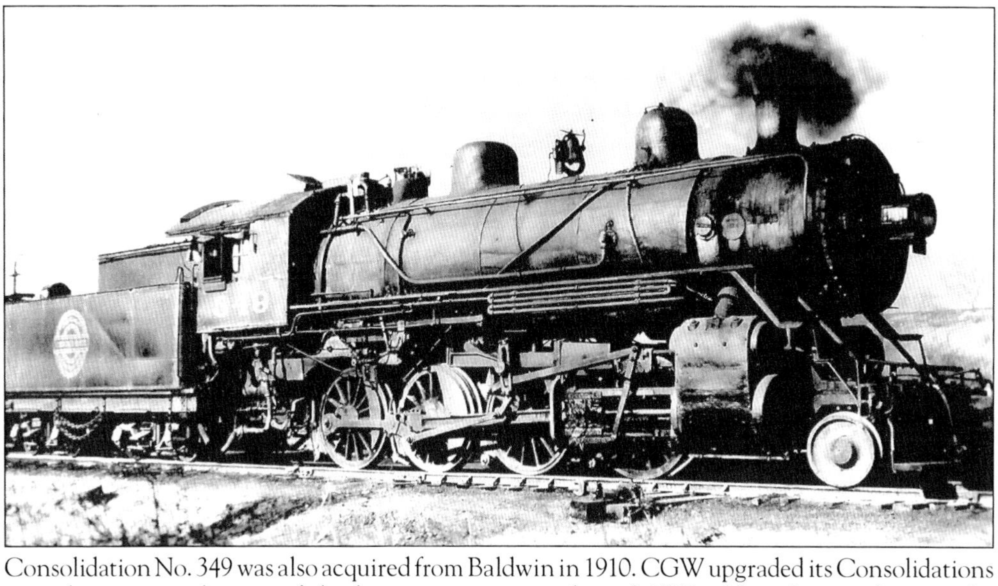

Consolidation No. 349 was also acquired from Baldwin in 1910. CGW upgraded its Consolidations over the years, and many of the locomotives survived until 1950, although out of service by that time. The Consolidations were used as switchers when replaced with more powerful locomotives. (Author's collection.)

Locomotive Rating in Tons of 2,000 Pounds between Tender and Caboose.

Engine Numbers	300 to 319	220 to 292	180 to 219	900 150 to to 920 175	100 to 148	90 to 95	70 to 85	15 to 69
Percentage D. B. Pull	132	110	100	83	65	60	50	44
East-Bound.								
Dyersville to Farley ... 6 miles	1450	1200	1075	925	750	675	560	490
Galena Junction to Stockton ... 26 miles	1200	1000	900	750	600	550	450	390
Oelwein to Chicago with helpers on above grades ... 245 miles	1900	1600	1400	1250	1000	925	750	650
West-Bound.								
Rodden to Winston ... 2 miles Kidder to Farley ... 4 miles	1200	1000	900	750	600	550	450	390
Chicago to Oelwein with helpers on above grades ... 245 miles	1500	1250	1100	950	775	700	575	500

Light Weights.

40,000 lb. flats and gondolas ... 10 tons
70,000 lb. flats or 40,000 lb. box ... 12 "
70,000 lb. gondolas, 50,000 lb. box cabooses ... 13 "
Stock cars ... 60,000 lb. box, tank cars ... 15 "
46 ft. furniture ... 70,000 lb. box ... 17 "
50 ft. furniture ... refrigerator ... 19 "
Engine tender ... 80,000 lb. box ... 20 "

Baggage cars, ... hand derrick cars ... 25 tons
8 wheel coaches and sleeping cars ... 30 "
12 wheel coaches and sleeping cars ... 40 "
Mogul engine and tender ... 70 "
... Steam derrick cars ... 80 "
Heavier engine and tender ... 110 "

This locomotive rating chart was published in Eastern Division employee timetable No. 20, effective August 8, 1909. Note Consolidations, Nos. 300 to 319, could haul more tonnage than Prairies, Nos. 180 to 292. CGW had not yet purchased the remainder of its Consolidations, including Nos. 340 and 349, when the chart was prepared. (Chicago and North Western Historical Society.)

Chicago Great Western Railroad Company

Locomotives Owned and Changes, Year Ended June 30, 1911

Exhibit 22

	Wheel Arrangement	Owned June 30, 1910	Added by purchase during the Year	Sold, Broken up or Condemned	Changed from another Class	Changed to another Class	Owned June 30, 1911
Switching:	OO						
Cylinders, 16 x 24		4		4			0
Switching:	OOO						
Cylinders, 17 x 24		8		2			6
Cylinders, 18 x 24		8		3			5
Cylinders, 19 x 26		5					5
Cylinders, 20 x 26			10				10
Switching:	OOOO						
Cylinders, 20½ x 30					1		1
Cylinders, 22 x 32		6			4		10
Total Switching		31	10	9	5		37
Transfer:	OOOOo						
Cylinders, 20½ x 30		10		2		8	0
Eight-Wheel:	OOoo						
Cylinders, 17 x 24		37		6			31
Cylinders, 18 x 24		12		2			10
Cylinders, 19 x 24		9					9
Total Eight-Wheel		58		8			50
Mogul:	OOOo						
Cylinders, 18 x 24		35		5			30
Cylinders, 19 x 28		2					2
Cylinders, 19 x 24		12		2			10
Mogul Cross Compound:	OOOo						
Cylinders, 21 and 32 x 24		2		2			0
Total Mogul		51		9			42
Ten-Wheel:	OOOoo						
Cylinders, 18 x 26		2					2
Cylinders, 19 x 26		4					4
Cylinders, 20 x 28		14			7		21
Cylinders, 26 x 28		4					4
Cylinders, 23 x 28			6				6
Ten-Wheel Cross Compound:	OOOoo						
Cylinders, 22 and 35 x 28		7				7	0
Total Ten-Wheel		31	6		7	7	37
Prairie:	oOOOo						
Cylinders, 20 x 26		15				6	9
Cylinders, 21 x 26		3					3
Cylinders, 21 x 28		26			4	3	27
Cylinders, 24 x 28		12			17		29
Prairie Cross Compound:	oOOOo						
Cylinders, 22 and 35 x 28		14				14	0
Prairie Tandem Compound:	oOOOo						
Cylinders, 16 and 28 x 28		20				7	13
Total Prairie		90			21	30	81
Consolidation:	OOOOo						
Cylinders, 24 x 30		20	20				40
Cylinders, 20½ x 30					7		7
Consolidation Cross Compound:	OOOOo						
Cylinders, 22 and 35 x 32		4				4	0
Total Consolidation		24	20		7	4	47
Pacific:	oOOOoo						
Cylinders, 20 x 26		3			3		6
Cylinders, 24 x 26		2			3		5
Total Pacific		5			6		11
Mallet Compound:	oOOOOOOo						
Cylinders, 23 and 35 x 32		0	10				10
Cylinders, 21 and 35 x 28		0			3		3
Total Mallet		0	10		3		13
Grand Total		300	46	28	49	49	318
Motor Cars		0	4				4
Total Motor Cars		0	4				4

38

CGW published this list of locomotives in the company's 1911 annual report. The motive power fleet consisted of 318 steam engines and four motorcars as of June 30, 1911. The motorcars were combination passenger-mail-express vehicles fueled by gasoline. (Author's collection.)

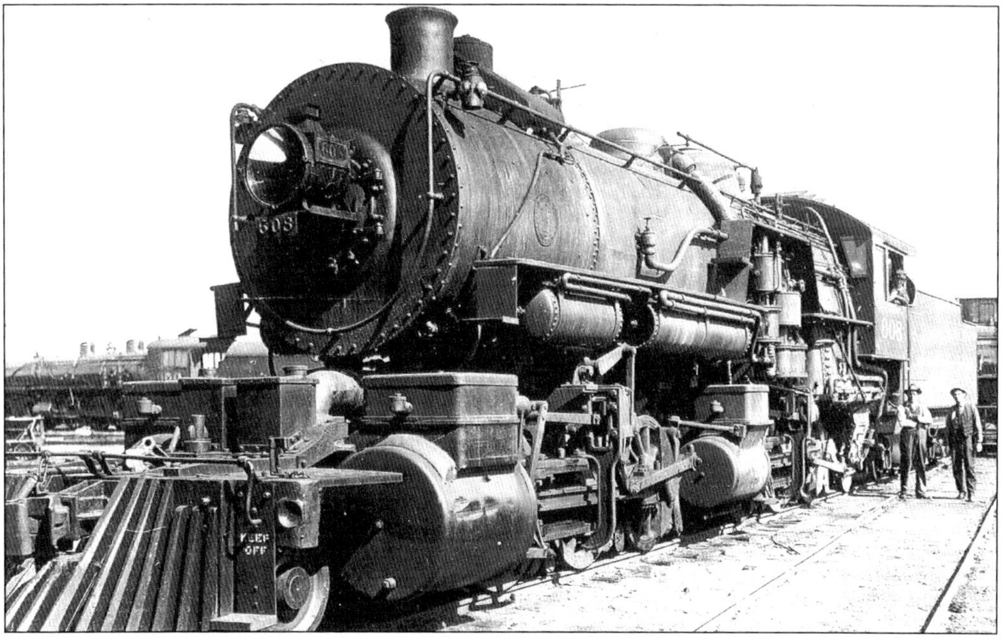

The Mallet 2-6-6-2 articulated locomotive was developed during the early 1900s for moving heavy tonnage over steep grades. CGW acquired 10 in 1910 from Baldwin for service between Stockton and Oelwein. The plan was to use Consolidations between Chicago and Stockton and Mallets between Stockton and Oelwein. Previously, train size was reduced west of Stockton if powered with a Consolidation or the company-assigned helper engines. The Mallet was powerful enough to pull the same train without reducing size or dispatching helpers. However, the Mallets were too slow and expensive to operate and maintain. All 10 were sold to the Clinchfield Railroad in 1916. No. 603, shown at Oelwein in 1912, was one of these behemoths. (James L. Rueber.)

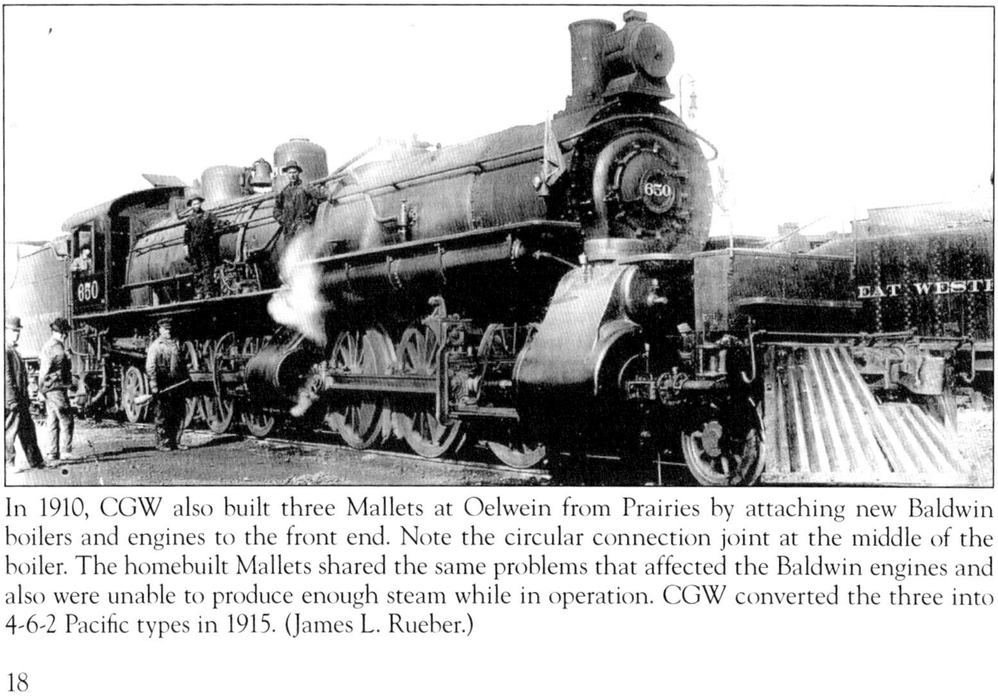

In 1910, CGW also built three Mallets at Oelwein from Prairies by attaching new Baldwin boilers and engines to the front end. Note the circular connection joint at the middle of the boiler. The homebuilt Mallets shared the same problems that affected the Baldwin engines and also were unable to produce enough steam while in operation. CGW converted the three into 4-6-2 Pacific types in 1915. (James L. Rueber.)

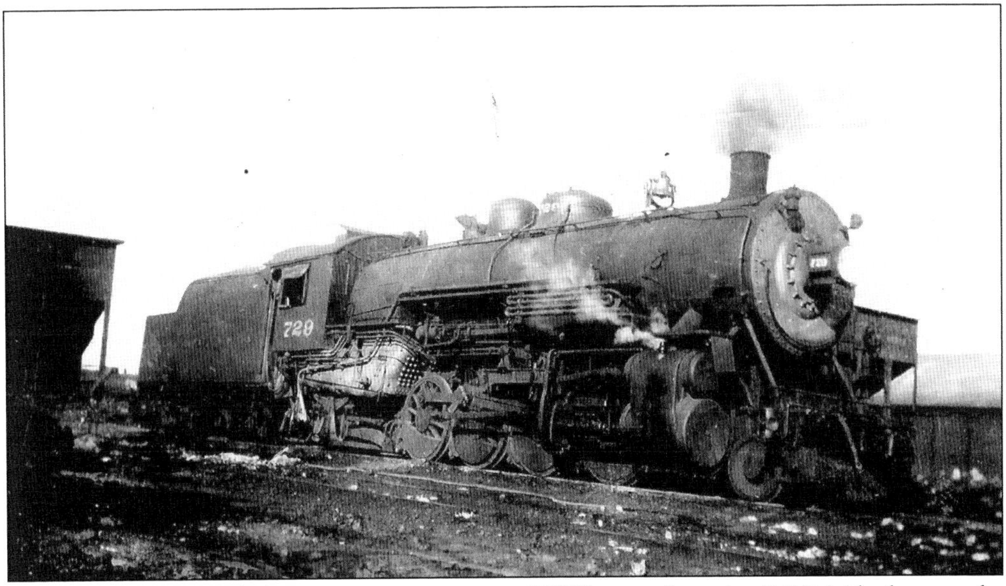

When the Mallet failed to meet expectations, CGW turned to the 2-8-2 Mikado type for moving heavy tonnage. The Mikado could haul more than the Consolidation, but the grades west of Stockton forced the CGW to resume reducing tonnage or assigning helper engines. CGW purchased 40 Mikados from Baldwin between 1912 and 1920. No. 729 was photographed at Oelwein in November 1934. (Author's collection.)

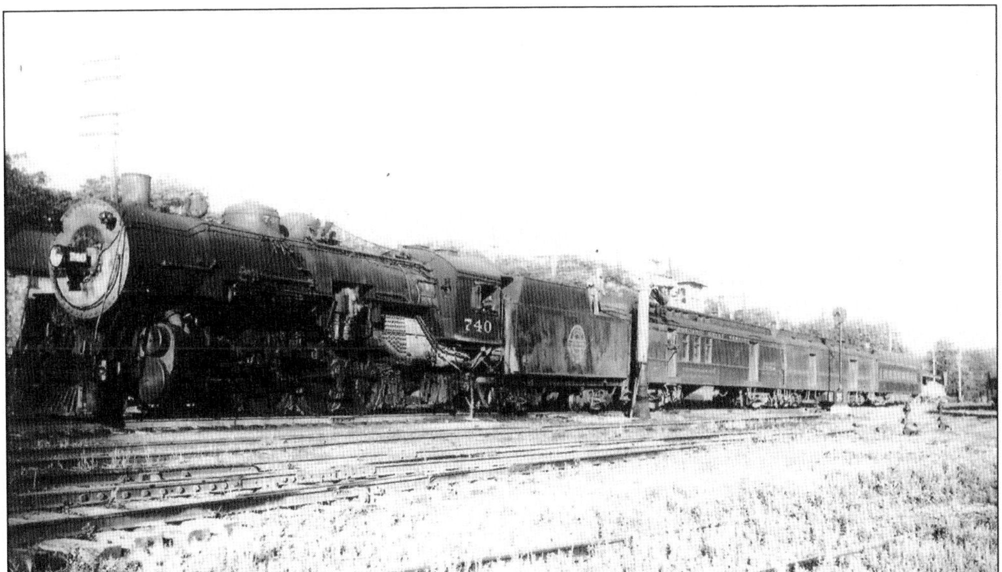

The versatility of the Mikado type to power either freight or passenger trains is shown in this photograph of No. 740 at Sycamore, Illinois. No. 740 was one of several Mikados rebuilt by CGW between 1937 and 1939 with automatic stokers, new frames, and disc-type main drivers. (Joiner History Room, Sycamore, Illinois.)

NEW LOCOMOTIVES SHOW EFFICIENCY

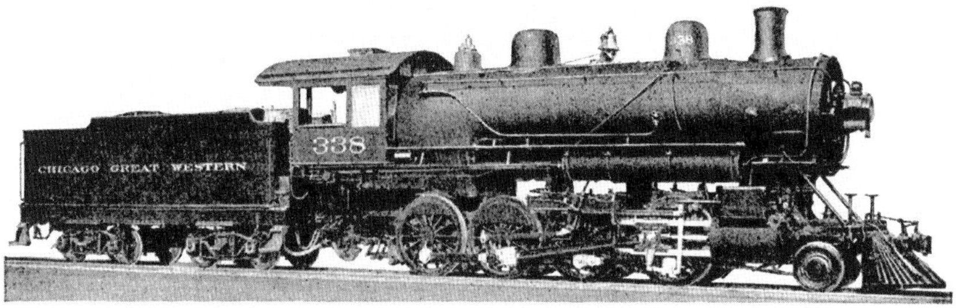

Consolidation Type Locomotive, Chicago Great Western Ry.

A recent test of twelve months duration, carried out on the Chicago Great Western Railway, illustrates the economies realized by using high power locomotives of modern design. This test was run on the Eastern Division where the maximum grades are one per cent. The locomotives tested included ten of the Consolidation type, built by The Baldwin Locomotive Works in 1909, and ten of the Mikado type, completed by the same builders in 1912. The former use saturated steam, while the latter are equipped with superheaters. The average train load hauled by the Mikado type engines was 53 per cent. greater than that hauled by the Consolidations, and this was done with a saving, on a ton-mile basis, of 37 per cent. in pounds of coal consumed, and 38 per cent. in cost of maintenance.

In this case the motive power was specially fitted for the work to be done. Similar results can be obtained on other roads, provided equal care is taken in selecting the locomotives. The Chicago Great Western test demonstrates the remarkable progress made in locomotive efficiency during the past few years.

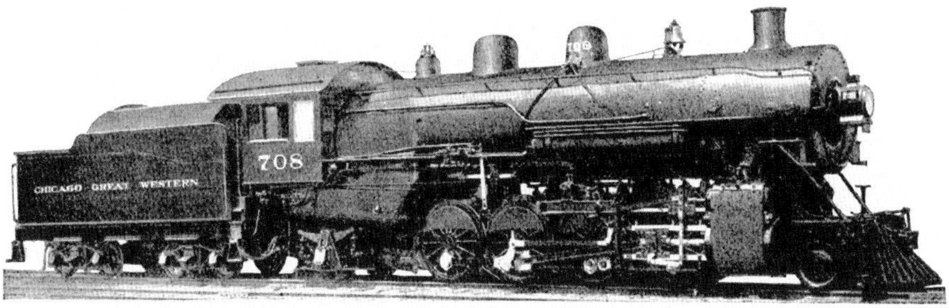

Mikado Type Locomotive, Chicago Great Western Ry.
G. M. Crownover, Supt. Motive Power.

THE BALDWIN LOCOMOTIVE WORKS

PHILADELPHIA, PA., U. S. A.

Represented by

F. W. Weston, 50 Church Street, New York, N. Y. Charles Riddell, 625 Railway Exchange, Chicago, Ill.
C. H. Peterson, 1610 Wright Building, St. Louis, Mo. A. Wm. Hinger, 722 Spalding Building, Portland, Ore.
George F. Jones, 407 Travelers Building, Richmond, Va.
Cable Address: "BALDWIN, PHILADELPHIA."

CGW frequently conducted comparison trials between locomotives to determine if it was using the most efficient engine. This 1915 Baldwin advertisement reported on the better performance of the Mikado than the Consolidation in freight service between Chicago and Oelwein. (Author's collection.)

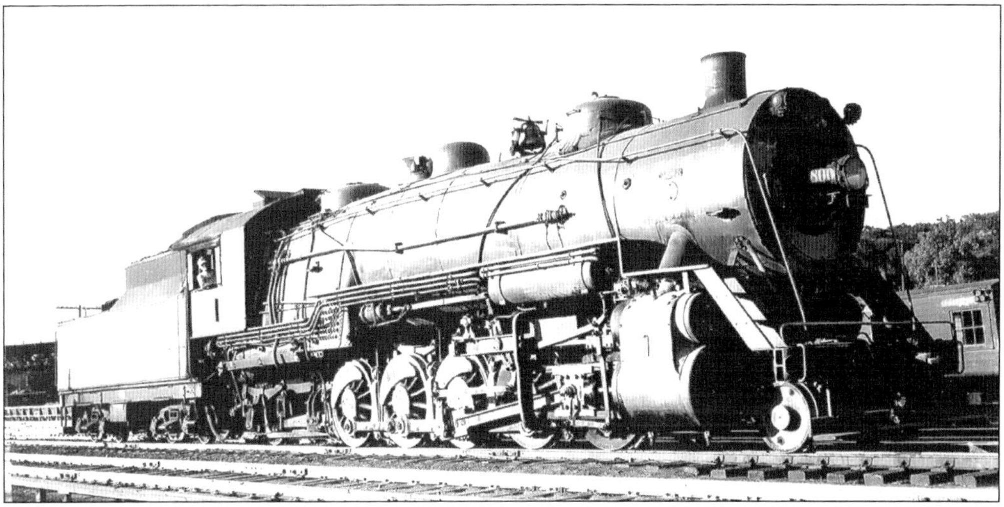

The 2-10-4 Texas–type locomotive was first built in 1925 for the Texas and Pacific Railway for hauling heavy tonnage at high speed over long distances. CGW found that the Texas had 30 percent more hauling capacity than the Mikado, with lower maintenance cost. Between 1929 and 1930, 36 were purchased from Lima Locomotive Works and Baldwin. The first Texas purchased from Baldwin, No. 800, was photographed at St. Paul, Minnesota, on July 18, 1947. (Author's collection.)

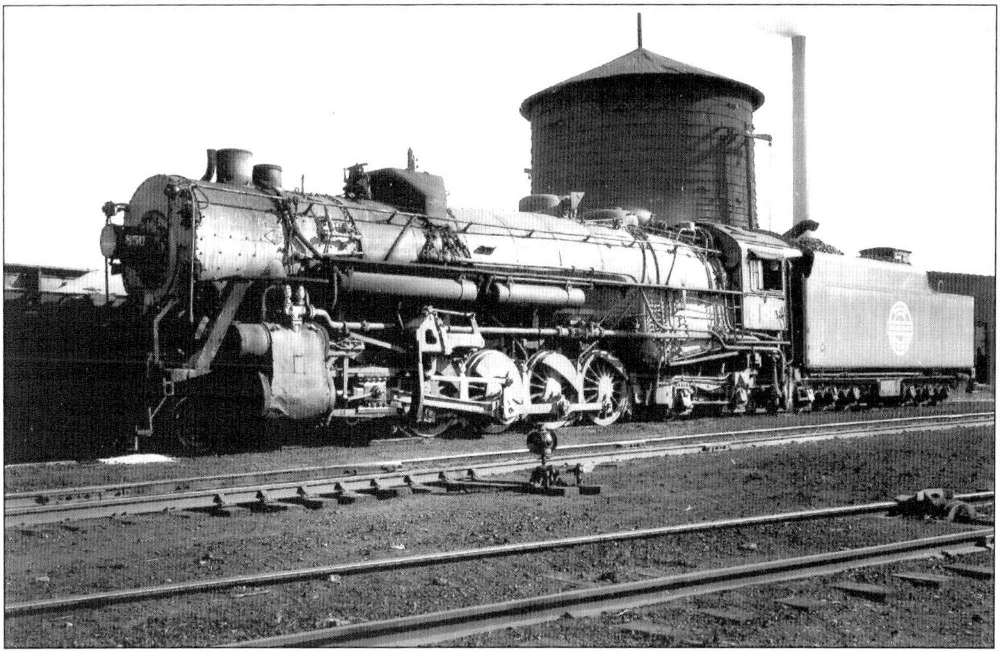

The Texas replaced the Mikado in heavy tonnage freight service between Chicago and St. Paul and between Oelwein and Kirmeyer, Missouri. The 2-10-4 produced enough power to pull freight trains over the steep grades west of Stockton with no reduction in train size or helpers. No. 850, the first CGW Texas built by Lima, was photographed at Chicago Transfer Yard on October 15, 1939. (James L. Rueber.)

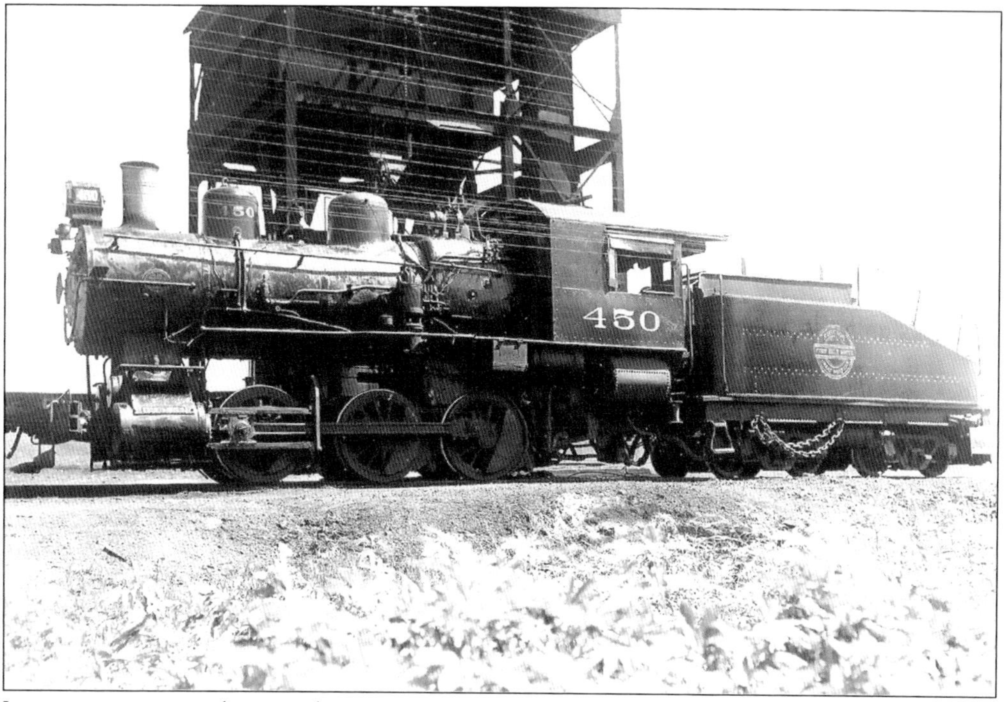

Locomotives assigned to switching service performed the highly important work of breakdown and makeup of trains in classification yards and pickup and delivery of freight cars at industries and interchanges. ALCO built No. 450, a 0-6-0 switcher, in 1902. (Joiner History Room, Sycamore, Illinois.)

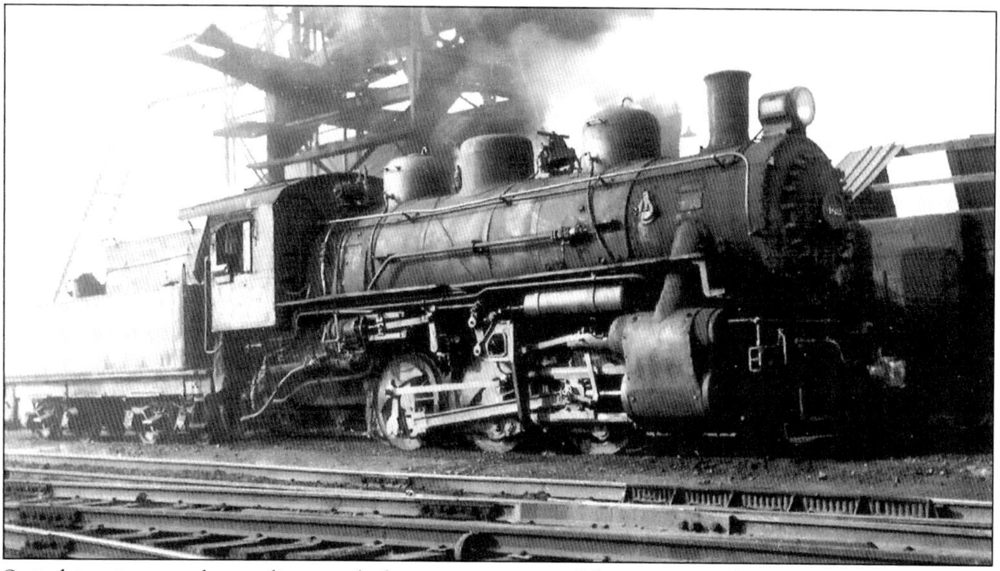

Switching is very demanding work for train crews and locomotives due to constant starting, stopping, and reversal of movement. Switcher No. 482 was photographed at Chicago Transfer Yard in 1937. (Joiner History Room, Sycamore, Illinois.)

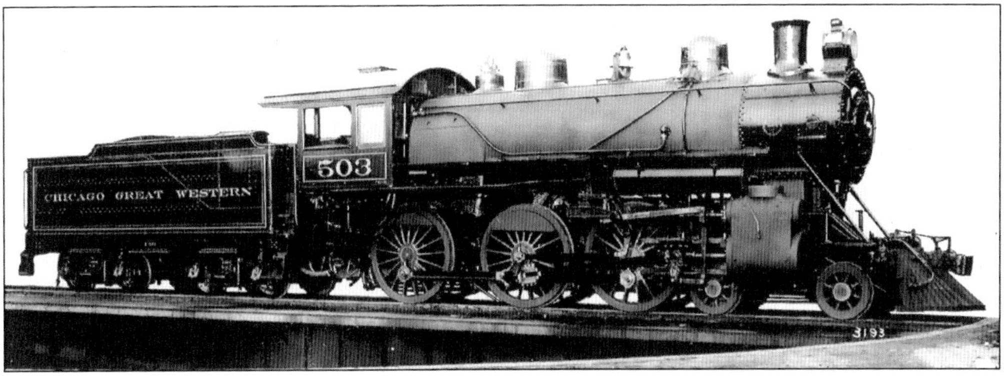

CGW acquired 37 4-6-0 Ten Wheelers from Baldwin, Lima, Rhode Island, and Richmond Locomotive Works between 1899 and 1910. The engines were assigned to power the company's premier passenger trains, including the Great Western Limited, which ran between Chicago and Minneapolis–St. Paul. No. 503 was painted dark green and black, and most of the external piping on the boiler was hidden under an outer casing for a streamlined appearance. (Joiner History Room, Sycamore, Illinois.)

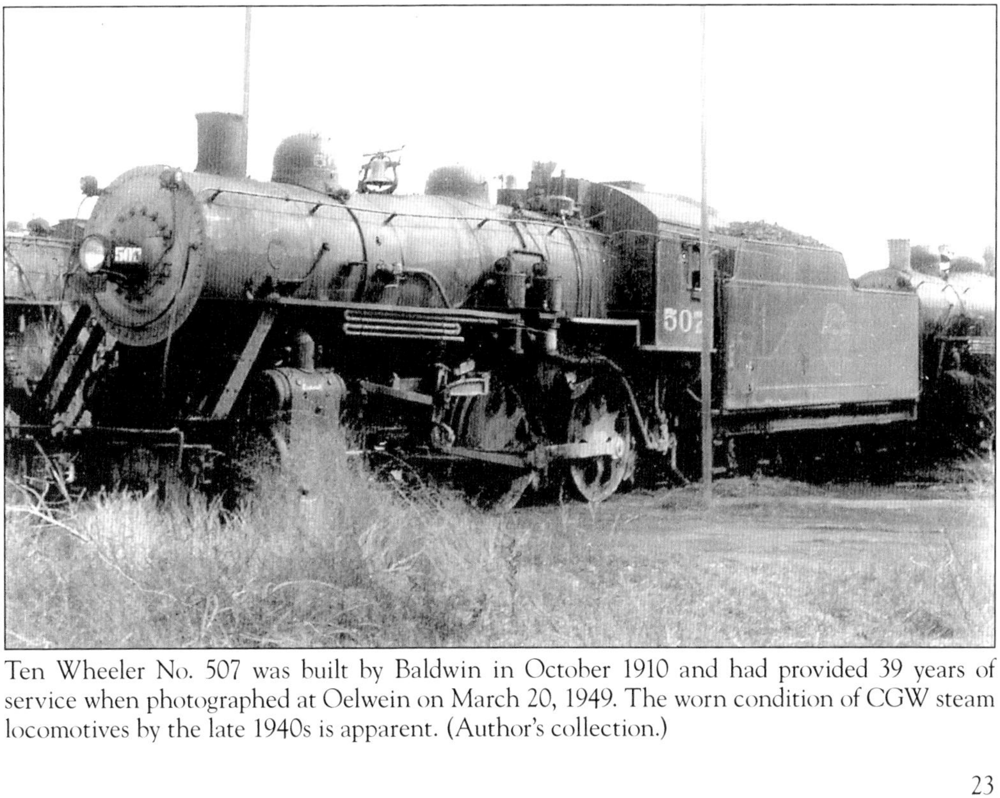

Ten Wheeler No. 507 was built by Baldwin in October 1910 and had provided 39 years of service when photographed at Oelwein on March 20, 1949. The worn condition of CGW steam locomotives by the late 1940s is apparent. (Author's collection.)

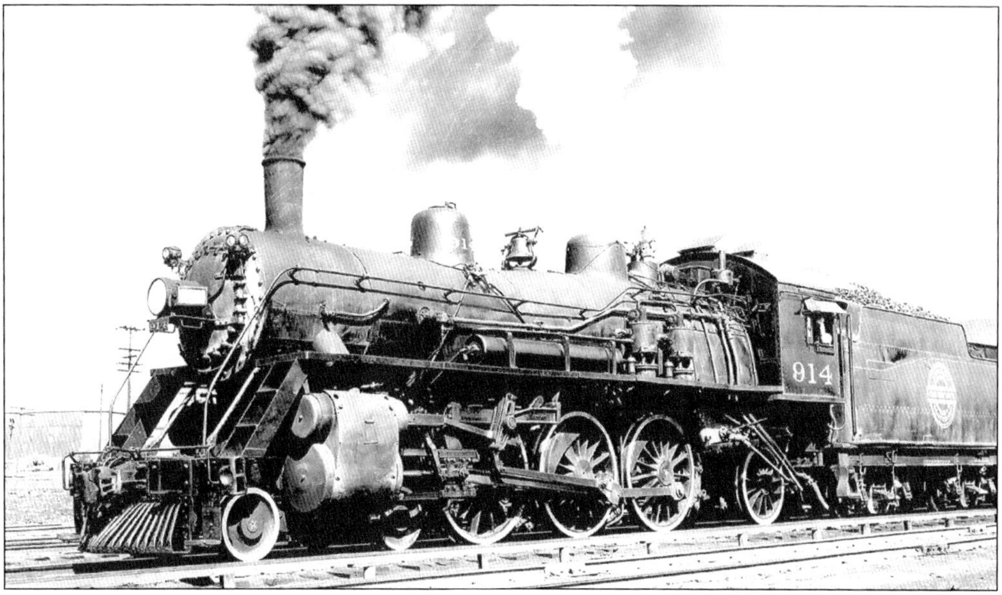

The 4-6-2 Pacific was also used to power passenger trains on the CGW, which had a fleet of 38. Eight were purchased from Baldwin in 1913 and 1916, and the remainder was built at Oelwein by modifying 2-6-2 Prairies and the homebuilt Mallets. No. 914 began as a Prairie type, rebuilt in 1916 and further modernized in 1923. The photograph was taken at St. Paul, Minnesota, on May 29, 1948. (Author's collection.)

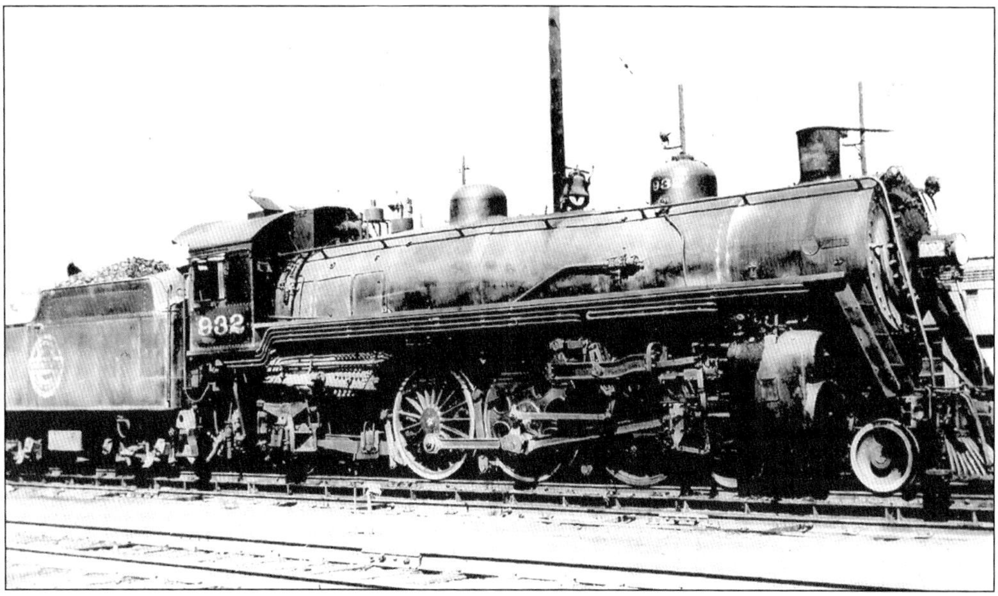

No. 932 was the last of the eight Pacific-type engines acquired from Baldwin. These locomotives were the most powerful 4-6-2s operated by CGW and were assigned to the fastest and heaviest passenger trains. (Author's collection.)

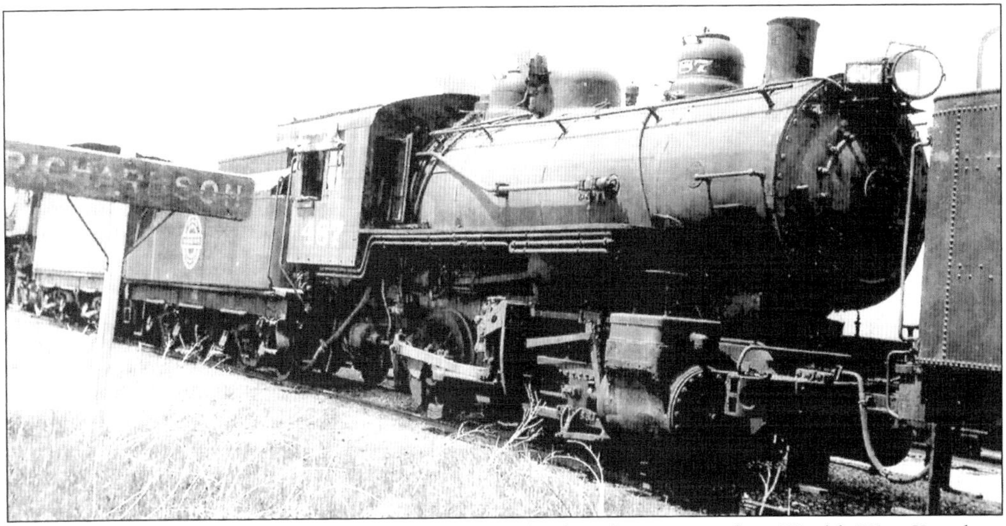

The CGW steam locomotive fleet was in need of replacement after World War II, when railroads were converting their motive power from steam to the more efficient diesel-electric. Electro-Motive Division (EMD) of General Motors provided CGW with diesel model F-3 No. 291 for test purposes during November 1946, and the railroad quickly became aware of the potential savings offered by this type of power. CGW ordered its first diesels on December 19, 1946, and began to retire its steam engines. This photograph shows "dead" steam locomotives passing through Richardson, Illinois, en route to Oelwein for sale to scrap dealers. (Joiner History Room, Sycamore, Illinois.)

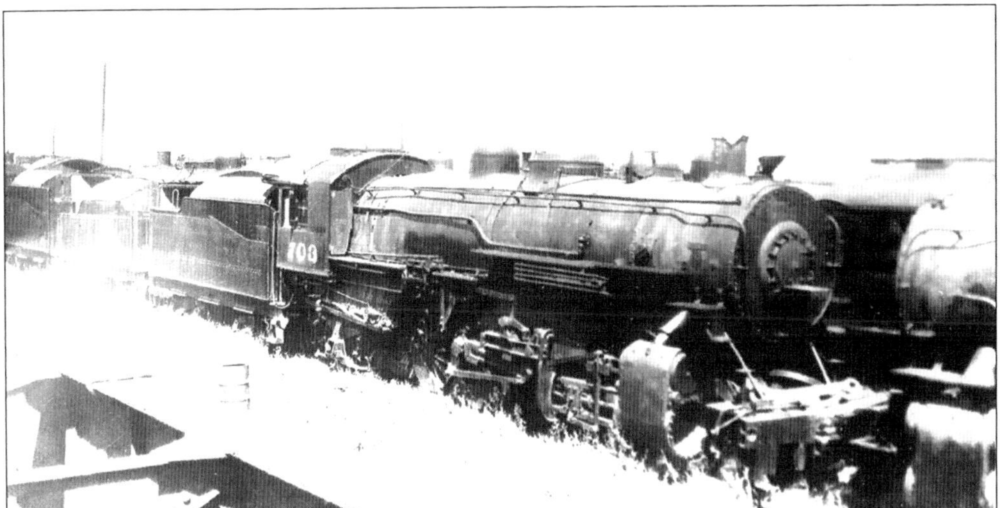

CGW began to power freight trains in Illinois with diesels on October 11, 1947. Steam locomotives were limited to switching service and local wayfreight, and motorcars powered passenger trains. The last active CGW steam locomotive in Illinois, No. 467, completed its final trip on July 9, 1949, and at that time, all CGW motive power in the Prairie State was diesel-electric. Later, in 1951, CGW dismantled all of the water tanks and coal chutes in Illinois that were previously used for steam engines. Oelwein became a steam locomotive graveyard as CGW completed the conversion of its motive power. (Author's collection.)

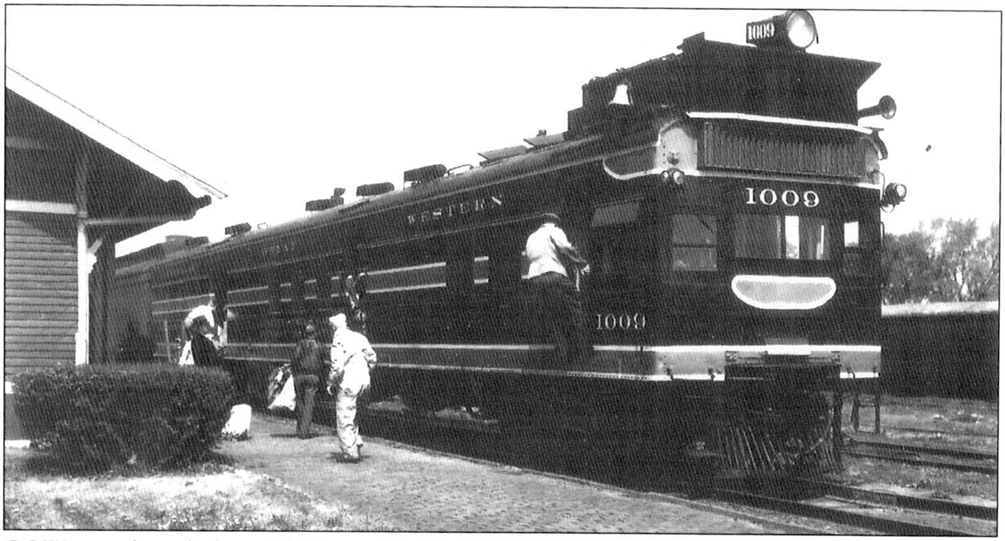

CGW purchased four McKeen Motor Car Company railcars in 1910 and the first Electro-Motive Company gas-electric car in 1924. The railcars were less expensive to operate than steam locomotives and were used to handle passenger business on lightly patronized lines. The CGW railcar fleet eventually totaled 16 vehicles. M-1009 was one of four purchased from Pullman Car and Manufacturing Company in 1932. It was a 450-horsepower combination mail-express-passenger coach with seating capacity for 22 passengers. The Pullmans were assigned to local passenger trains that operated between Chicago and Oelwein. The first railcar placed in this service made the maiden voyage on April 1, 1932. (Joiner History Room, Sycamore, Illinois.)

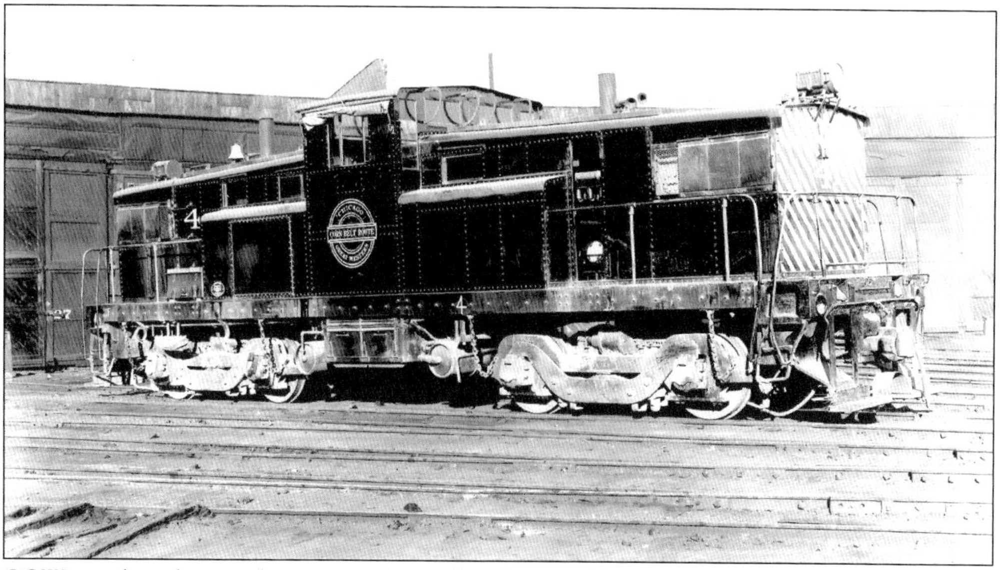

CGW purchased a gasoline-powered switcher from Baldwin in 1925 and assigned it No. 1. The company acquired its first diesel-electric locomotive from Westinghouse Electric and Manufacturing Company for yard switching at Oelwein in 1934 and designated it No. 2. It was placed on public display at Grand Central Station, Chicago, during December 1934. Two more diesel-electric switchers, Nos. 3 and 4, were also acquired from Westinghouse in April 1936. All four were rated at 800 horsepower. This is a photograph of No. 4 at Oelwein. (James L. Rueber.)

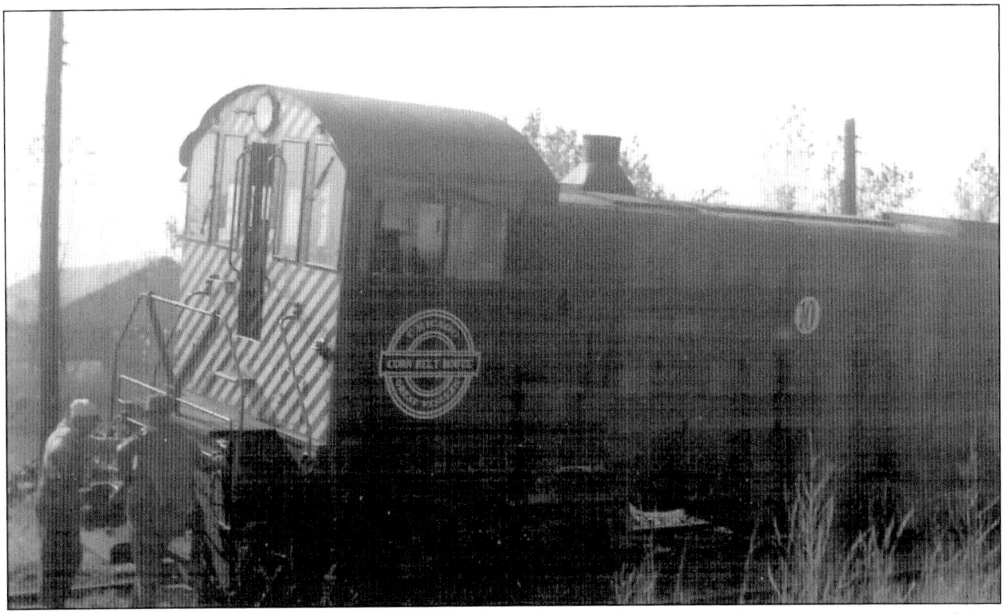

The diesel-electric locomotive was first developed to replace steam locomotives in switching service because it provides full power immediately and consumes less fuel when stopped and idling. A steam locomotive does not have these capabilities. The first CGW diesels were acquired for switching work and included No. 10, one of three model S-2 1,000-horsepower units purchased from ALCO in 1947. The locomotive has derailed, and the train crew is waiting for assistance. (Joiner History Room, Sycamore, Illinois.)

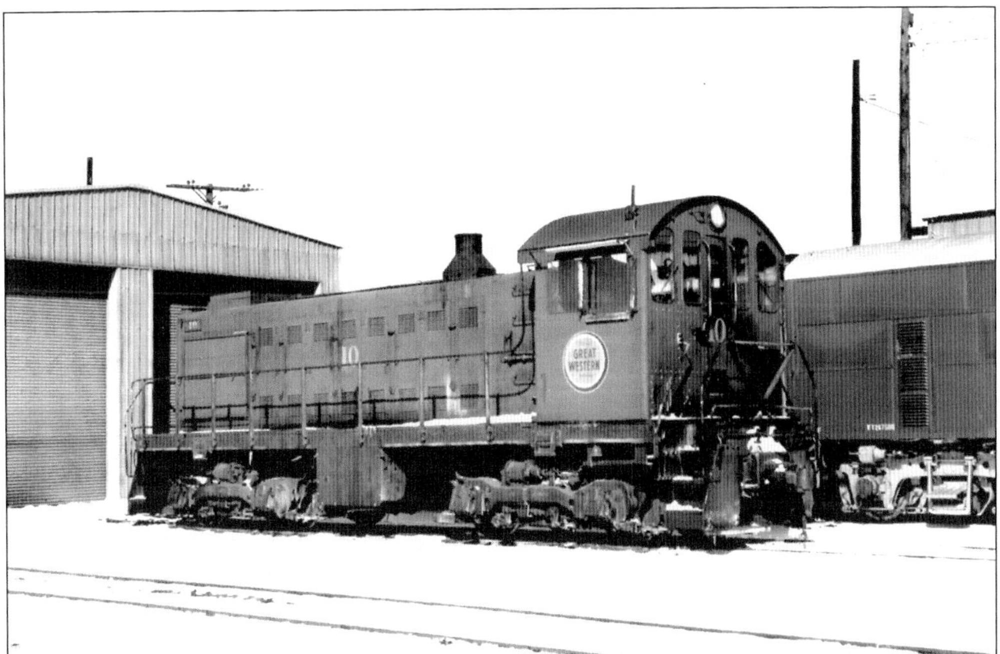

Here is No. 10 again but in better circumstances. Note the different CGW emblem on the cab side. This photograph was taken on February 25, 1967, at Chicago Transfer Yard. (Joseph Piersen.)

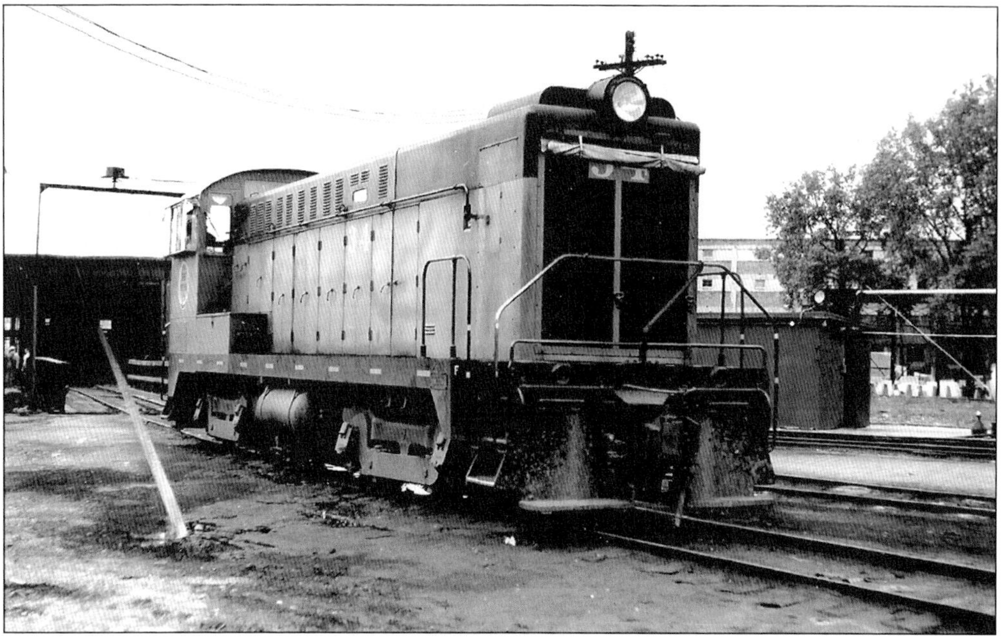

No. 34 is one of 10 Baldwin model DS-4-4-1000, 1,000-horsepower engines acquired in 1949 for switching service. It was photographed on May 28, 1968, at St. Paul. CGW became completely dieselized in September 1949 and was the first railroad in its territory to achieve this status. (Author's collection.)

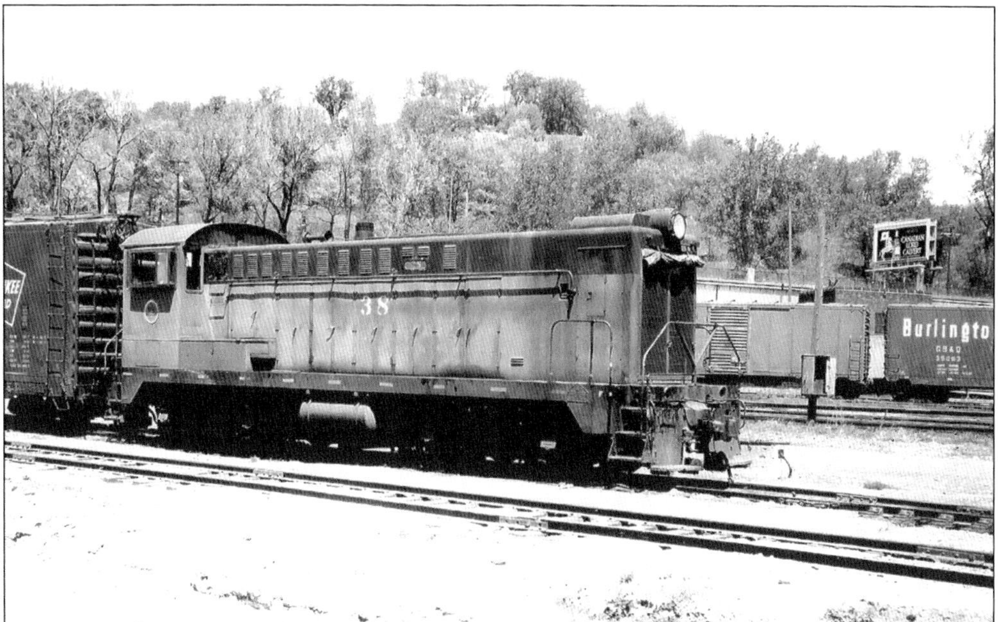

The 10 Baldwin DS-4-4-1000 switchers also included No. 38. CGW reported to the Association of American Railroads on January 1, 1950, that it owned 137 diesel-electric locomotives at that time, which represented 87 percent of its motive power fleet. (Author's collection.)

This information on CGW diesel-electric locomotives was published in employee timetable No. 3, effective October 1, 1965. The Cooper's Rating table was used to determine if a bridge was designed to support the weight of a particular locomotive. Diesels with boilers were assigned to passenger trains because the boiler provided heating. (Author's collection.)

21

CLASSIFICATION OF LOCOMOTIVES

Class	Units	Locomotive Numbers
D-1	1	2
D-2	6	6, 11, 12, 13, 14, 15
D-3	31	5, 8, 9, 10 and 16 to 42, inc.
D-4	18	58 A-B to 66 A-B, Inc.
D-5	8	50 to 57, inc.
D-6	2	120-121
D-7	4	101 A-B-C-D
"	2	102 B-D
"	3	103 A-B-D
"	3	104 A-B-D
"	2	105 B-D
"	4	106 A-B-C-D
"	4	107 A-B-C-D
"	4	108 A-B-C-D
"	4	109 A-B-C-D
"	4	110 A-B-C-D
"	4	111 A-B-C-D
"	4	112 A-B-C-D
"	4	113 A-B-C-D
"	4	114 A-B-C-D
"	4	115 A-B-C-D
"	7	116 A-B-C-D-E-F-G
"	5	150, 152, 153, 155, 156
D-8	8	201 to 208 inc.
Total..........	140	

COOPER'S RATING OF C.G.W. LOCOMOTIVES

D-1	E-47
D-2	E-40
D-3	E-49
D-4	E-49
D-5	E-46
D-6	E-50
D-7	E-47
D-8	E-57

Diesel Units Equipped With Steam Boilers

114-B	115-B	115-D	116-A	116-B	116-C
116-D	116-E	116-F	116-G	150	
152	153		155	156	

Diesel Units Equipped With Steam Connections But No Boilers

102-D	104-D	112-D	113-B	113-D	114-D
		120	121		

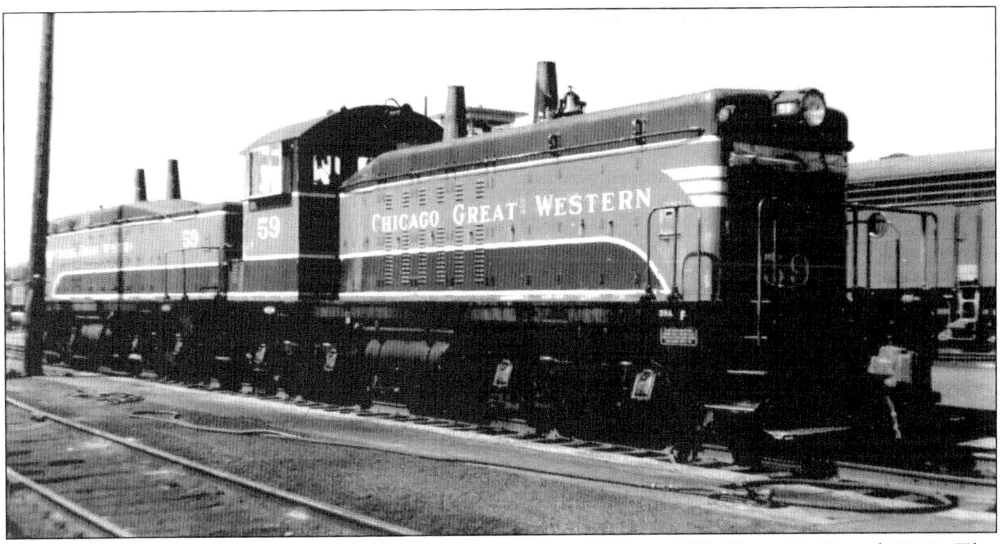

CGW purchased 18 model TR-2 engines from General Motors' EMD in 1948 and 1949. The designation TR referred to transfer service, which is moving trains from one railroad to another within yard limits. The engine was connected to a booster unit that provided extra power. The configuration was nicknamed "cow and calf." No. 59 and its calf were photographed at Oelwein on April 26, 1962. (James L. Rueber.)

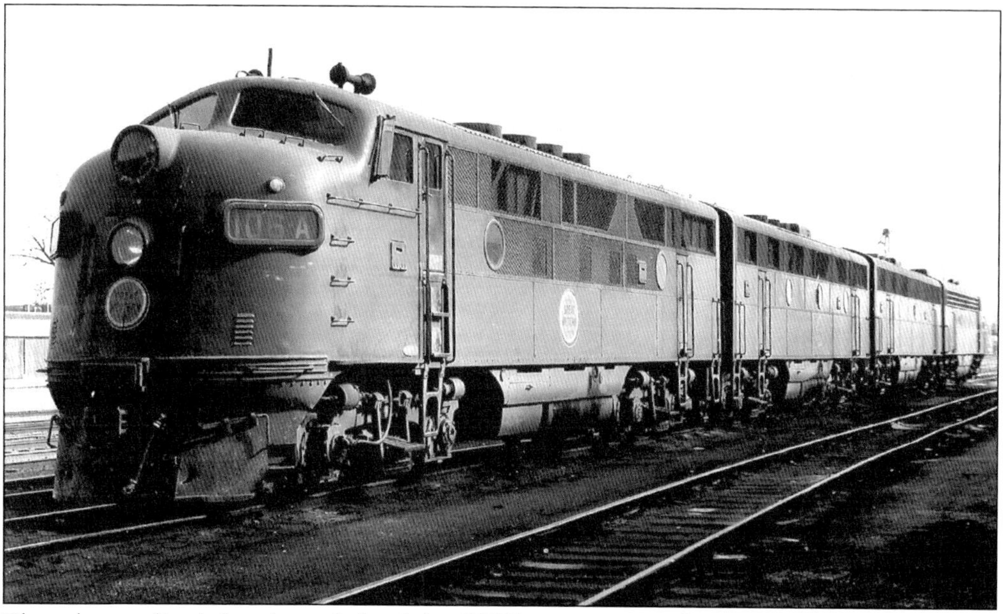

The cab-type diesel-electric symbolized the CGW motive power fleet as it existed between 1949 and 1968. All of the cab types were purchased from EMD between 1947 and 1951, primarily for freight service. The diesel-electric permitted CGW to achieve efficiency by powering trains with fewer locomotives. (Author's collection.)

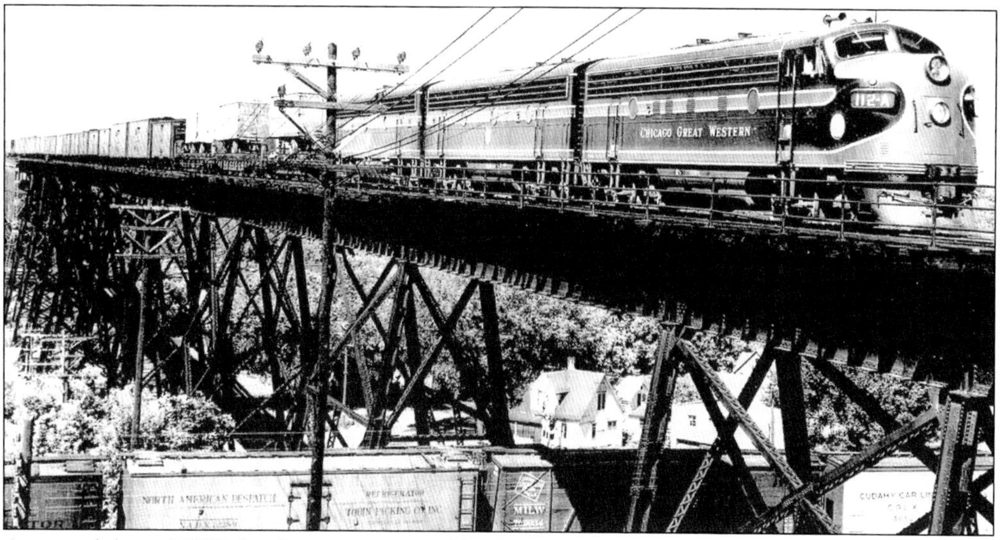

A typical, long CGW freight train powered by four cab-type diesels was photographed crossing the Des Moines River Valley Bridge at Fort Dodge, Iowa. EMD estimated the diesel-electric locomotive would return 17.2 percent annually in savings on the investment in new power. William Deramus III, CGW president, informed shareholders in 1950 that the return exceeded expectations and was 30 percent. (James L. Rueber.)

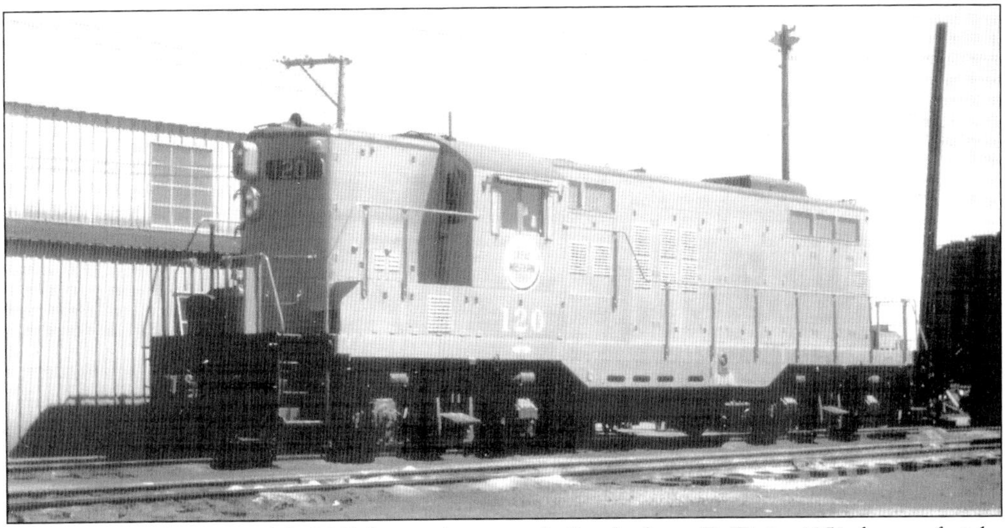

CGW acquired two model GP-7 (general purpose) diesels from EMD in 1951 for wayfreight service, including No. 120. This particular engine was almost destroyed in a fire at the Forty-sixth Street roundhouse near Chicago Transfer Yard on September 15, 1955. It was rebuilt the following year as an updated version designated GP-9. The photograph was taken on September 5, 1965, at Chicago Transfer Yard. (James L. Rueber.)

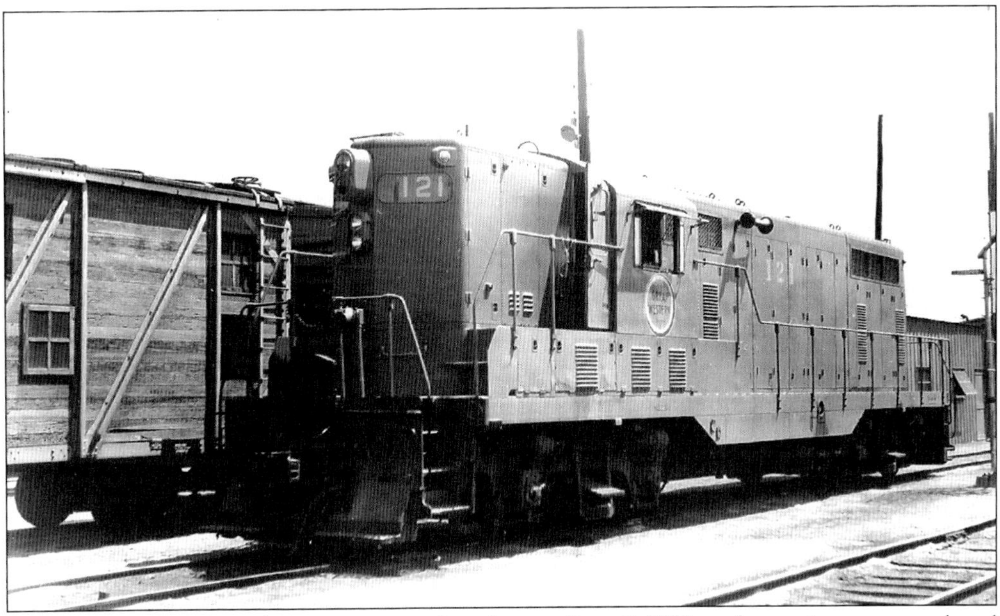

Here is GP-7 No. 121. The units were referred to as "jeeps" (GP) and were just as rugged and reliable. Nos. 120 and 121 are the author's favorite CGW motive power. No. 121 was photographed at Chicago Transfer Yard on July 17, 1966. (Author's collection.)

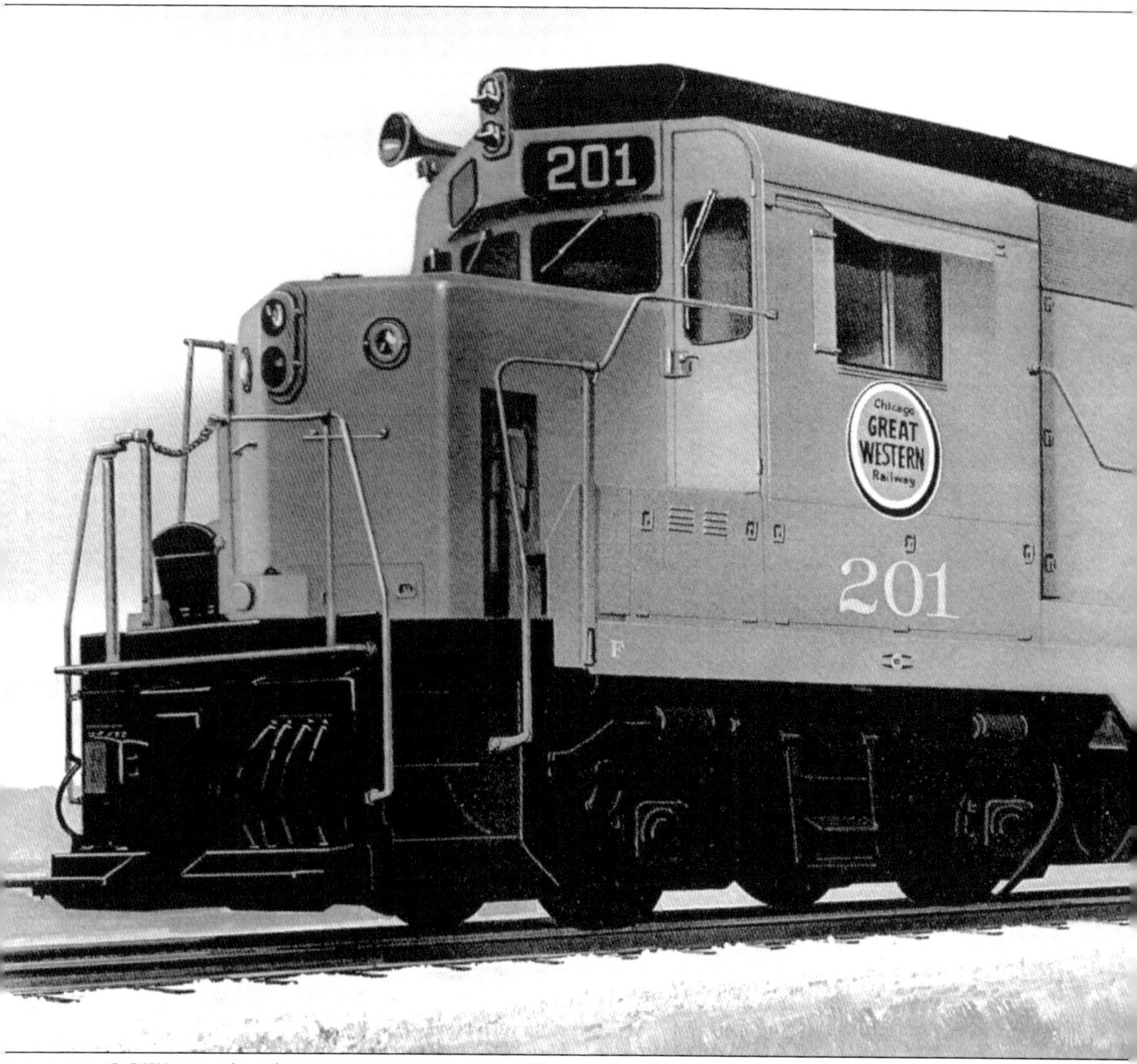

CGW completed its initial acquisition of diesel-electric locomotives in 1951, and at that time, the fleet consisted of 102 road locomotives, 39 switchers, and two railcars. The next purchase of diesels occurred in 1963, when CGW acquired model GP-30 locomotives from EMD. A drawing of the first unit, No. 201, was featured on the cover of the company's 1963 annual report. (Author's collection.)

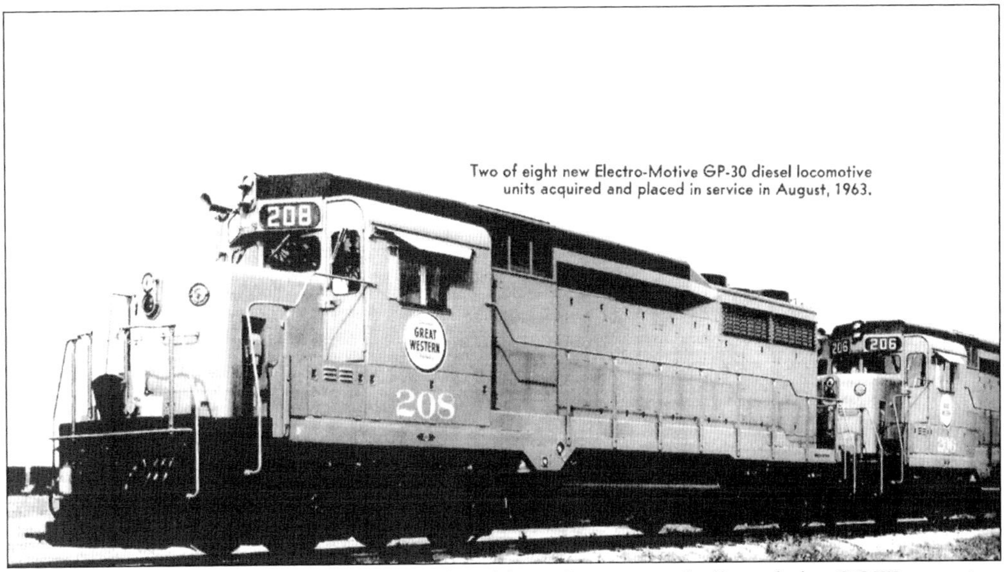

The GP-30 produced more power than the older cab units and allowed the CGW to assign fewer engines to a heavy tonnage train. For example, six cab units coupled together produced 9,000 horsepower, which was the same as four GP-30s coupled together. An article in the September and October 1963 issue of *Safety News* reported that the new GP-30s made a distinctive sound when running, and the sound of the air horn chime was also unique. (Author's collection.)

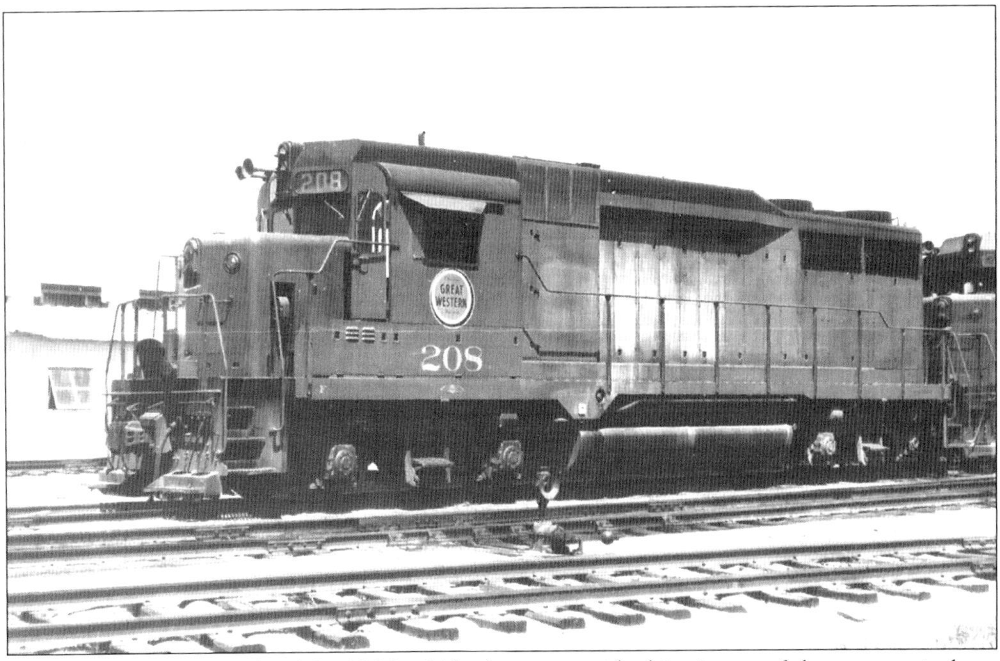

Compare the photograph of GP-30 No. 208 when new with this picture of the same unit three years later. Wear and tear and faded paint are the result of continual operation pulling heavy tonnage trains day after day through all types of weather. This photograph of No. 208 was taken at Kansas City, Missouri, on May 28, 1966. (Author's collection.)

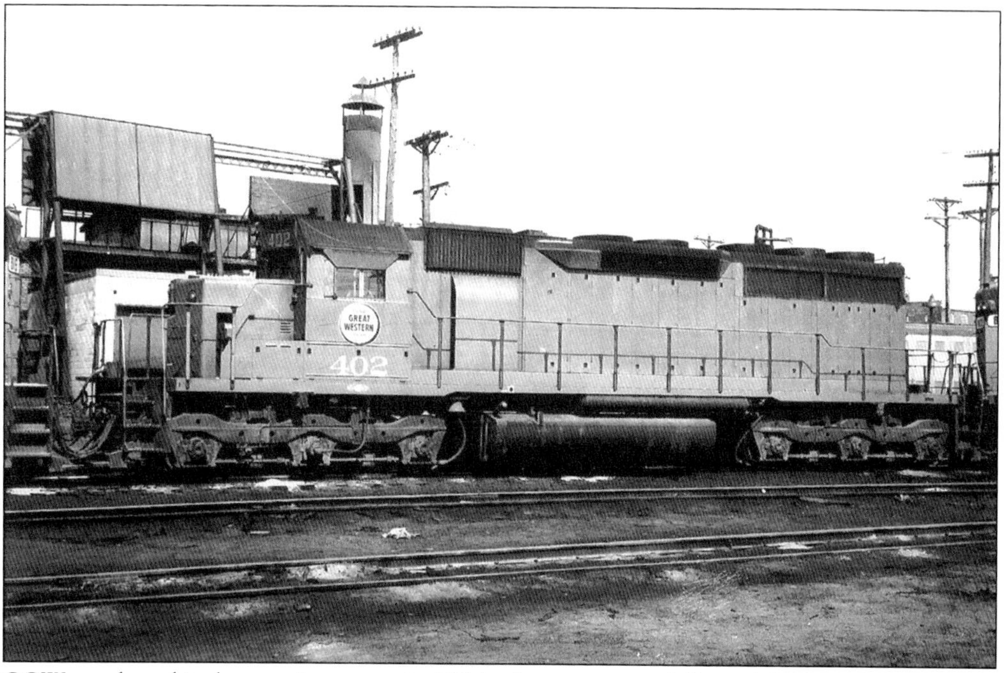

CGW purchased its last motive power in 1966, when it acquired 10 model SD-40 (special duty) locomotives built by EMD. The SD-40s were rated at 3,000 horsepower each. No. 402 was photographed at C&NW shops in Minneapolis in July 1968. (Author's collection.)

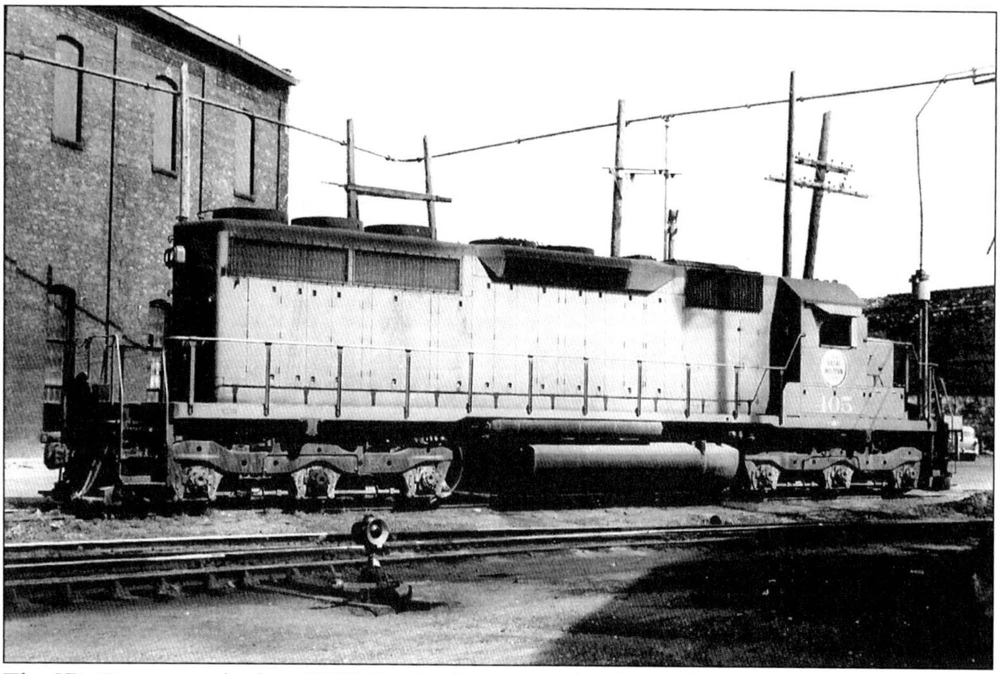
The SD-40 type was the first CGW diesel to be equipped with six-wheel trucks, and the company described the engines as the finest in modern motive power. No. 405 was also photographed at the C&NW Minneapolis shops in July 1968. (Author's collection.)

Three

FREIGHT SERVICE

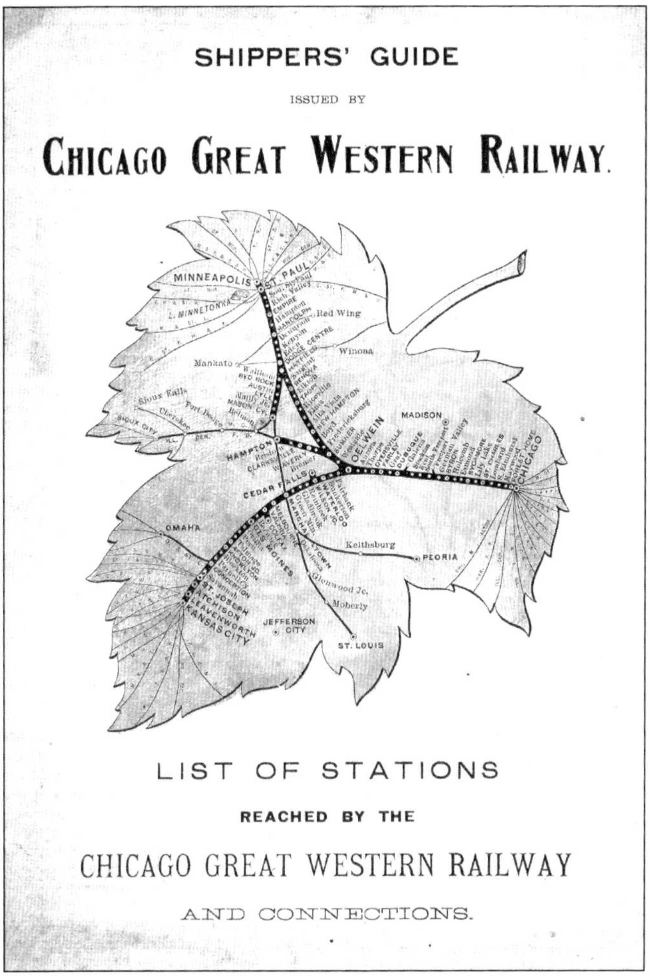

This is a CGW shippers' guide published during the 1890s. The guide contained a list of stations served by CGW and connecting railroads. Note the maple leaf trademark. Predecessor company CStP&KC conducted a nationwide trademark contest among ticket agents in 1889, and the winning submission was a sugar maple leaf that depicted the company's lines as veins on the leaf. The winner of the contest was a Wabash Railroad employee who received a prize of $100 for his entry. (Author's collection.)

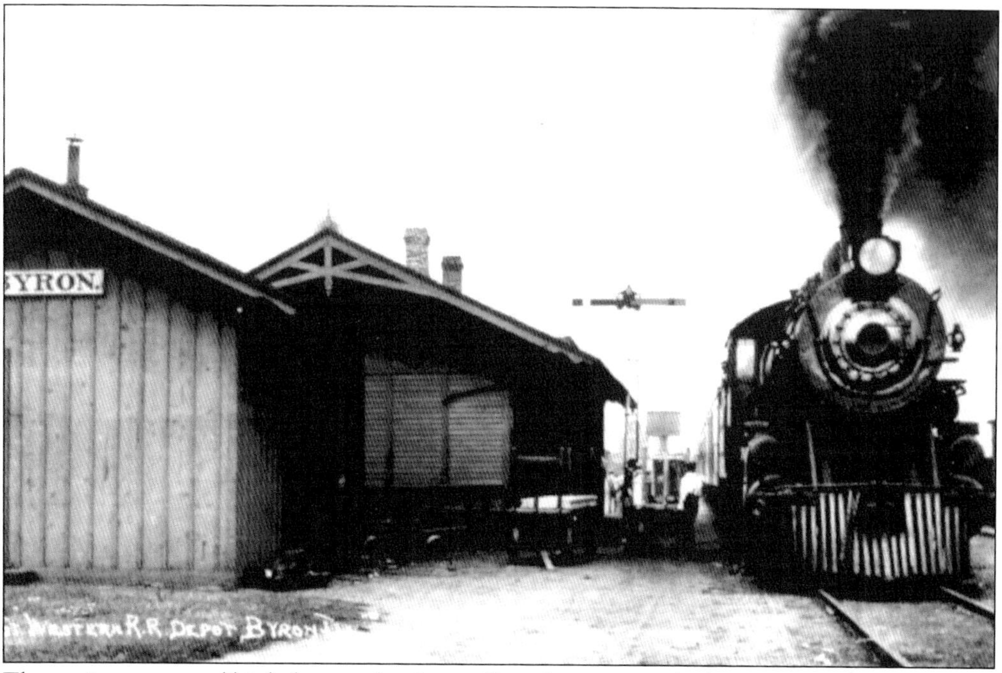

The station agent and his helper are loading milk and express in the baggage car of an eastbound train at Byron, Illinois. This scene was repeated frequently at stations all along the CGW system over the years. (Byron Museum of History.)

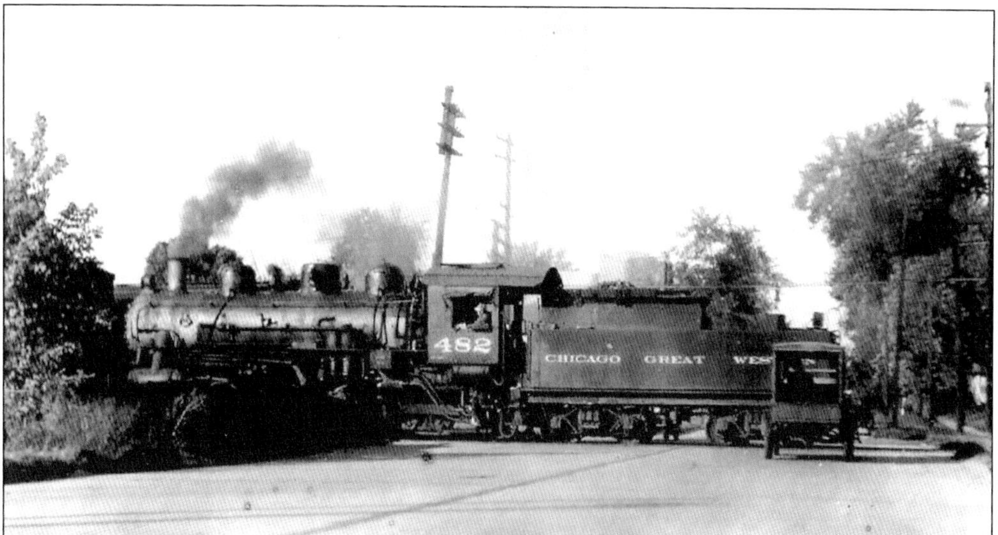

Railroad freight service includes switching cars at industries and interchanges. Switcher No. 482 is pushing a freight car across a grade crossing. Note the engineer leaning out the cab window, watching for hand signals from his brakeman. Also note the absence of crossing gates or flagmen. (Joiner History Room, Sycamore, Illinois.)

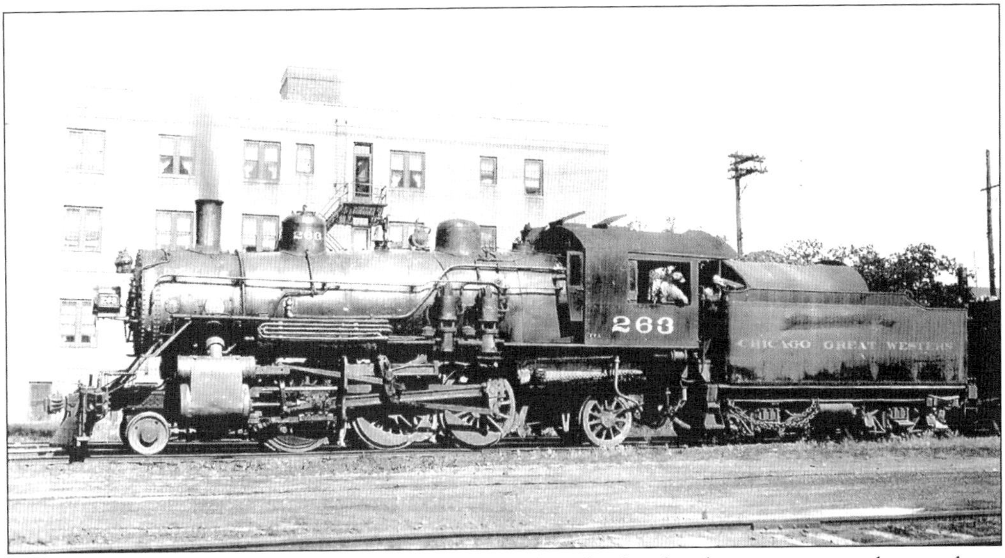

The crew of locomotive No. 263 appears to be ready to back a freight car onto another track, or else something of interest has caught their attention. The photograph was taken at Minneapolis, and the weather must have been warm. The ventilators on the cab roof are opened as well as the cab door. (Author's collection.)

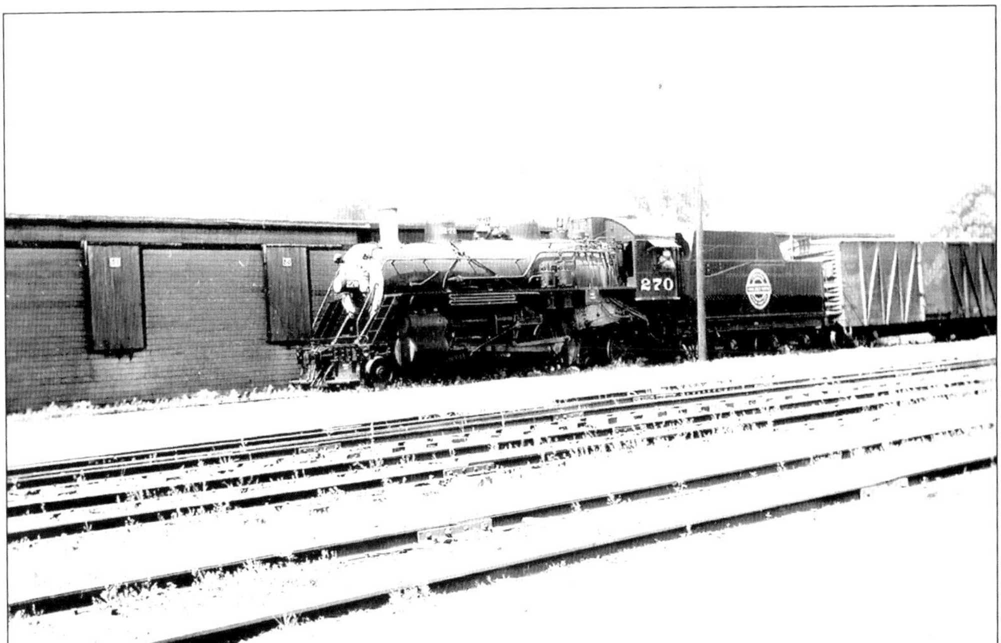

CGW operated a complex system of freight activities, including switching at industries and interchanges, moving freight trains between terminals, and classifying freight cars in yards at Oelwein, Chicago, Minneapolis, St. Paul, Omaha, and Kansas City. Locomotive No. 270 was photographed switching an industry siding. (Author's collection.)

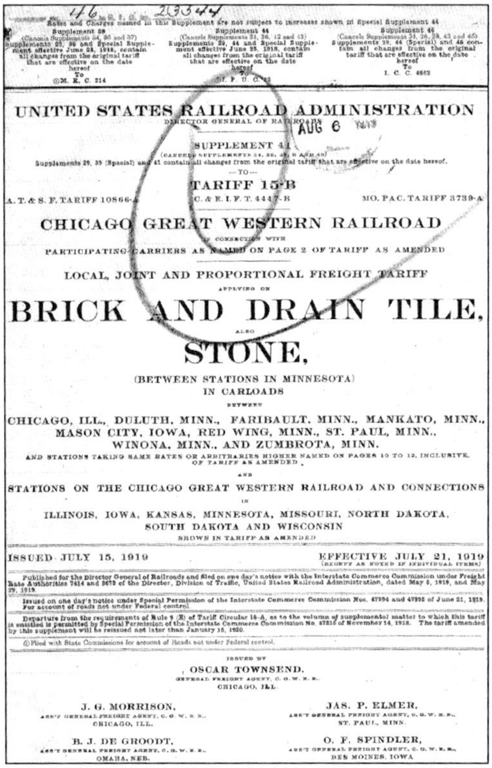

46 ... 23344

Rates and Charges named in this Supplement are not subject to increases shown in Special Supplement 44

Supplement 38	Supplement 44	Supplement 46
(Cancels Supplements 34, 36 and 37) Supplements 29, 36 and Special Supplement effective June 25, 1918, contain all changes from the original tariff that are effective on the date hereof To ⓐM. R. C. 214	(Cancels Supplements 34, 36, 12 and 43) Supplements 29, 44 and Special Supplement effective June 25, 1918, contain all changes from the original tariff that are effective on the date hereof To ⓐI. P. U. C. 32	(Cancels Supplements 34, 36, 38, 43 and 45) Supplements 29, 44 (Special) and 46 contain all changes from the original tariff that are effective on the date hereof To I. C. C. 4863

UNITED STATES RAILROAD ADMINISTRATION

DIRECTOR GENERAL OF RAILROADS

AUG 6 1919

SUPPLEMENT 41

(CANCELS SUPPLEMENTS 34, 36, 38, 8 AND 40)

Supplements 29, 39 (Special) and 41 contain all changes from the original tariff that are effective on the date hereof.

—TO—

TARIFF 15-B

A. T. & S. F. TARIFF 10866-A C. & E. I. F. T. 4447-B MO. PAC. TARIFF 3739-A

CHICAGO GREAT WESTERN RAILROAD

IN CONNECTION WITH

PARTICIPATING CARRIERS AS NAMED ON PAGE 2 OF TARIFF AS AMENDED

LOCAL, JOINT AND PROPORTIONAL FREIGHT TARIFF

APPLYING ON

BRICK AND DRAIN TILE,

ALSO

STONE,

(BETWEEN STATIONS IN MINNESOTA)
IN CARLOADS

BETWEEN

CHICAGO, ILL., DULUTH, MINN., FARIBAULT, MINN., MANKATO, MINN., MASON CITY, IOWA, RED WING, MINN., ST. PAUL, MINN., WINONA, MINN., AND ZUMBROTA, MINN.

AND STATIONS TAKING SAME RATES OR ARBITRARIES HIGHER NAMED ON PAGES 10 TO 12, INCLUSIVE, OF TARIFF AS AMENDED.

AND

STATIONS ON THE CHICAGO GREAT WESTERN RAILROAD AND CONNECTIONS

IN

ILLINOIS, IOWA, KANSAS, MINNESOTA, MISSOURI, NORTH DAKOTA, SOUTH DAKOTA AND WISCONSIN

SHOWN IN TARIFF AS AMENDED

ISSUED JULY 15, 1919 EFFECTIVE JULY 21, 1919
(EXCEPT AS NOTED IN INDIVIDUAL ITEMS)

Published for the Director General of Railroads and filed on one day's notice with the Interstate Commerce Commission under Freight Rate Authorities 7414 and 8679 of the Director, Division of Traffic, United States Railroad Administration, dated May 5, 1919, and May 29, 1919.

Issued on one day's notice under Special Permission of the Interstate Commerce Commission Nos. 47994 and 47995 of June 21, 1919. For account of roads not under Federal control.

Departure from the requirements of Rule 9 (E) of Tariff Circular 18-A, as to the volume of supplemental matter to which this tariff is entitled is permitted by Special Permission of the Interstate Commerce Commission No. 47515 of November 14, 1918. The tariff amended by this supplement will be reissued not later than January 15, 1920.

ⓐFiled with State Commissions for account of Roads not under Federal control.

ISSUED BY

OSCAR TOWNSEND,
GENERAL FREIGHT AGENT, C. G. W. R. R.
CHICAGO, ILL.

J. G. MORRISON,
ASS'T GENERAL FREIGHT AGENT, C. G. W. R. R.,
CHICAGO, ILL.

JAS. P. ELMER,
ASS'T GENERAL FREIGHT AGENT, C. G. W. R. R.,
ST. PAUL, MINN.

B. J. DE GROODT,
ASS'T GENERAL FREIGHT AGENT, C. G. W. R. R.,
OMAHA, NEB.

O. F. SPINDLER,
ASS'T GENERAL FREIGHT AGENT, C. G. W. R. R.,
DES MOINES, IOWA

Railroads publish freight rates in schedules such as CGW tariff No. 15-B, which contained charges on shipping brick, drain tile, and stone. Increases, decreases, and other revisions were published in supplements. (Author's collection.)

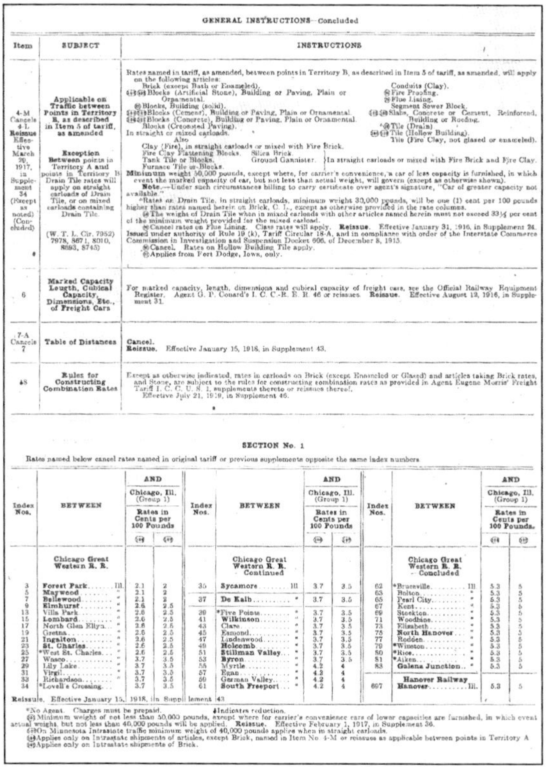

GENERAL INSTRUCTIONS—Concluded

Item	SUBJECT	INSTRUCTIONS
4-M Cancels 4-L Reissue Effective March 29, 1917, in Supplement 34 (Except as noted) (Concluded)	Applicable on Traffic between Points in Territory B, as described in Item 5 of tariff, as amended Exception Between points in Territory A and points in Territory B Drain Tile rates will apply on straight carloads of Drain Tile, or on mixed carloads containing Drain Tile. (W. T. L. Cir. 7952) 7978, 8671, 8010, 8693, 8745)	Rates named in tariff, as amended, between points in Territory B, as described in Item 5 of tariff, as amended, will apply on the following articles: Brick (except Bath or Enameled). Blocks (Artificial Stone), Building or Paving, Plain or Ornamental. Blocks, Building (solid). Blocks (Cement), Building or Paving, Plain or Ornamental. Blocks (Concrete), Building or Paving, Plain or Ornamental. Blocks (Creosoted Paving). Conduits (Clay). Fire Proofing. Flue Lining. Segment Sewer Block. Slabs, Concrete or Cement, Reinforced, Building or Roofing. *Tile (Drain). Tile (Hollow Building). Tile (Fire Clay, not glazed or enameled). In straight or mixed carloads. Also Clay (Fire), in straight carloads or mixed with Fire Brick. Fire Clay Flattening Blocks. Silica Brick. Tank Tile or Blocks. Ground Gannister. Furnace Tile or Blocks. In straight carloads or mixed with Fire Brick and Fire Clay. Minimum weight 50,000 pounds, except where, for carrier's convenience, a car of less capacity is furnished, in which event the marked capacity of car, but not less than actual weight, will govern (except as otherwise shown). Note.—Under such circumstances billing to carry certificate over agent's signature, "Car of greater capacity not available." *Rates on Drain Tile, in straight carloads, minimum weight 30,000 pounds, will be one (1) cent per 100 pounds higher than rates named herein on Brick, C. L., except as otherwise provided in the rate columns. The weight of Drain Tile when in mixed carloads with other articles named herein must not exceed 33⅓ per cent of the minimum weight provided for the mixed carload. Cancel rates on Flue Lining. Class rates will apply. Reissue. Effective January 31, 1916, in Supplement 24. Issued under authority of Rule 19 (k), Tariff Circular 18-A, and in compliance with order of the Interstate Commerce Commission in Investigation and Suspension Docket 606, of December 8, 1915. Cancel. Rates on Hollow Building Tile apply. Applies from Fort Dodge, Iowa, only.
6	Marked Capacity Length, Cubical Capacity, Dimensions, Etc., of Freight Cars	For marked capacity, length, dimensions and cubical capacity of freight cars, see the Official Railway Equipment Register. Agent G. P. Conard's I. C. C.-R. E. R. 46 or reissues. Reissue. Effective August 12, 1916, in Supplement 31.
7-A Cancels 7	Table of Distances	Cancel. Reissue. Effective January 15, 1918, in Supplement 43.
♦8	Rules for Constructing Combination Rates	Except as otherwise indicated, rates in carloads on Brick (except Enameled or Glazed) and articles taking Brick rates, and Stone, are subject to the rules for constructing combination rates as provided in Agent Eugene Morris' Freight Tariff I. C. C. U. S. 1, supplements thereto or reissues thereof. Effective July 21, 1919, in Supplement 46.

SECTION No. 1

Rates named below cancel rates named in original tariff or previous supplements opposite the same index numbers

Index Nos.	BETWEEN	AND Chicago, Ill. (Group 1) Rates in Cents per 100 Pounds		Index Nos.	BETWEEN	AND Chicago, Ill. (Group 1) Rates in Cents per 100 Pounds		Index Nos.	BETWEEN	AND Chicago, Ill. (Group 1) Rates in Cents per 100 Pounds	
		(68)	(69)			(68)	(69)			(68)	(69)
	Chicago Great Western R. R.				Chicago Great Western R. R. Continued				Chicago Great Western R. R. Concluded		
3	Forest Park ... Ill.	2.1	2	35	Sycamore ... Ill.	3.7	3.5	62	*Bruceville ... Ill.	5.3	5
5	Maywood ... "	2.1	2					63	Bolton ... "	5.3	5
7	Bellewood ... "	2.1	2	37	De Kalb ... "	3.7	3.5	65	Pearl City ... "	5.3	5
9	Elmhurst ... "	2.6	2.5					67	Kent ... "	5.3	5
13	Villa Park ... "	2.6	2.5	39	*Five Points ... "	3.7	3.5	69	Stockton ... "	5.3	5
15	Lombard ... "	2.6	2.5	41	Wilkinson ... "	3.7	3.5	71	Woodbine ... "	5.3	5
17	North Glen Ellyn ... "	2.6	2.5	43	Clare ... "	3.7	3.5	73	Elizabeth ... "	5.3	5
19	Gretna ... "	2.6	2.5	45	Esmond ... "	3.7	3.5	75	North Hanover ... "	5.3	5
21	Ingalton ... "	2.6	2.5	47	Lindenwood ... "	3.7	3.5	77	Rodden ... "	5.3	5
23	St. Charles ... "	2.6	2.5	49	Holcomb ... "	3.7	3.5	79	*Winston ... "	5.3	5
25	*West St. Charles ... "	2.6	2.5	51	Stillman Valley ... "	3.7	3.5	80	*Rice ... "	5.3	5
27	Wasco ... "	3.7	3.5	53	Byron ... "	3.7	3.5	81	*Aiken ... "	5.3	5
29	Lily Lake ... "	3.7	3.5	55	Myrtle ... "	4.2	4	83	Galena Junction ... "	5.3	5
31	Virgil ... "	3.7	3.5	57	Egan ... "	4.2	4		Hanover Railway		
33	Richardson ... "	3.7	3.5	59	German Valley ... "	4.2	4				
34	*Lovell's Crossing ...	3.7	3.5	61	South Freeport ... "	4.2	4	697	Hanover ... Ill.	5.3	5

Reissue. Effective January 15, 1918, in Supplement 43.

*No Agent. Charges must be prepaid. ♦Indicates reduction.

(68) Minimum weight of not less than 50,000 pounds, except where for carrier's convenience cars of lower capacities are furnished, in which event actual weight, but not less than 40,000 pounds will be applied. Reissue. Effective February 1, 1917, in Supplement 36.

(69) On Minnesota Intrastate traffic minimum weight of 40,000 pounds applies when in straight carloads.

(68) Applies only on Intrastate shipments of articles, except Brick, named in Item No. 4-M or reissues as applicable between points in Territory A.

(69) Applies only on Intrastate shipments of Brick.

CGW published a revised rate schedule on shipping brick between Chicago and other Illinois stations in supplement No. 41 to tariff 15-B, effective July 21, 1919. The list of stations indicates no agent at West St. Charles, Lovell's Crossing, Five Points, Bruceville, Winston, Rice, and Aiken. Therefore, charges had to be prepaid when shipping to these points. (Author's collection.)

This is a 1914 advertisement on CGW fast freight service. Railroads had to offer this type of service to meet shipper demands. For example, in 1911, the railroads lengthened transit times between Chicago and western cities from second-morning delivery to third after the ICC refused to allow an increase in freight rates. Chicago merchants and produce dealers quickly lodged a strenuous protest and vowed to boycott any road that failed to resume second-morning service. The railroads held firm, but their resolve ended several months later when CGW decided to comply with shipper demands and reinstated second-morning service. (Author's collection.)

THROUGH FAST FREIGHT SERVICE

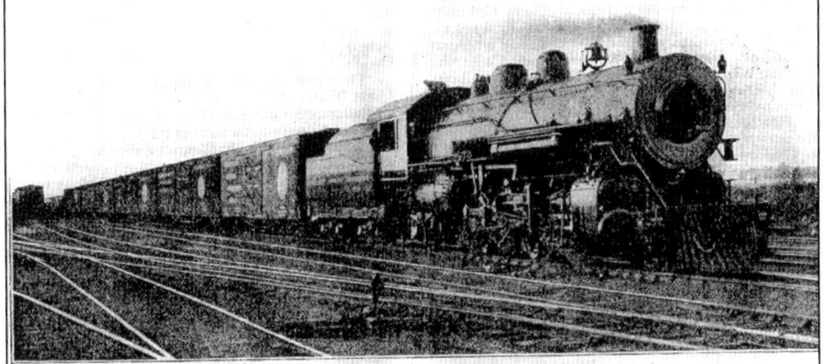

BETWEEN

NORTH AND SOUTH

NORTHBOUND

Leave KANSAS CITY..........6.25 P.M.
Arrive ST. PAUL................7.00 A.M.
Arrive MINNEAPOLIS.........11.00 A.M.

Time in transit—
To St. Paul, 36 hours, 35 minutes.
To Minneapolis, 40 hours, 35 minutes.

SOUTHBOUND

Leave MINNEAPOLIS..........6.00 P.M.
Leave ST. PAUL...............11.00 P.M.
Arrive KANSAS CITY..........5.20 A.M.

Time in transit—
From Minneapolis, 59 hours, 20 minutes.
From St. Paul, 54 hours, 20 minutes.

These expedited through trains offer unexcelled service for the handling of perishable freight and other commodities in both carload and less than carload quantities, between points in the South and Southwest and points in Minnesota, the Dakotas, Montana, North Pacific Coast States and the Canadian Northwest. The exchange of commodities between these sections is rapidly increasing, and the needs of this traffic for a prompt through service have been anticipated by this Company in the arrangement of its schedules between the southwest Missouri River Crossings and the Twin Cities.

BETWEEN

EAST AND WEST

Fast freight trains are operated daily in both directions between Chicago and the Missouri River and the Twin Cities, handling carload and less than carload traffic.

WESTBOUND: Trains depart from Chicago at 7.00 P. M., arriving St. Joseph at 6.30 A. M. Leavenworth 11.30 A. M., Kansas City 2.00 P. M. Council Bluffs 4.30 P.M., and St. Paul 2.00 P.M. of the second day. Deliveries in Omaha and Minneapolis are made immediately following arrival of trains at Council Bluffs and St. Paul respectively.

EASTBOUND: Trains leave Kansas City at 6.25 P.M., Leavenworth 8.15 P.M., St. Joseph 10.50 P.M., Council Bluffs 9.00 P. M., and St. Paul 11.00 P.M., reaching Chicago 6.00 A.M. of the second day.

Close connections are made at Chicago with lines operating to the East, Southeast and South, and at the Missouri River and St. Paul with lines operating in all directions, insuring the prompt interchange of through traffic and its expeditious movement.

Details concerning service, rates or other information will be furnished by any of the Company's representatives whose names and addresses appear on page 4, or by

OSCAR TOWNSEND, General Freight Agent,
1129 Peoples Gas Building,
CHICAGO, ILL.

FREIGHT SCHEDULES

From Chicago

To

Stations	Lv/Ar	Train	Time	Day	Lv/Ar	Train	Time	Day
Chicago	Lv	143	7 00	0	Lv	91	11 00	0
Bellwood	Lv	143	7 55	0	Lv	91	12 15	1
Ingalton	Lv	143	8 40	0	Lv	91	1 10	1
Sycamore	Lv	143	9 25	0	Lv	91	2 00	1
South Freeport	Lv	143	11 30	0	Lv	91	3 35	1
Galena Junction	Lv	143	1 15	0	Lv	91	5 15	1
Dubuque	Lv	143	1 45	0	Lv	91	5 45	1
Oelwein	Ar	143	4 15	0	Ar	91	8 15	1
Oelwein	Lv	42	6 00	0	Lv	92	8 30	1
McIntire	Lv	42	9 20	0	Lv	92	11 15	1
Hayfield	Lv	42	11 15	0	Lv	92	1 00	1
Randolph	Ar	42	1 45	1	Ar	92	3 15	1
South Saint Paul	Ar	42	2 45	1	Ar	92	4 25	1
Saint Paul	Ar	42	3 00	1	Ar	92	4 45	1
Oelwein	Lv	43	8 00	0	Lv	41	11 00	1
Waterloo	Ar	43	9 30	0	Ar	41	12 45	1
Marshalltown	Ar	43	12 01	1	Ar	41	2 55	1
Des Moines	Ar	43	2 20	1	Ar	41	5 15	1
Des Moines	Lv	43	3 20	1	Lv	41	6 15	1
Conception	Lv	43	8 00	1	Lv	41	11 20	1
Saint Joseph	Ar	43	10 10	1	Ar	41	12 30	2
Kansas City	Ar	43	2 00	1	Ar	41	4 00	2
Oelwein					Lv	91	4 00	1
Waverly					Lv	91	5 10	1
Hampton					Lv	91	6 50	1
Clarion					Ar	91	8 10	1
Fort Dodge					Ar	91	9 05	1
Council Bluffs					Ar	91	2 00	2

From Minneapolis-St. Paul

To

Stations	Lv/Ar	Train	Time	Day	Lv/Ar	Train	Time	Day
St. Paul	Lv	43	6 00	0	Lv	41	4 45	0
So. St. Paul	Lv	43	6 30	0	Lv	41	5 30	0
Randolph	Lv	43	8 15	0	Lv	41	7 01	0
Hayfield	Lv	43	11 00	0	Lv	41	8 55	0
McIntire	Lv	43	12 15	0	Lv	41	10 40	0
Oelwein	Ar	43	3 00	0	Ar	41	1 00	1
Oelwein	Lv	90	4 00	0	Lv	192	2 00	1
Dubuque	Ar	90	7 05	0	Ar	192	6 15	1
Galena Jct.	Lv	90	7 35	0	Lv	192	6 45	1
So. Freeport	Lv	90	9 40	0	Lv	192	8 40	1
Sycamore	Lv	90	11 20	0	Lv	192	10 13	1
Ingalton	Ar	90	12 10	1	Ar	192	11 10	1
Bellwood	Ar	90	1 00	1	Ar	192	12 10	1
Chicago	Ar	90	1 45	1	Ar	192	1 00	1
Oelwein	Lv	43	8 00	0	Lv	41	11 00	1
Waterloo	Ar	43	9 30	0	Ar	41	12 45	1
Marshalltown	Ar	43	12 01	1	Ar	41	2 55	1
Des Moines	Ar	43	2 20	1	Ar	41	5 15	1
Des Moines	Lv	43	3 20	1	Lv	41	6 15	1
Conception	Lv	43	8 00	1	Lv	41	11 20	1
St. Joseph	Ar	43	10 10	1	Ar	41	12 30	2
Kansas City	Ar	43	2 00	1	Ar	41	4 00	2
Oelwein	Lv	91	4 00	0				
Waverly	Lv	91	5 10	0				
Hampton	Lv	91	6 50	0				
Clarion	Ar	91	8 10	0				
Fort Dodge	Ar	91	9 05	0				
Council Bluffs	Ar	91	2 00	1				

From Kansas City

To

Stations	Lv/Ar	Train	Time	Day	Lv/Ar	Train	Time	Day
Kansas City	Lv	92	7 00	0	Lv	42	7 00	0
St. Joseph	Lv	92	10 10	0	Lv	42	10 30	0
Conception	Lv	92	11 35	0	Lv	42	12 15	1
Des Moines	Ar	92	3 45	0	Ar	42	4 30	1
Des Moines	Lv	92	5 30	0	Lv	42	5 15	1
Marshalltown	Ar	92	8 20	0	Ar	42	8 15	1
Waterloo	Ar	92	11 00	0	Ar	42	10 45	1
Oelwein	Ar	92	12 15	1	Ar	42	11 59	1
Oelwein	Lv	92	8 30	1	Lv	42	6 00	1
McIntire	Lv	92	11 15	1	Lv	42	9 20	1
Hayfield	Lv	92	1 00	1	Lv	42	11 15	1
Randolph	Ar	92	3 15	1	Ar	42	1 45	2
So. St. Paul	Ar	92	4 25	1	Ar	42	2 45	2
St. Paul	Ar	92	4 45	1	Ar	42	3 00	2
Oelwein	Lv	192	2 00	1	Lv	90	4 00	1
Dubuque	Ar	192	6 15	1	Ar	90	7 05	1
Galena Jct.	Lv	192	6 45	1	Lv	90	7 35	1
So. Freeport	Lv	192	8 40	1	Lv	90	9 40	1
Sycamore	Lv	192	10 13	1	Lv	90	11 20	1
Ingalton	Ar	192	11 10	1	Ar	90	12 10	2
Bellwood	Ar	192	12 10	1	Ar	90	1 00	2
Chicago	Ar	192	1 00	1	Ar	90	1 45	2
Oelwein					Lv	91	4 00	1
Waverly					Lv	91	5 10	1
Hampton					Lv	91	6 50	1
Clarion					Ar	91	8 10	1
Fort Dodge					Ar	91	9 05	1
Council Bluffs					Ar	91	2 00	2

SHIP VIA CHICAGO GREAT WESTERN RAILWAY

A.M. Figures Light
P.M. Figures Dark

Further details may be secured from traffic representatives listed herein.

From Omaha-Council Bluffs

To

Stations	Lv/Ar	Train	Time	Day
Council Bluffs	Lv	90	7 00	0
Fort Dodge	Ar	90	12 00	0
Clarion	Ar	90	12 55	0
Hampton	Ar	90	1 55	0
Waverly	Ar	90	3 25	0
Oelwein	Ar	90	4 00	0
Oelwein	Lv	90	4 00	0
Dubuque	Ar	90	7 05	0
Galena Jct.	Ar	90	7 35	0
So. Freeport	Lv	90	9 40	0
Sycamore	Lv	90	11 20	0
Ingalton	Ar	90	12 10	1
Bellwood	Ar	90	1 00	1
Chicago	Ar	90	1 45	1
Oelwein	Lv	42	6 00	0
McIntire	Lv	42	9 20	0
Hayfield	Lv	42	11 15	0
Randolph	Ar	42	1 45	1
So. St. Paul	Ar	42	2 45	1
St. Paul	Ar	42	3 00	1
Oelwein	Lv	43	8 00	0
Waterloo	Ar	43	9 30	0
Marshalltown	Ar	43	12 01	1
Des Moines	Ar	43	2 20	1
Des Moines	Lv	43	3 20	1
Conception	Lv	43	8 00	1
St. Joseph	Ar	43	10 10	1
Kansas City	Ar	43	2 00	1

Shown is a CGW freight schedule effective April 27, 1952. The company completed an extensive rehabilitation program during the early 1950s to modernize freight operations in conjunction with dieselization. The capacity of the classification yard at Oelwein was increased to 3,000 cars when rebuilt in 1952. (Author's collection.)

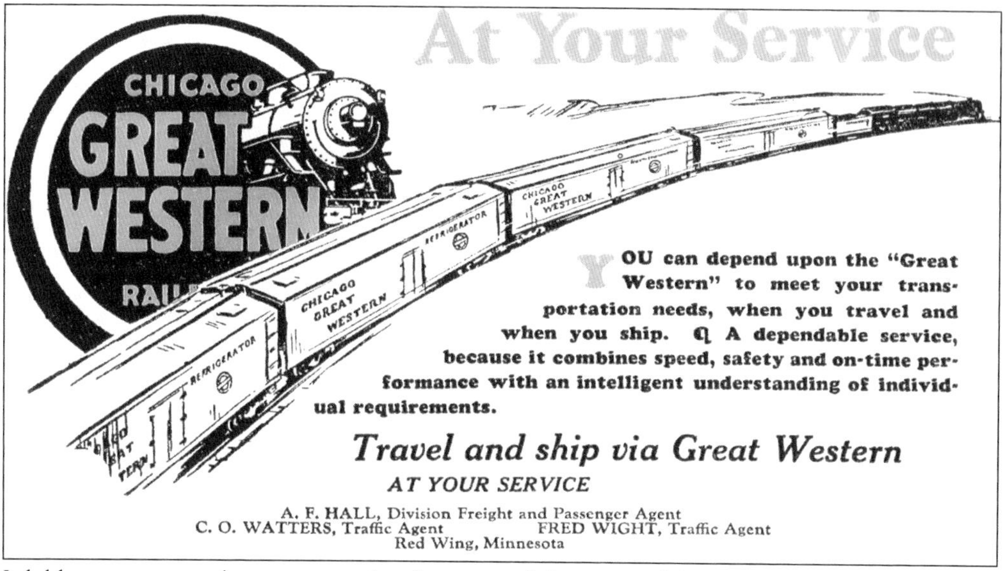

Ink blotters were used years ago to absorb excess ink from pens. Many companies used them as a form of advertising, such as this particular blotter provided to CGW patrons as a reminder that the company was "At Your Service." (Author's collection.)

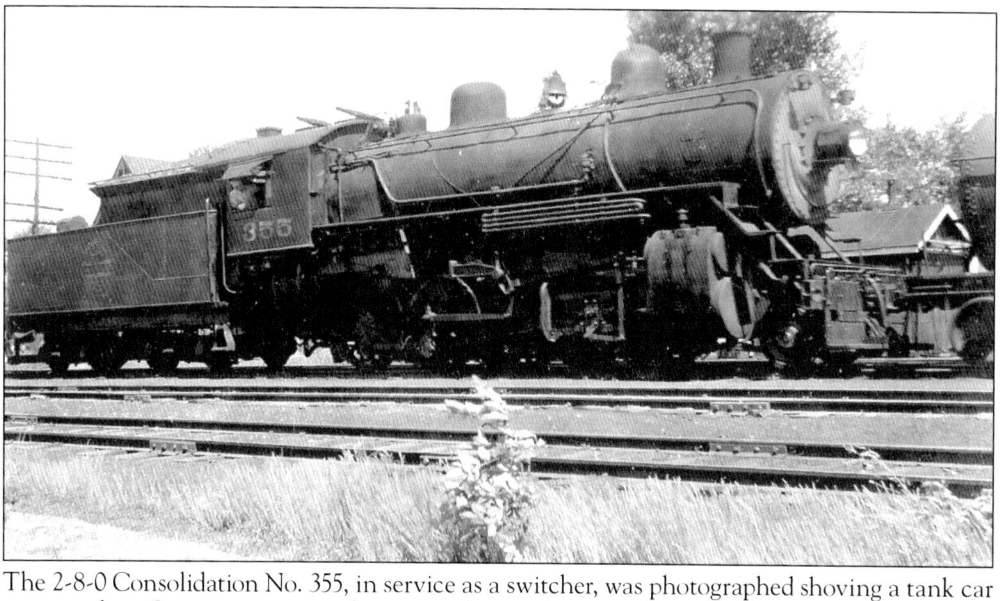

The 2-8-0 Consolidation No. 355, in service as a switcher, was photographed shoving a tank car onto a siding. Spotting cars at industries and interchanges required skill and careful handling. Sometimes other cars had to be moved out of the way in order to get to one car. Also, industry sidings were not always well maintained, and it was not unusual to end up derailing a car while moving it along an old rusty spur track. (Author's collection.)

This list of junction points was published in 1914 to show travelers where they could make connections with other railroads. The information was also useful to identify track connections with other railroads for the interchange of freight cars. (Author's collection.)

Junction Points and Track Connections

POP.	Junction	Connections	
....	AFTON JCT., IOWA	*C. B. & Q. R. R.	U
6,960	AUSTIN, MINN.	C. M. & St. P. Ry	T
....	BEE CREEK, MO.	A. T. & S. F. Ry	U
200	BELLEWOOD, ILL.	Ind. Harbor R. R.	T
1,224	BELMOND, IOWA	C. R. I. & P. Ry. and M. & St.L. R.R.	T
....	BENNING, MINN	C. M. & St. P. Ry	U
932	BYRON, ILL.	C. M. & St. P. Ry	T
1,875	CANNON FALLS, MINN.	*C. M. & St. P. Ry	T
3,546	CARROLL, IOWA	C. & N. W. Ry	T
5,012	CEDAR FALLS, IOWA	Ill. Cent. R.R. and C.R.I.&P.Ry., W.C.F. & N.Ry.	T
2,185,283	CHICAGO, ILL.	Lines diverging	U and T
2,065	CLARION, IOWA	C. R. I. & P. Ry	T
865	CLARKSVILLE, IOWA	C. R. I. & P. Ry	T
....	CLEAR LAKE JCT., IOWA	St. P. & D.M.R.R. and M.C. & C.L. Ry. (electric)	U
150	CONCEPTION, MO.	Wabash R. R.	U
29,292	COUNCIL BLUFFS, IOWA	Ill. Cent. R. R., U. P. R. R., C. & N. W. Ry., C. M. & ST. P. Ry., C. B. & Q. R. R., C. R. I. & P. Ry. and Wabash R. R.	T
775	DEARBORN, MO.	*C. R. I. & P. Ry	T
8,112	DE KALB, ILL.	C. M. & G. Ry	A
		C. & N. W. Ry	T
86,368	DES MOINES, IOWA	Wabash R. R., M. & St.L. R. R., C. B. & Q. R.R. and C. M. & St. P. Ry	U
		C. R. I. & P. Ry., C. & N. W. Ry., St. P. & D. M. R. R., Inter-Urban and Ft. D. D. M. & S. R. R.	T
509	DIAGONAL, IOWA	C. B. & Q. R. R.	T
1,025	DODGE CENTER, MINN.	C. & N. W. Ry	U
38,494	DUBUQUE, IOWA	C.B.&Q.R.R., Ill.Cent.R.R. and C.M.&St.P.Ry	T
550	DUMONT, IOWA	*C. & N. W. Ry	T
450	DUNDAS, MINN.	C. M. & St. P. Ry. and C. R. I. & P. Ry	T
1,511	DYERSVILLE, IOWA	Ill. Cent. R. R.	T
3,387	EAGLE GROVE, IOWA	C. & N. W. Ry	T
2,360	ELMHURST, ILL.	Ill. Cent. R. R.	T
9,001	FARIBAULT, MINN.	C. M. & St. P. Ry and C. R. I. & P. Ry	T
678	FARLEY, IOWA	*Ill. Cent. R. R. and C. M. & St. P. Ry	T
6,594	FOREST PARK, ILL.	C. T. T. Ry. and M. St. P. & S. S. M. Ry	T
15,543	FORT DODGE, IOWA	Ill. Cent. R. R., M. & St. L. R. R. and Ft. D. D. M. & S. R. R. (electric). *Transfer of cars to Ill. Cent. R. R. and M. & St. L. R. R. made at Gypsum, 4 miles distant*	T
....	GALENA JCT., ILL.	C. B. & Q. R. R.	U
869	GLADBROOK, IOWA	C. & N. W. Ry	T
25	GYPSUM, IA.	Ill. Cent. R. R. and M. & St. L. R. R.	T
2,617	HAMPTON, IOWA	M. & St.L. R. R. and St. P. & D. M. R. R.	T
2,570	HARLAN, IOWA	C. & N. W. Ry. and C. R. I. & P. Ry	T
....	HICKS, IOWA	*C. & N. W. Ry	U
160	HOLCOMB, ILL.	C. B. & Q. R. R. and C. M. & St. P. Ry	T
50	INGALTON, ILL.	E. J. & E. Ry	T
248,381	KANSAS CITY, MO.	K.C.So.Ry., St.J.&G.I.Ry. and Q.O. & K.C.R.R.	U
		A. T. & S. F. Ry., K. C. Term. Ry., C. & A. R. R., C. R. I. & P. Ry., C. B. & Q. R. R., Frisco Ry., M. K. & T. Ry., Mo. Pac. Ry., U. P. R. R. and Wabash R. R.	T
1,650	KENYON, MINN.	*C. M. & St. P. Ry	T
928	LEHIGH, IOWA	W. C. & C. C. R. R.	T
1,025	LE ROY, MINN.	C. M. & St. P. Ry	T
750	LOMBARD, ILL.	*C. & N. W. Ry	T
674	LOHRVILLE, IOWA	*C. & N. W. Ry. and *C. M. & St. P. Ry	T
850	LYLE, MINN.	*C. M. & St. P. Ry. and Ill. Cent. R. R.	T
10,365	MANKATO, MINN.	C. M. & St. P. Ry	U
		C. & N. W. Ry. and C. St. P. M. & O. Ry	T
846	MANLY, IOWA	M. & St.L.R. R.	T
		C. R. I. & P. Ry	U
1,434	MANNING, IOWA	*C. & N. W. Ry. and *C. M. & St. P. Ry	T
13,374	MARSHALLTOWN, IOWA	C. & N. W. & Ia. Cent. Ry	T
11,230	MASON CITY, IOWA	St. P. & D. M. Ry	U
		C. & N. W. Ry., C. M. & St. P. Ry., M. & St.L. and M. C. & C. L. Ry	T
8,682	MAYWOOD, ILL.	*C. & N. W. Ry	T
423	MELBOURNE, IOWA	C. M. & St. P. Ry	T
423	MINDEN, IOWA	*C. R. I. & P. Ry	T
301,408	MINNEAPOLIS, MINN.	Lines diverging	U and T
208	MINNESOTA CITY, MINN.	*C. M. & St. P. Ry. and C. & N. W. Ry	T
177	MOORLAND, IOWA	M. & St. L. R. R.	T
2,275	NEW HAMPTON, IOWA	C. M. & St. P. Ry	T
3,488	NORTHFIELD, MINN.	*C. M. & St. P. Ry	T
....	NORTH HANOVER, ILL.	Hanover R. R.	U
6,028	OELWEIN, IOWA	C. R. I. & P. Ry	T
124,096	OMAHA, NEB.	C.R.I.&P.Ry., C.M.&St.P.Ry., Mo.Pac.Ry., U.P.R.R., C.&N.W.Ry., Ill.Cent.R.R., Wabash R.R. and C.St.P.M.&O.Ry.	U
		C. B. & Q. R. R.	T
200	ONEIDA, IOWA	C. M. & St. P.	T
		M. & O. Ry	U
2,445	OSAGE, IOWA	Ill. Cent. R. R.	T
1,125	PINE ISLAND, MINN.	*C. & N. W. Ry	T
250	RANDOLPH, MINN.	*C. M. & St. P. Ry	T
9,048	RED WING, MINN.	C. M. & St. P. Ry	T
1,205	REINBECK, IOWA	C. R. I. & P. Ry	T
200	RINARD, IOWA	Ft. D. D. M. & S. Ry	U
7,844	ROCHESTER, MINN.	C. & N. W. Ry	T
256	ROWAN, IOWA	C. R. I. & P. Ry	T
1,886	SAVANNAH, MO.	*C. B. & Q. R. R.	T
....	SO. FREEPORT, ILL.	Ill. Cent. R. R.	T
169	SOMERS, IOWA	C. R. I. & P. Ry	T
1,925	SPRING VALLEY, MINN.	*C. M. & St. P. Ry	T
1,575	ST. CHARLES, MINN.	*C. & N. W. Ry	T
500	STILLMAN VALLEY, ILL.	*C. M. & St. P. Ry	T
77,403	ST. JOSEPH, MO.	A. T. & S. F. Ry., C. R. I. & P. Ry., C. B. & Q. R. R., Mo. Pac. Ry. and St. J. & G. I. Ry	U
214,744	ST. PAUL, MINN.	G. N. Ry., N. P. Ry., C. M. & St. P. Ry., C. St. P. M. & O. Ry., C. B. & Q. R. R., M. St. P. & S. S. M. Ry., M. & St. L. R. R. and C. R. I. & P. Ry	U
3,659	SYCAMORE, ILL.	C. & N. W. Ry	T
180	TAOPI, MINN.	*C. M. & St. P. Ry	T
250	VALERIA, IOWA	C. N. R. R.	U
104	WATERFORD, MINN.	C. M. & St. P. Ry	T
26,693	WATERLOO, IA. (eastside)	Ill. Cent. R. R. and W. C. F. & N. Ry	T
26,693	WATERLOO, IA. (westside)	W. C. F. & N. Ry	T
		C. R. I. & P. Ry	U
1,475	WATERVILLE, MINN.	M. & St. L. R. R.	T
3,205	WAVERLY, IOWA	Ill. Cent. R. R. and *C. R. I. & P. Ry	T
....	WILKINSON, ILL.	C. M. & G. R. R.	U
18,583	WINONA, MINN.	C. M. & St. P. Ry	U
		G. B. & W. R. R., C. & N. W. Ry. and C. B. & Q. R. R.	T
1,800	ZUMBROTA, MINN.	C. & N. W. Ry. and C. M. & St. P. Ry	T

(U) Union Depot. (T) Transfer necessary. (*) No track connections. (A) Adjacent.

CHICAGO GREAT WESTERN RAILWAY

ALPHABETICAL LIST OF JUNCTIONS AT WHICH

FREIGHT TRAFFIC

MAY BE DIRECTLY INTERCHANGED WITH CONNECTING LINES (Except as noted)

JUNCTIONS	CONNECTING LINES (See bottom of page for Explanation of Numbers)
Austin, Minn.	17.
Bellwood, Ill.	2, 3, 7, 8, 9, 11, 13, 14, 15, 17, 21, 23, 24, 25, 29, 32, 35, 36, 38, 51, 55, 56, 58, 59, 60, 68 (via I. H. B.)
Belmond, Iowa	21, 47.
Beverly, Mo.	14.
Byron, Ill.	17.
Cannon Falls, Minn.	17.
Carroll, Iowa	11.
Cedar Falls, Iowa	21, 36, 69.
Chicago, Ill.	2, 3, 4, 5, 7, 8, 9, 10, 11, 12, 14, 15, 16, 17, 19, 20, 21, 23, 24, 25, 29, 32, 35, 36, 37, 46, 51, 55, 56, 58, 59, 60, 68.
Clarion, Iowa	21.
Clarksville, Iowa	21.
Conception, Mo.	68.
Council Bluffs, Iowa	11, 14, 17, 21, 36, 66, 58.
DeKalb, Ill.	11, 17.
Des Moines, Iowa	11, 14, 17, 21, 26, 27, 31, 47, 68.
Dodge Center, Minn.	11.
Dubuque, Iowa	14, 17, 30, 36.
Dyersville, Iowa	36.
Eagle Grove, Iowa	11.
Elmhurst, Ill.	36.

JUNCTIONS	CONNECTING LINES (See bottom of page for Explanation of Numbers)
Faribault, Minn.	17, 21.
Fort Dodge, Iowa	31, 36, 47.
Galena Junction, Ill.	14.
Gladbrook, Iowa	11.
Hampton, Iowa	21, 47.
Harlan, Iowa	11, 21.
Holcomb, Ill.	14, 17.
Ingalton, Ill.	2, 3, 7, 9, 11, 14, 15, 17, 18, 21, 28, 32, 35, 36, 51, 55, 56, 58, 59, 60, 68 (via E. J. & E.)
Kansas City, Kan.	2, 21, 39, 41, 42, 43, 53, 54, 54, 55.
Kansas City, Mo.	2, 14, 17, 21, 30, 35, 40, 42, 43, 53, 54, 64, 66, 68.
Leavenworth, Kan.	2, 14, 54, 66.
Le Roy, Minn.	17.
Lyle, Minn.	17, 36.
Mankato, Minn.	11, 17, 22.
Manly, Iowa	21, 47.
Marshalltown, Iowa	11, 47.
Mason City, Iowa	11, 17, 21, 45, 47.
Melbourne, Iowa	17.
Minneapolis, Minn.	6, 14, 17, 21, 22, 30, 33, 47, 48, 49, 50, 51, 52, 57, 61.
Minnesota Transfer, Minn.	14, 17, 21, 22, 33, 47, 51, 57.
Moorland, Iowa	47.

JUNCTIONS	CONNECTING LINES (See bottom of page for Explanation of Numbers)
New Hampton, Iowa	17.
Northfield, Minn.	17, 21.
Oelwein, Iowa	21.
Omaha, Neb.	11, 14, 17, 21, 22, 36, 54, 66, 68 (via UP).
Osage, Iowa	36.
Randolph, Minn.	50.
Red Wing, Minn.	17.
Reinbeck, Iowa	21.
Rinard, Iowa	31.
Rochester, Minn.	11.
Rowan, Iowa	21.
St. Joseph, Mo.	2, 14, 21, 54, 62, 63, 66, 67.
St. Paul, Minn.	6, 14, 17, 21, 22, 30, 33, 47, 51, 57.
Somers, Iowa	21.
South Freeport, Ill. (Dunbar)	36.
South Omaha, Neb.	11, 14, 17, 21, 22, 36, 54, 65, 66, 68.
South St. Paul, Minn.	21.
Sycamore, Ill.	11.
Waterloo, Iowa	21, 36, 69.
Waterville, Minn.	47.
Waverly, Iowa	36, 69.
Winona, Minn.	11, 14, 17, 34.
Zumbrota, Minn.	17.

Interchange is made via B&OCT, BRC, CJ, CR&I, IN or IHB Bellwood or EJ&E Ingalton.
Interchanged direct for industries east of Cicero Ave (4800 West). For industries west of Cicero Ave. (4800 West) interchange is made via BRC.
Interchanged direct or via B&OCT, BRC, CJ, CR&I, IN or IHB Bellwood or EJ&E Ingalton.
Interchange is made via B&OCT, BRC, CJ, CR&I, IN or IHB Bellwood or EJ&E Ingalton, except on potatoes and onions consigned to the C&NW Wood St. Terminal, may be interchanged direct.
Interchange is made via B&OCT, BRC, CJ, CR&I or IHB Bellwood or EJ&E Ingalton, except perishable freight reconsigned from CGW team track may be interchanged direct at 16th St.
Interchange is made via B&OCT, BRC, CJ, CR&I or IHB Bellwood or EJ&E Ingalton.

Via B&OCT.
Via BRC.
Via B&OCT or BRC.
Via B&OCT, BRC or CJ.
Via CB&Q.
Via DMU.
Via IC.
Via FtDDM&S.
Via KCS.
Via MP.
Via GN and MStP&SSM or NP and MStP&SSM.
Via GN.
Via GN, NP or RTC.
Via CMStP&P.
Via Highland Junction, Iowa.
Via NP.
Via SOT.
Via CB&Q or CMStP&P.
Via MC&CL.
Via GN or RTC.
Via RTC.

EXPLANATION OF RAILROADS REFERRED TO ABOVE BY NUMBERS

2—AT&SF
3—B&O
4—B&OCT
5—BRC
6—CBC (Cen. Barge Co.)
7—C&O
8—C&CR
9—C&EI
10—C&IW
11—C&NW
13—CA&E
14—CB&Q
15—CI&L
16—CJ
17—CMStP&P
18—CNS&M
19—CPT (Chgo. Produce Terminal)
20—CR&I
21—CRI&P
22—CStPM&O
24—CSS&SB
25—CWP&S
26—DM&CI
27—DMU
28—EJ&E
29—Erie
30—FBL
31—FtDDM&S
32—GTW
33—GN
34—GB&W
36—IC
37—IN
38—IHB
39—K&MR&T
40—KCC
41—KCKV
42—KCS
43—KCT
45—MC&CL
46—MJ
47—M&StL
49—ME
50—MN&S
51—MStP&SSM
52—MW
53—MKT
54—MP
55—NYC
56—NYC&StL
57—NP
58—PENN
59—PM
61—RTC (Ry. Transfer Co.)
62—StJB
63—StPT
64—StL-SF
65—SOT
66—UP
67—UT
68—WAB
69—WCF&N

Interchange connections with other roads is vital because 75 percent of rail shipments involve at least two railroads. CGW published this list of junctions and connecting railroads in 1952. The company also relied upon intermediate switching roads to complete connections, such as the Indiana Harbor Belt Railroad at Bellwood, Illinois, which facilitated interchange between CGW and 26 other railroads in Chicago. (Author's collection.)

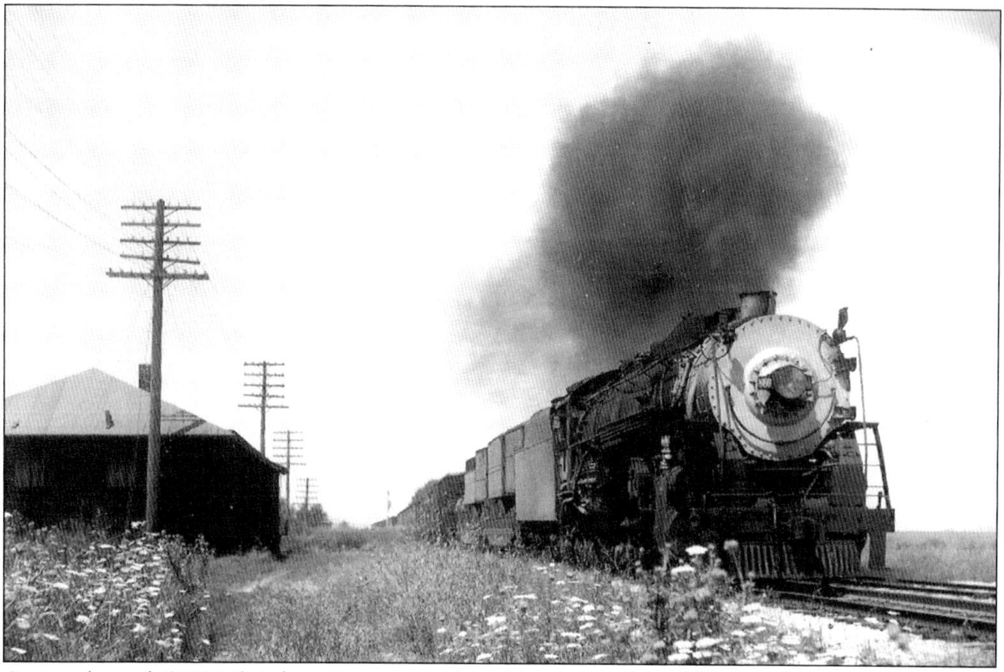

An eastbound CGW freight train powered by locomotive No. 860 is rushing past the depot at Wilkinson, Illinois, in 1935. Note the semitrailers on flatcars behind the tender. CGW was a pioneer in providing shippers with TOFC, or trailer-on-flatcar service, also referred to as "piggyback." (Joiner History Room, Sycamore, Illinois.)

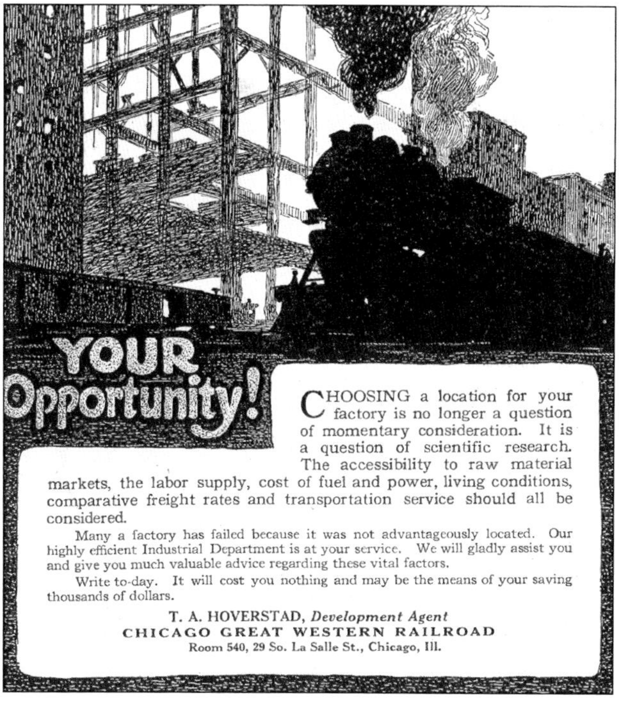

CGW established an industrial department to develop online freight business, as shown in this 1921 advertisement. Aggressive solicitation efforts resulted in hundreds of large and small businesses locating warehouses, factories, lumberyards, and bulk oil storage facilities along the CGW. (Author's collection.)

The company promoted the operation of fast freight trains and terminal facilities as incentives to ship by the CGW. Freight facilities included team tracks and warehouses at terminals and stations for receipt and delivery of shipments. (Author's collection.)

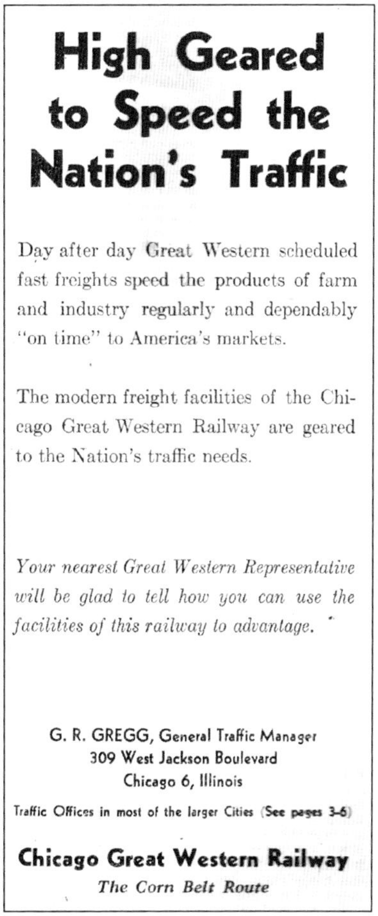

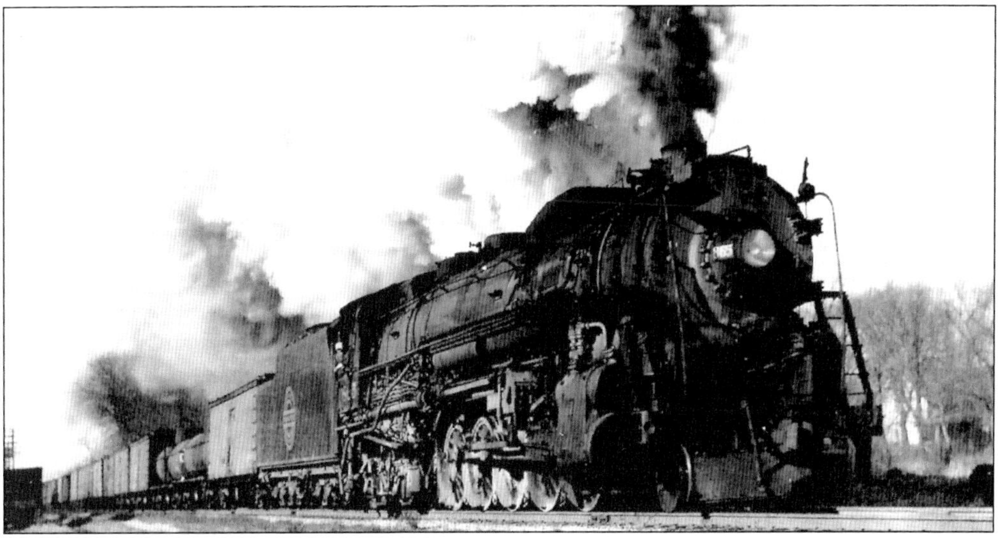

Locomotive No. 865, with engineer Herb Brown at the throttle, roars through Lombard, Illinois, with an eastbound freight train on November 7, 1940. CGW transported 6,069,807 tons of freight in 1940. (James L. Rueber.)

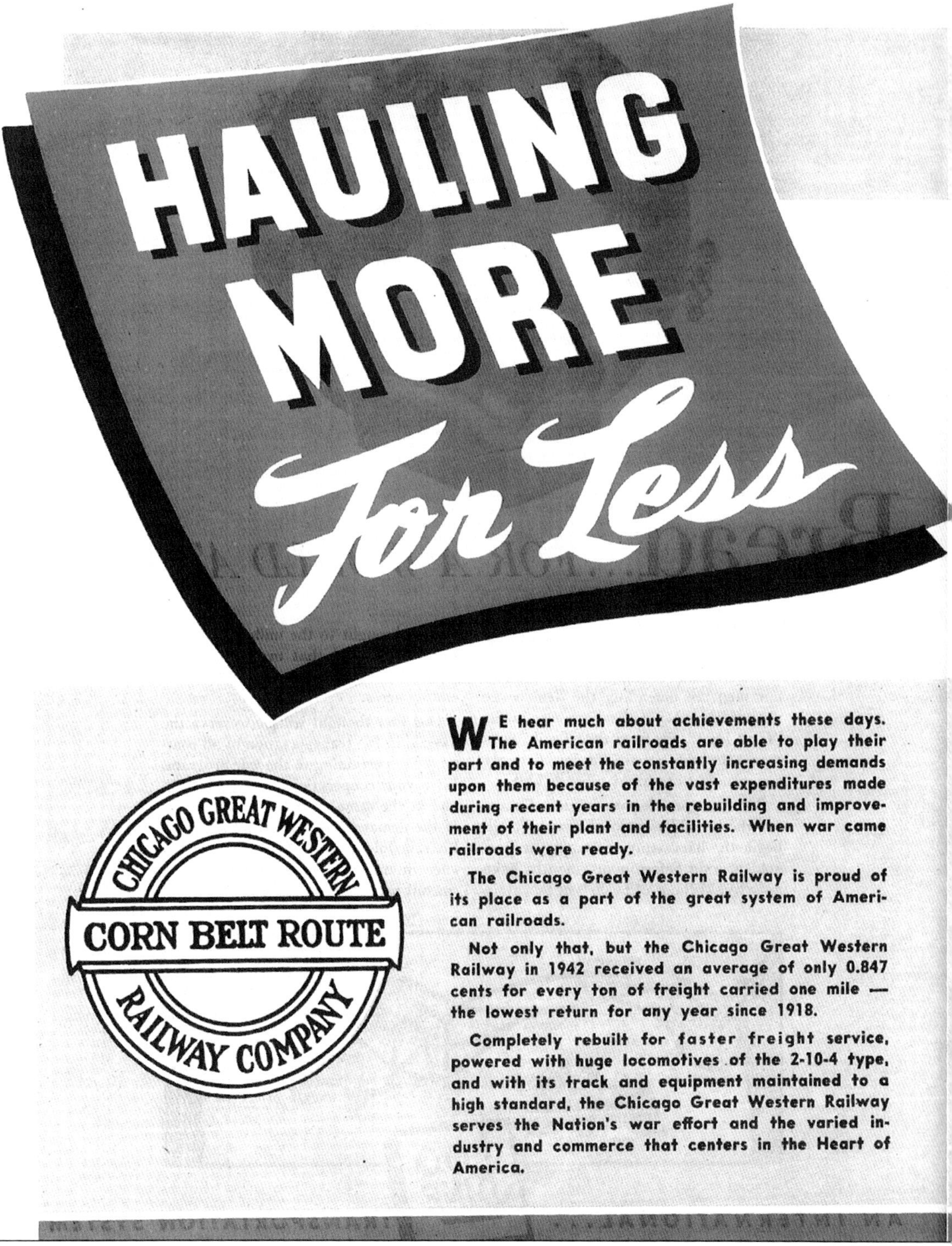

The company transported the highest volume of freight traffic in its history in 1943, when it hauled

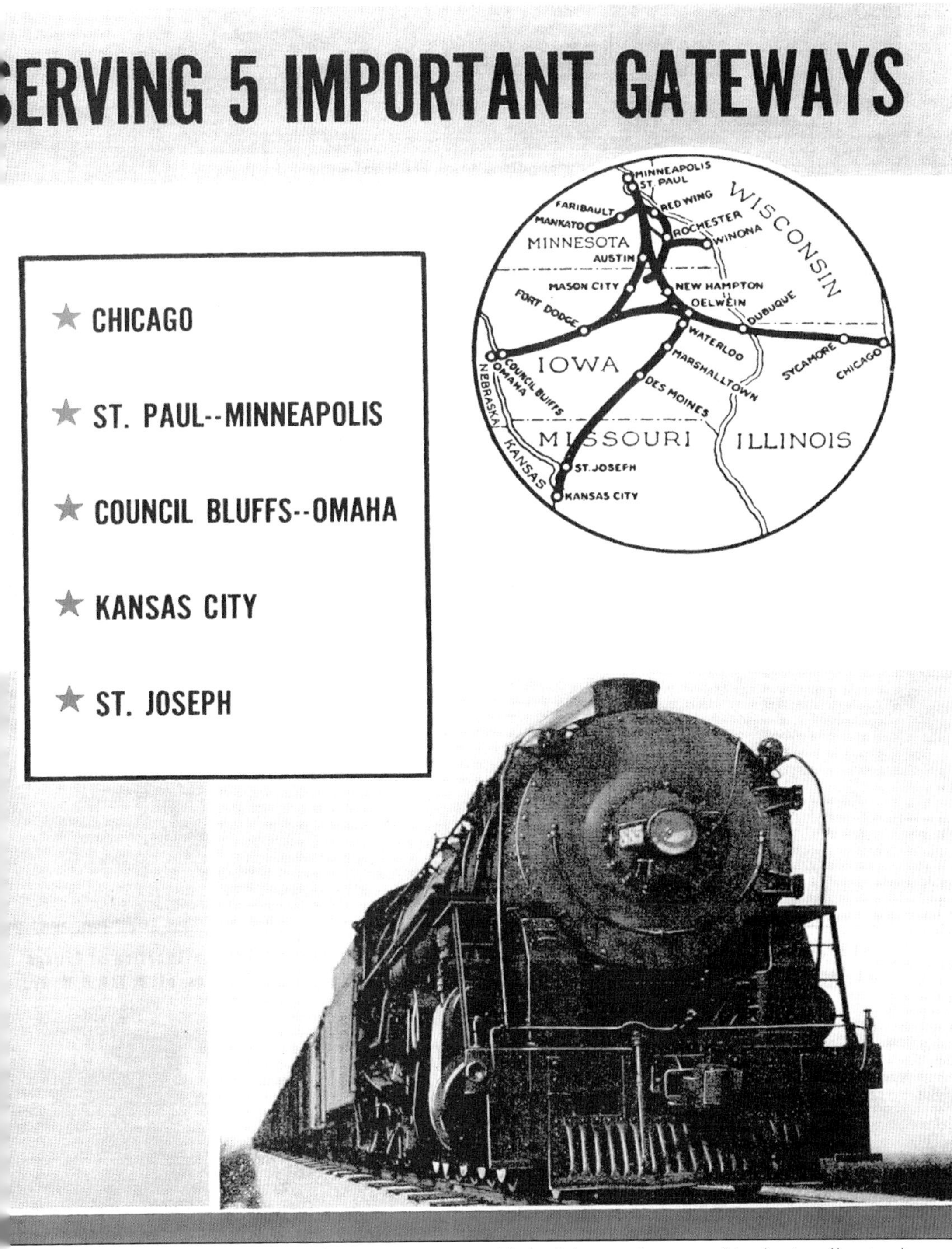

9,286,188 tons. This freight advertisement was published during that year. (Author's collection.)

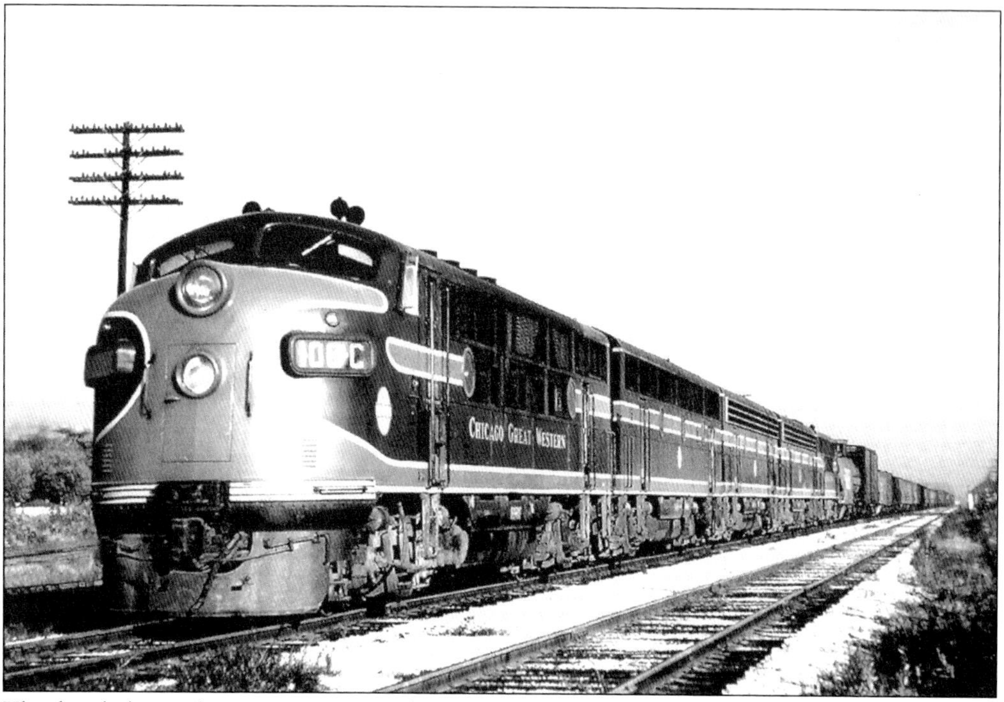

The diesel-electric locomotive possessed operating features that enabled it to move heavier trains than with steam engines. CGW took advantage of these capabilities by making up massive freight trains with as many as 275 freight cars in one train, thereby reducing the number of freight trains operated. This photograph shows one of these heavy-tonnage trains heading west through Bellwood in 1951. (Author's collection.)

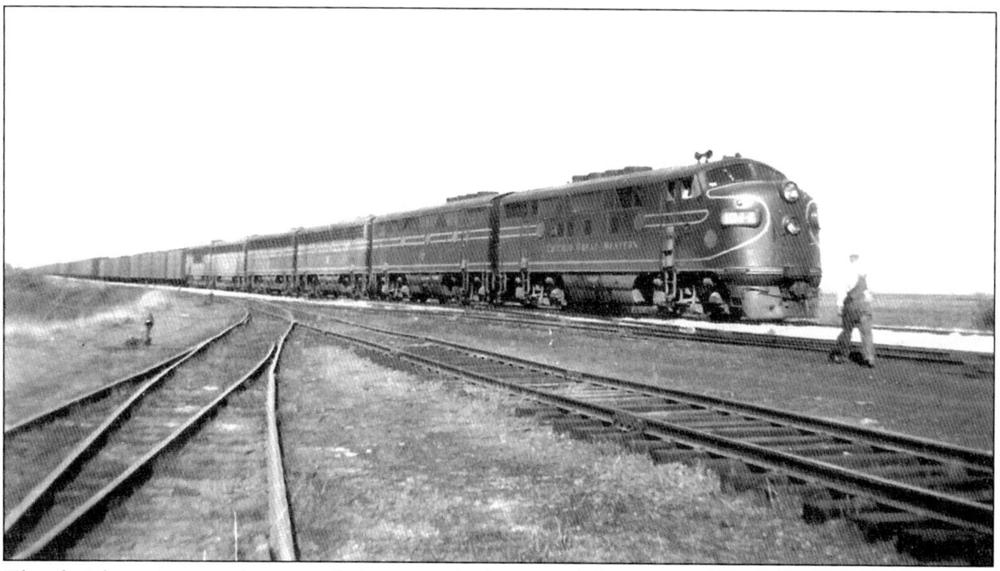

This freight train stretches out of view into the horizon. Movement of such heavy trains placed a tremendous amount of strain on couplers and required expert control of throttle and brake. The photograph was taken at Hayfield, Minnesota, in 1955. (Author's collection.)

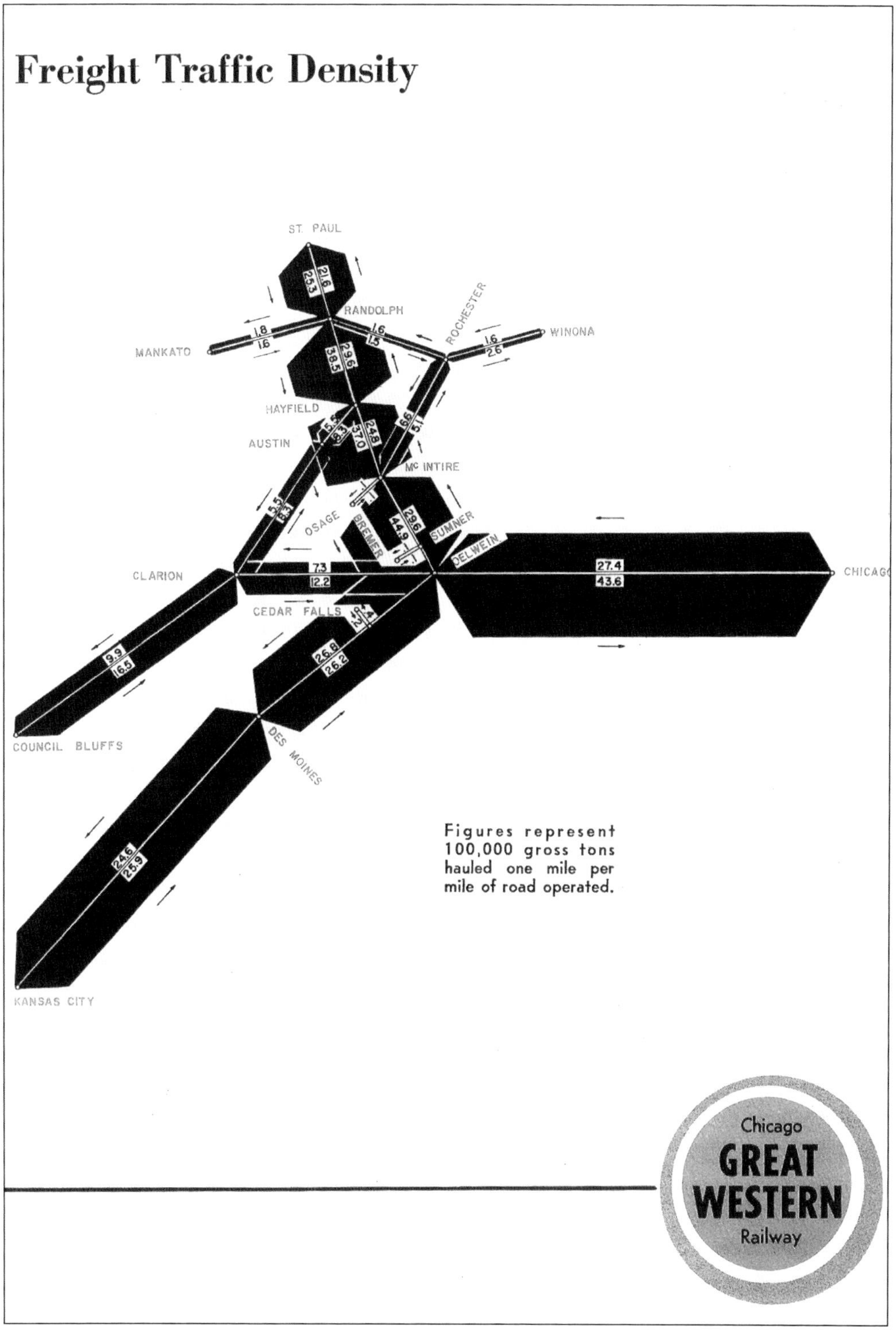

CGW published this freight traffic density map in the 1961 annual report. The main line from and to Chicago usually carried the heaviest amount of traffic, as shown. (Author's collection.)

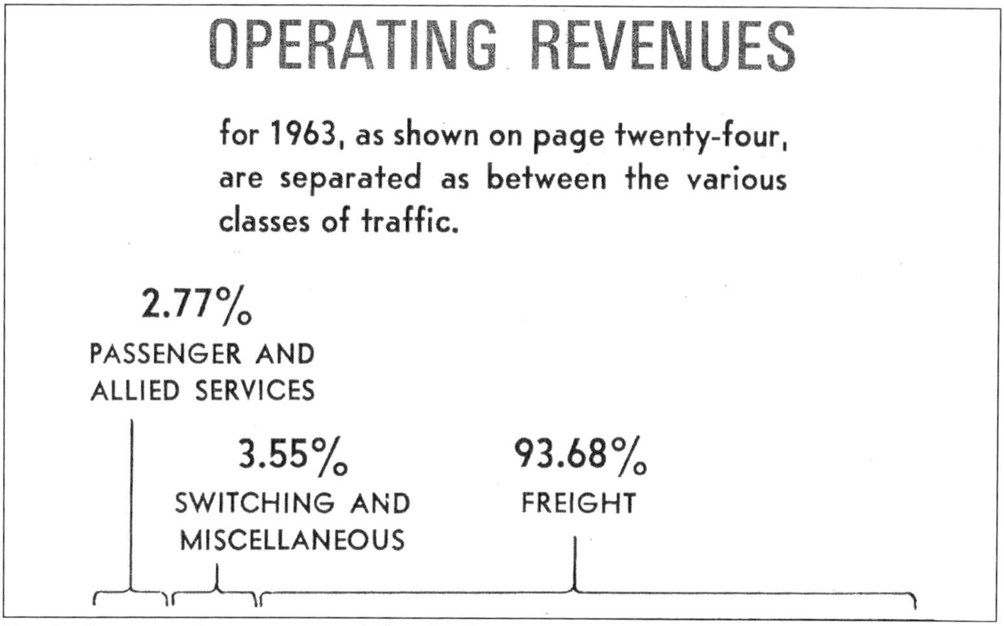

Freight business always accounted for the largest percentage of annual earnings, as shown in this graph from the 1963 annual report. The small percentage attributed to passenger service was similar for most railroads. In 1960, the railroad industry handled only 27 percent of intercity commercial passenger traffic, with the remainder divided among airlines and bus companies. (Author's collection.)

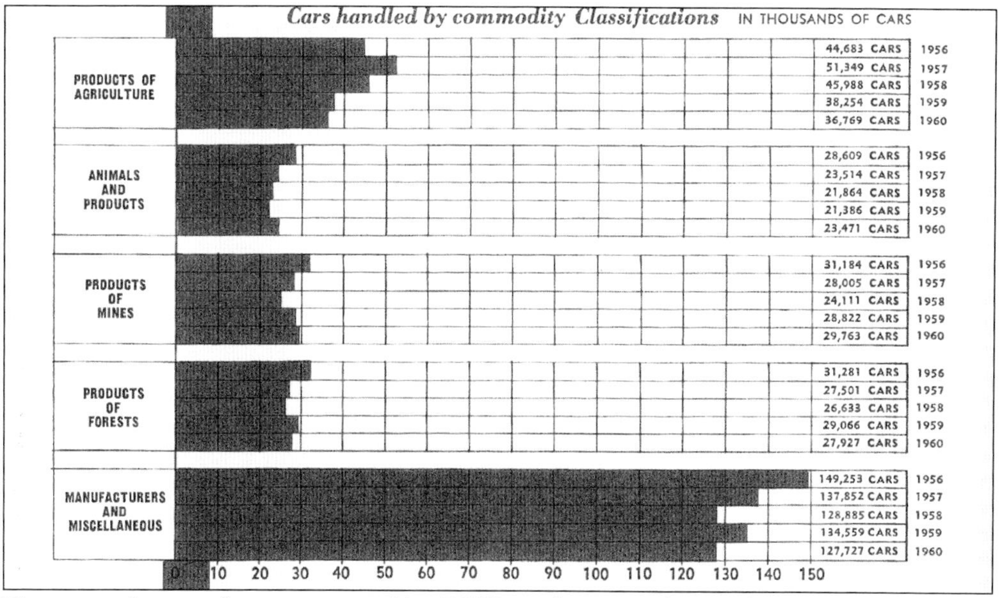

The types of commodities transported by CGW are shown on this graph published in the 1961 annual report. Products of agriculture were always an important source of business because the company served the country's breadbasket. In 1920, CGW established an agricultural development department, which solicited business from farmers and conducted institutes on better farming practices. Eighty-seven institutes were held in 1925, as an example, attended by 17,016 people. (Author's collection.)

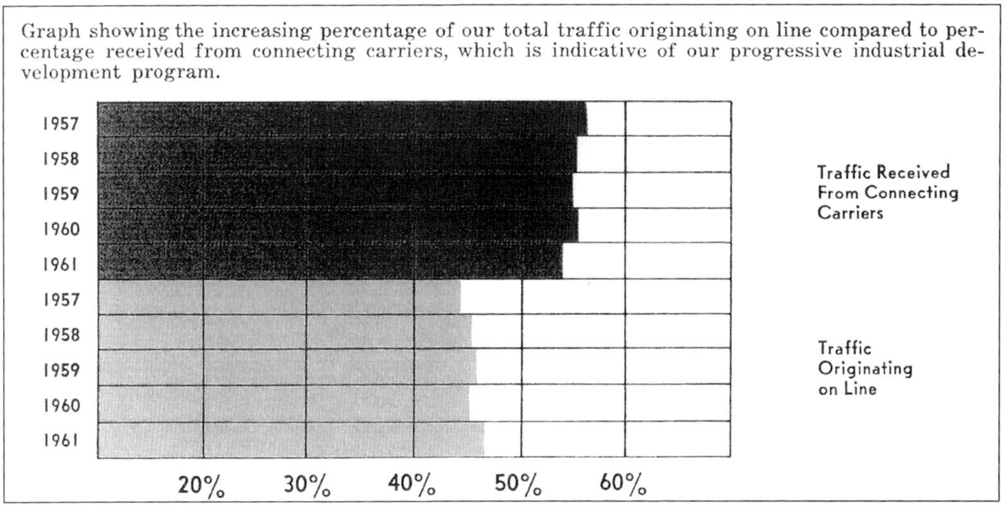

Efforts to develop online industries began years before this chart was published in the 1961 annual report. Examples of this activity include the acquisition of a large tract of land west of St. Charles, Illinois, in 1893 for an industrial town and development of a 6,250-acre industrial district at Roseport, Minnesota, in 1954. (Author's collection.)

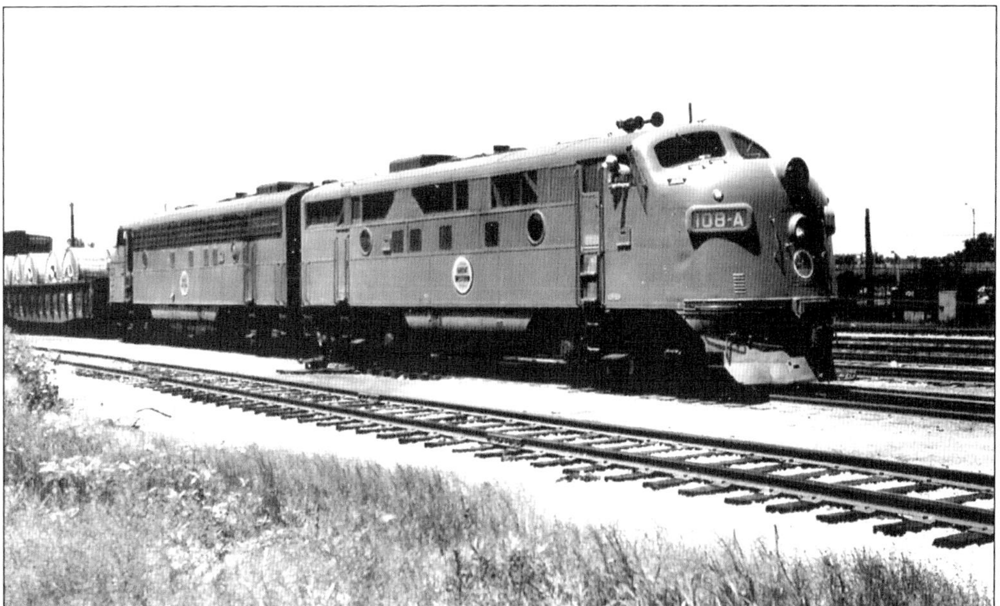

Locomotive Nos. 108-A and 116-A were photographed pushing freight cars onto a yard track at Chicago Transfer Yard on July 15, 1967. Note the load of steel coils in the gondola car behind the last engine. (Author's collection.)

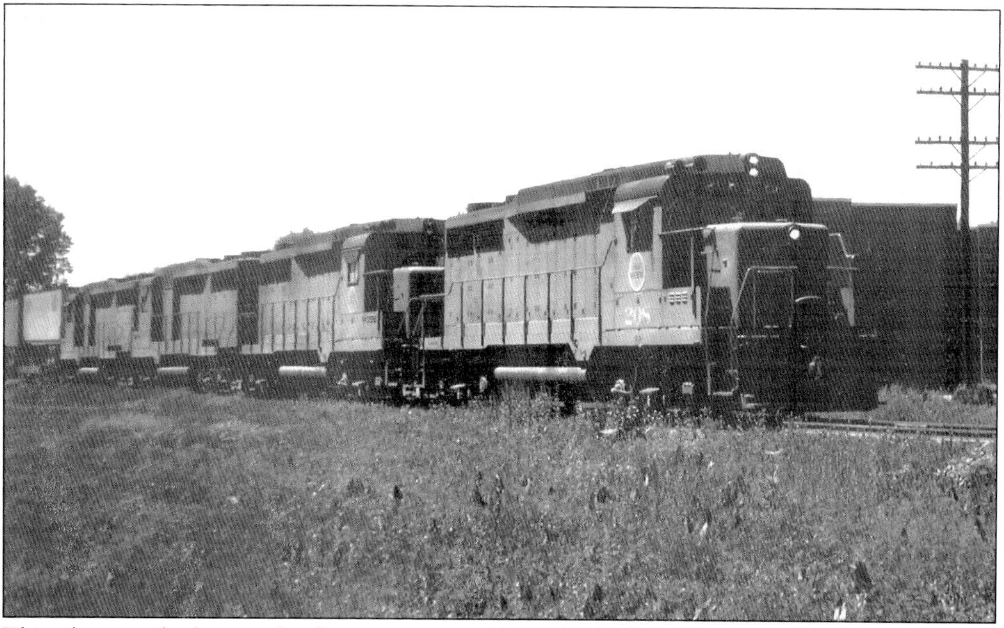

This photograph shows a freight train passing through Elmhurst, Illinois, in 1966. Four of the company's fleet of eight GP-30 diesels were assigned to this particular train. (Author's collection.)

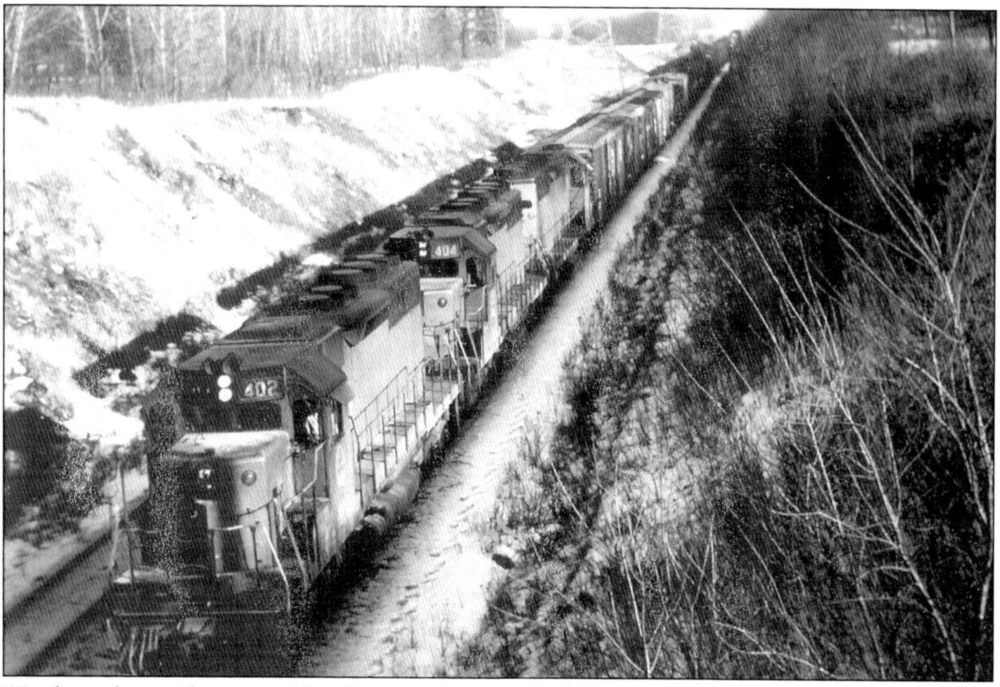

Westbound manifest train No. 91 was photographed at Ingalton, Illinois, in January 1968. This image clearly shows the benefits of using more powerful locomotives. Only three SD-40 diesels were required to power this freight train instead of four GP-30 engines or six cab units. (Author's collection.)

CGW was one of the first railroads to provide trailer-on-flatcar (TOFC) service when it began transporting semitrailers between Chicago and Minneapolis–St. Paul on July 6, 1936. The company also patented equipment to secure the trailer on the flatcar, as depicted in this patent drawing. Note the use of chains and turnbuckles to attach the trailer to anchor rails on the flatcar deck. (Author's collection.)

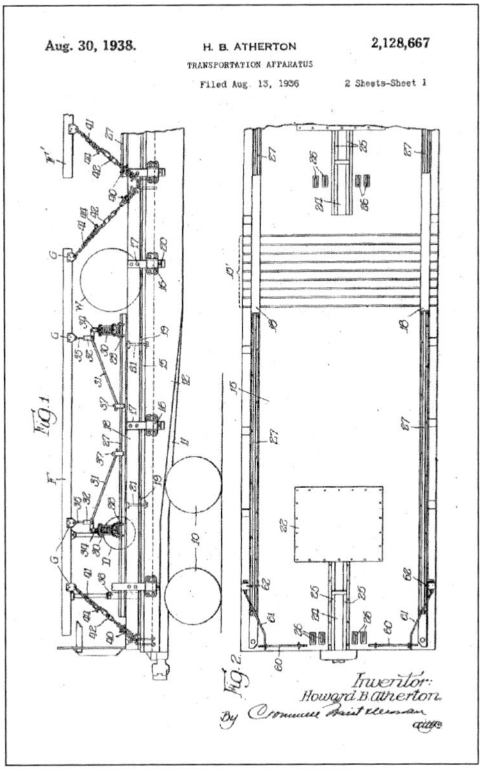

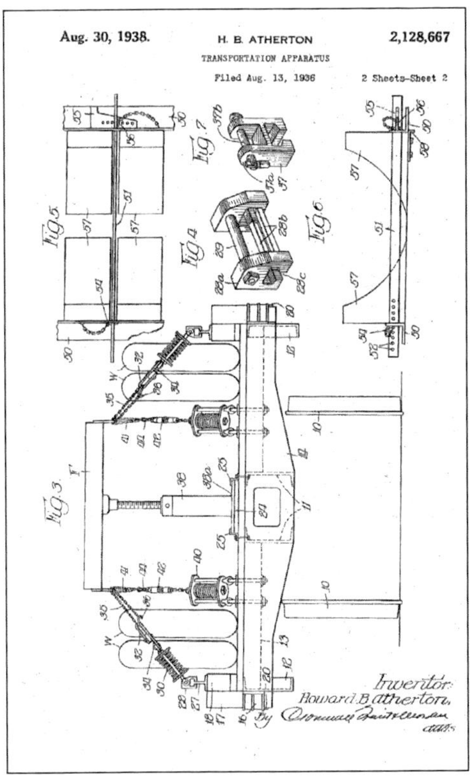

This is the second sheet of the patent drawing, and it shows the use of an adjustable jack to support the front end of the trailer. Other components included wheel chocks and ramps for loading and unloading the trailer. The patent was No. 2,128,667, dated August 30, 1938. (Author's collection.)

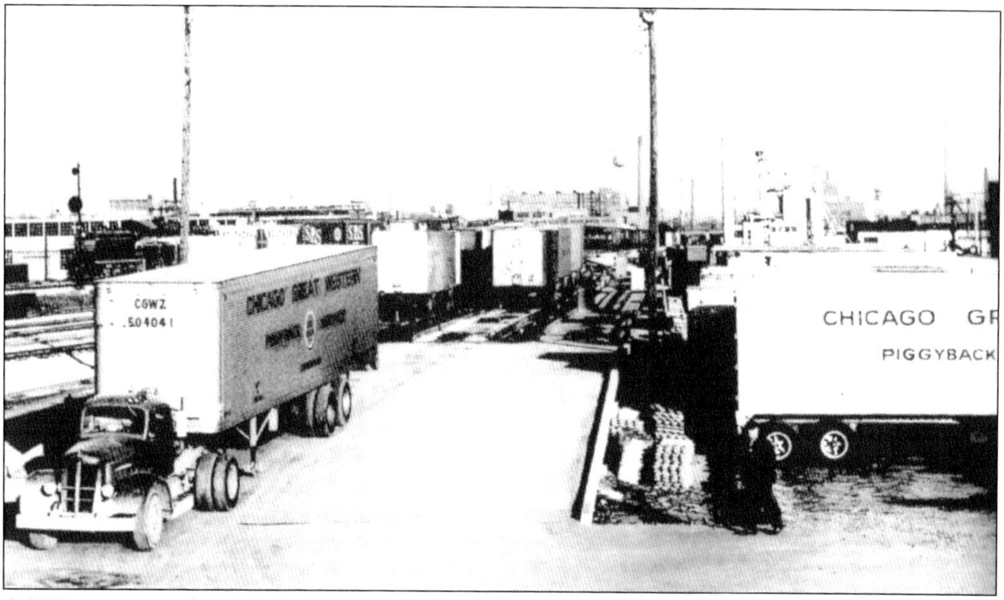

CGW transported 10,296 trailers for 20 motortruck companies during the first year of TOFC service from July 1936 to July 1937. The operation was considered a success, with 96 percent on-time delivery, no pilferage, and only minimal damage to freight. This photograph shows the trailer ramp at Chicago Transfer Yard. (Author's collection.)

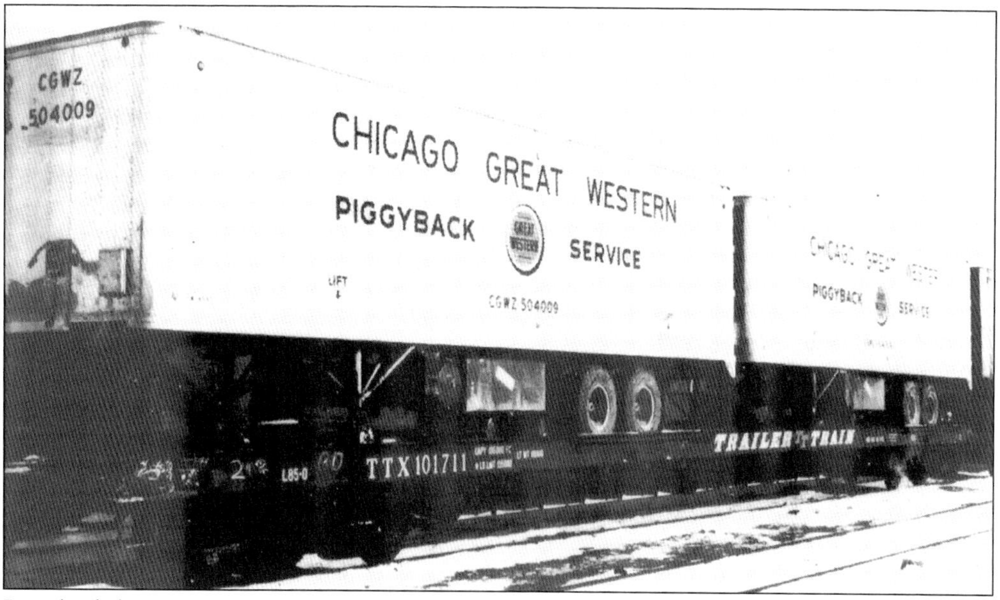

Piggyback business was actively promoted and expanded starting in 1962. To accommodate shipments, CGW joined the national piggyback pool of Trailer Train in February 1961 to obtain flatcars and leased 100 refrigerated trailers in 1963 for transporting perishables. Also in 1963, trailer ramps were constructed at several stations, which resulted in a total of 16 terminals equipped with ramps to load and unload trailers. (Author's collection.)

Four

PASSENGER SERVICE

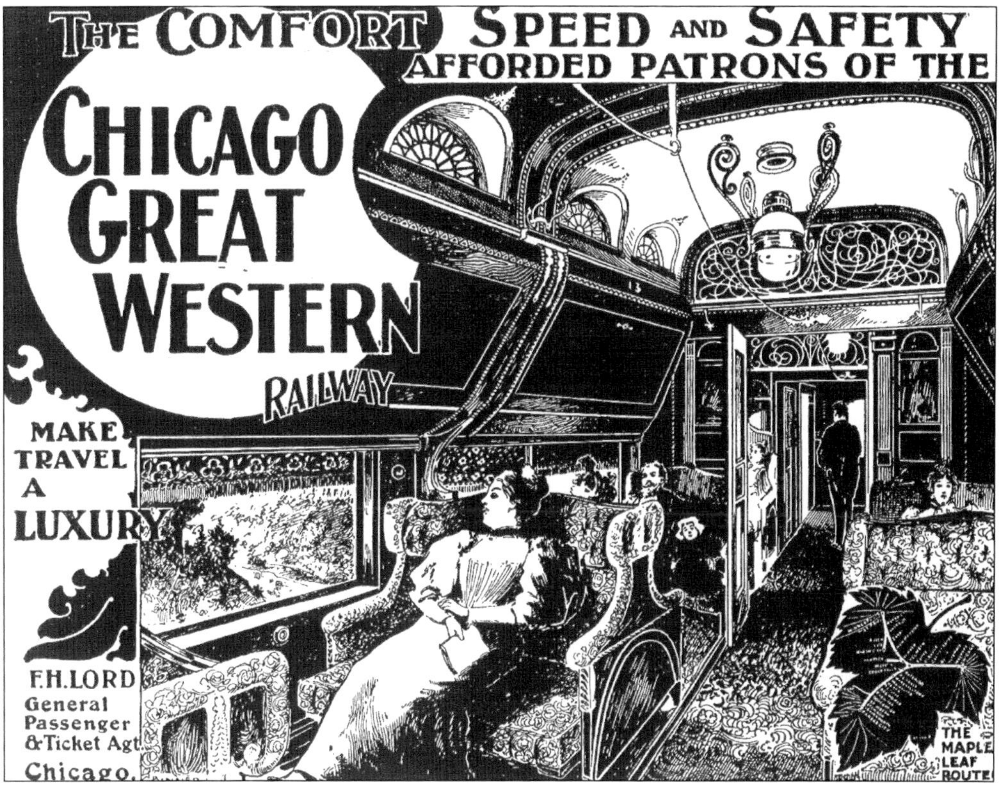

This advertisement from 1896 informed patrons that CGW made traveling a luxury. The lady gazing out the window seems relaxed and ready for a peaceful nap. A time card effective May 10, 1896, shows that daily (except Sunday) passenger service at Chicago consisted of six eastbound and seven westbound trains. Only four trains were operated in either direction on Sunday. (Author's collection.)

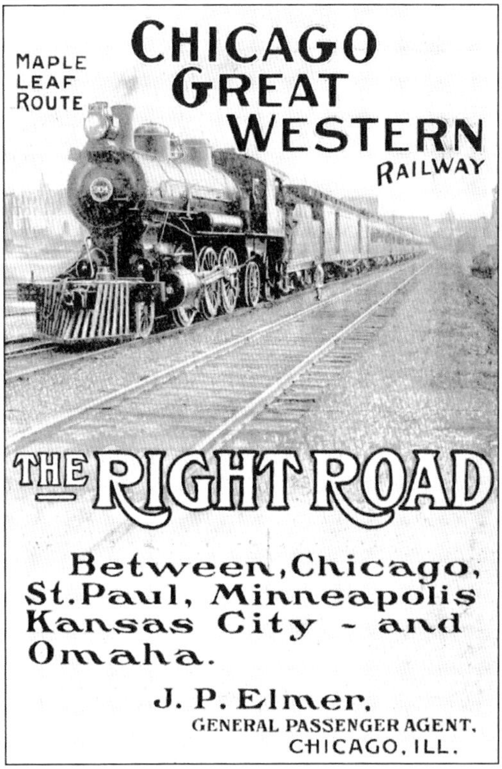

CGW began an advertising campaign in the summer of 1905, promoting itself as "the Right Road" for traveling from Chicago to Minnesota, Iowa, and other western destinations. The advertisements featured this slogan and a caricature of a Pullman porter who symbolized attentive service. The promotion ceased in 1908, when the company was in receivership. This particular advertisement includes the Pullman porter watching a passenger train, with locomotive No. 904 at the head end, departing Grand Central Station, Chicago. (Author's collection).

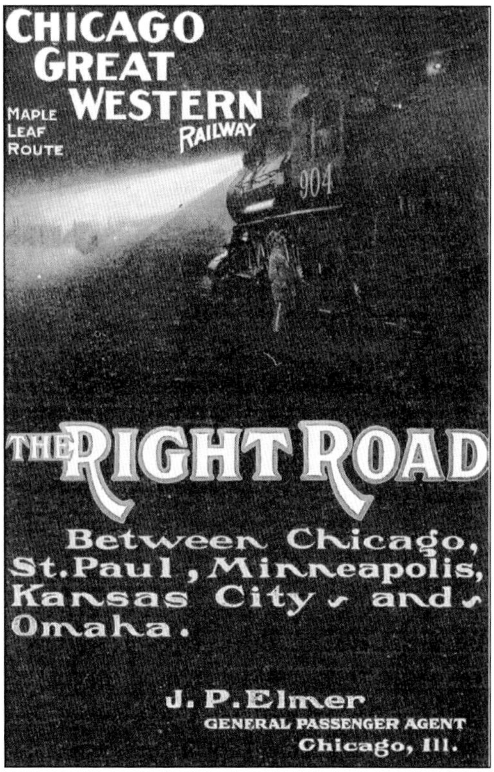

Another 1905 advertisement again shows locomotive No. 904 at night with a city landscape illuminated by its headlight. Note the Pullman porter is also present, chatting with the train crew. One can imagine that this advertisement and the one above depicted passenger train No. 3, the daily Twin City Day Express, which departed Chicago at 8:45 a.m. and arrived at Minneapolis at 9:50 p.m. (Author's collection).

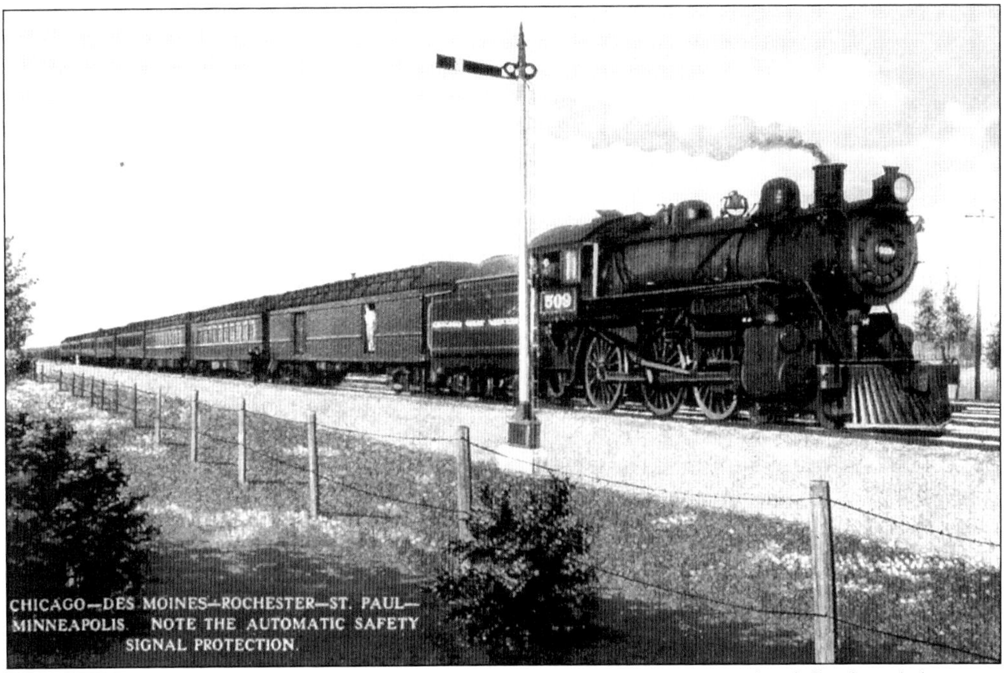

The Great Western Limited, consisting of locomotive No. 509, a tender full of coal, baggage car, and coaches, travels along a substantial ballasted right-of-way protected with fencing and automatic signals. Only a small amount of smoke belches from the smokestack due to skillful firing by an experienced fireman and a locomotive that is properly maintained, sparing passengers from soot and cinders. The Great Western Limited was a daily overnight luxury train that entered service in July 1898 between Chicago and Minneapolis–St. Paul. (James L. Rueber.)

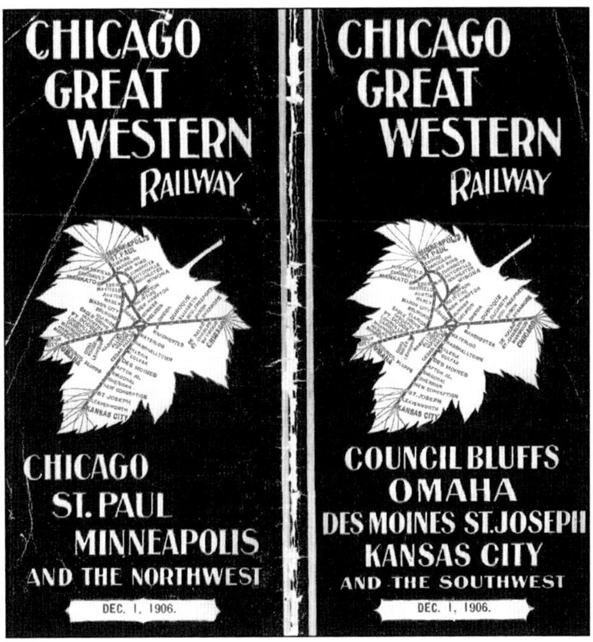

Front and back covers of the December 1, 1906, passenger timetable are shown here. The system map in the maple leaf shows the extent of the company's expansion efforts during the early years of the 20th century. There are now branch lines in Minnesota and Iowa and an extension to Omaha. (Author's collection.)

CHICAGO GREAT WESTERN RY.

"The Maple Leaf Route"

LOCAL TIME TABLES

Chicago to Dubuque, St. Paul and Minneapolis.

Mls. fr. Chic'go	STATIONS	1 LIMITED DAILY	5 EXPRESS DAILY	3 MAIL DAILY	7 DAILY	13 DAILY EX. SUN.
0	Lv CHICAGO	D 8.80 PM	11.30 PM	8.45 AM	3 00 PM	7 00 AM
5	Lv FOREST HOME		A 11.55 PM		F 3 25 PM	F 7 25 AM
7	Lv MAYWOOD		A 11.57 PM		F 3 27 PM	7 28 AM
12	Lv SOUTH ELMHURST		A 12 04 AM		3 38 PM	F 7 38 AM
16	Lv LOMBARD		A 12.10 AM		3 46 PM	7 46 AM
18	Lv N. GLEN ELLYN		A 12.13 AM		3 50 PM	F 7 49 AM
21	Lv GRETNA		A 12 16 AM		3 59 PM	F 7 56 AM
26	Lv INGALTON		A 12.23 AM		4 14 PM	F 8 04 AM
31	Lv ST. CHARLES		12.33 AM	A 9.41 AM	4 28 PM	8 14 AM
36	Lv WASCO		A 12.41 AM		4 42 PM	8 25 AM
40	Lv LILY LAKE		A 12.49 AM		4 55 PM	8 33 AM
44	Lv VIRGIL		A 12.53 AM		5 05 PM	F 8 38 AM
46	Lv RICHARDSON		A 12.56 AM		5 14 PM	8 42 AM
58	Lv DE KALB					
52	Lv SYCAMORE	8.00 PM	1.08 AM	10.13 AM	5 28 PM	8 55 AM
59	Lv CLARE		A 1.18 AM		5 43 PM	F 9 06 AM
65	Lv ESMOND		A 1.27 AM		5 52 PM	9 16 AM
70	Lv LINDENWOOD		A 1.35 AM		6 01 PM	9 24 AM
74	Lv HOLCOMB		F 1.40 AM		6 07 PM	9 30 AM
78	Lv STILLMAN VALLEY		F 1.48 AM		6 17 PM	9 40 AM
83	Lv BYRON	8.50 PM	1.58 AM	A 10.55 AM	6 25 PM	9 50 AM
89	Lv MYRTLE				ARRIVE	F 10 00 AM
91	Lv EGAN					F 10 05 AM
96	Lv GERMAN VALLEY		A 2.14 AM			10 14 AM
102	Lv SOUTH FREEPORT	E 9.17 PM	2.27 AM	A 11.24 AM		10 28 AM
109	Lv BOLTON					10 43 AM
115	Lv PEARL CITY		F 2.45 AM			10 53 AM
119	Lv KENT		A 2.52 AM			11 02 AM
126	Lv STOCKTON	9.58 PM	3.08 AM	11.59 AM		11 20 AM
133	Lv WOODBINE		A 3.18 AM			11 31 AM
138	Lv ELIZABETH		3.28 AM	A 12.19 PM		11 41 AM
141	Lv NORTH HANOVER		A 3.33 AM			11 47 AM
146	Lv RODDEN		A 3.37 AM			F 11 53 AM
153	Lv GALENA JUNCTION		F 3.53 AM			12 11 PM
167	Lv DUBUQUE	11.20 PM	4.25 AM	1.15 PM		12 35 PM
175	Lv DURANGO		F 4.41 AM	F 1.31 PM		ARRIVE
183	Lv GRAF		F 4.55 AM	F 1.45 PM		
187	Lv KIDDER			F 1.51 PM		
191	Lv FARLEY		F 5.10 AM	F 2.00 PM		
197	Lv DYERSVILLE	E 12 20 AM	5.25 AM	2.13 PM		
208	Lv ALMORAL		F 5.37 AM	F 2.24 PM		
210	Lv ONEIDA		5.47 AM	2.32 PM		
218	Lv MANCHESTER		† 5.15 AM	2.00 PM		
218	Ar MANCHESTER		† 6.15 AM	3 45 PM		
215	Lv THORPE		F 5.55 AM	F 2.40 PM		
220	Lv DUNDEE		F 6.03 AM	F 2.48 PM		
225	Lv LAMONT		6.13 AM	2.55 PM		
230	Lv AURORA		6.22 AM	3.04 PM		
235	Lv STANLEY		6.30 AM	3.13 PM		
240	Lv OELWEIN	1.45 AM	M 7.25 AM	3.38 PM		
248	Lv WESTGATE		7.37 AM	3.52 PM		
256	Lv SUMNER	2.13 AM	7.50 AM	4.05 PM		
266	Lv FREDERICKSBURG		8.07 AM	4.24 PM		
270	Lv BOYD		F 8.15 AM	F 4.32 PM		
274	Lv NEW HAMPTON	2.48 AM	8.23 AM	4.40 PM		
279	Lv DEVON		F 8.30 AM	4.48 PM		
285	Lv ALTA VISTA		8.41 AM	5.00 PM		
289	Lv ELMA	3.15 AM	8.40 AM	5.07 PM		
294	Lv LOWTHER			F 5.16 PM		
299	Lv RICEVILLE	B 3.33 AM	9.05 AM	5.24 PM		
305	Lv McINTIRE	F 3.45 AM	9.15 AM	5.34 PM		
307	Lv BAILEY			F 5.38 PM		
314	Lv TAOPI		9.30 AM	5.50 PM		
322	Lv ELKTON		F 9.43 AM	F 6.03 PM		
324	Lv SUTTON			F 6.06 PM	7 DAILY	
328	Lv RENOVA		F 9.54 AM	F 6.14 PM		
333	Lv SARGEANT		F 10.08 AM	6.23 PM		
339	Lv HAYFIELD	4.55 AM	10.19 AM	6.39 PM	7 10 AM	
344	Lv VLASATY				F 7 20 AM	
348	Lv DODGE CENTER	5.11 AM	10.38 AM	0.55 PM	7 28 AM	
353	Lv EDEN		10.47 AM	7.04 PM	7 38 AM	
358	Lv WEST CONCORD		10.56 AM	7 12 PM	7 48 AM	
362	Lv SKYBURG				7 57 AM	
367	Lv KENYON	5.46 AM	11.16 AM	7.30 PM	8 11 AM	
374	Lv NERSTRAND				8 36 AM	
379	Lv DENNISON				8 57 AM	
384	Lv STANTON				9 15 AM	
388	Lv RANDOLPH	6.21 AM	11.50 AM	8.05 PM	9 35 AM	
415	Ar RED WING	† 10.45 AM			† 10.45 AM	
394	Lv HAMPTON, MINN.				9.48 AM	
398	Lv EMPIRE				F 9.57 AM	
402	Lv COATES				F 10.07 AM	
404	Lv RICH VALLEY				F 10.12 AM	
412	Lv INVER GROVE				F 10 28 AM	
415	Lv SOUTH ST. PAUL			8.57 PM	10 32 AM	
420	Ar ST. PAUL	7.20 AM	12.50 PM	9.10 PM	10 45 AM	
430	Ar MINNEAPOLIS	8 00 AM	1.20 PM	9 50 PM	11 20 AM	

A Stops to receive passengers for Dubuque and beyond or discharge passengers from Chicago. B Stops to discharge passengers from beyond Oelwein and to take passengers for St. Paul and Minneapolis. D Dining Car attached. E Stops to receive passengers for points beyond Oelwein, at which train stops. F Stops only on signal. G Stops to receive passengers for Dubuque and stations beyond. M Stops for meals. † Except Sunday. Trains Nos. 1, 3 and 5 are solid through trains Chicago to Minneapolis. For equipment see page 7.

13

CHICAGO GREAT WESTERN RY.

LOCAL TIME TABLES

Minneapolis and St. Paul to Dubuque and Chicago.

Mls. fr. St. P'l	STATIONS	2 LIMITED DAILY	4 EXPRESS DAILY	6 CHIC'O SP'L DAILY	8 DAILY	14 DAILY EX. SUN.
....	Lv MINNEAPOLIS	8 00 PM	9 10 AM	10 45 PM	4.35 PM	
0	Lv ST. PAUL	8 35 PM	9 40 AM	11 20 PM	5.10 PM	
1	Lv WEST ST. PAUL					
5	Lv SOUTH ST. PAUL			11 35 PM	5.23 PM	
8	Lv INVERGROVE			F 11 40 PM	F 5.28 PM	
16	Lv RICH VALLEY			F 11 56 PM	F 5.43 PM	
18	Lv COATES			F 12 02 AM	F 5.48 PM	
22	Lv EMPIRE			F 12 15 AM	F 5.59 PM	
26	Lv HAMPTON MINN.			12 26 AM	6.08 PM	
59	Lv RED WING	† 4 40 PM				
33	Lv RANDOLPH	9 39 PM	10 40 AM	12 40 AM	6.25 PM	
36	Lv STANTON		F 10 46 AM	F 12 48 AM	6.38 PM	
41	Lv DENNISON		10 55 AM	F 12 58 AM	6.53 PM	
46	Lv NERSTRAND		11 05 AM	F 1 09 AM	†7.08 PM	
53	Lv KENYON	10 14 PM	11 16 AM	1 23 AM	7.30 PM	
58	Lv SKYBURG		F 11 26 AM		7.43 PM	
62	Lv WEST CONCORD		11 35 AM	1 45 AM	7.55 PM	
67	Lv EDEN		11 43 AM		8.07 PM	
72	Lv DODGE CENTER	10 45 PM	11 53 AM	2 08 AM	8.18 PM	
76	Lv VLASATY		F 11 59 AM		F 8.25 PM	
81	Lv HAYFIELD	11 07 PM	12 13 PM	2 30 AM	8.35 PM	
87	Lv SARGEANT		F 12 25 PM	F 2 44 AM		
92	Lv RENOVA		F 12 35 PM			
96	Lv SUTTON		F 12 43 PM			
98	Lv ELKTON		F 12 47 PM			
106	Lv TAOPI		1 00 PM	3 22 AM		
113	Lv BAILEY		F 1 11 PM			
115	Lv McINTIRE	12 01 AM	1 16 PM	3 45 AM		
121	Lv RICEVILLE	E 12 10 AM	1 27 PM	3 59 AM		
126	Lv LOWTHER		F 1 35 PM			
131	Lv ELMA	12 28 AM	1 45 PM	4 24 AM		
135	Lv ALTA VISTA		1 53 PM	F 4 34 AM		
141	Lv DEVON		2 04 PM			
146	Lv NEW HAMPTON	12 54 AM	2 12 PM	5 00 AM		
150	Lv BOYD		F 2 20 PM	F 5 11 AM		
154	Lv FREDERICKSBURG		2 29 PM	5 23 AM		
164	Lv SUMNER	1.25 AM	2 46 PM	5 45 AM		
172	Lv WESTGATE		2 58 PM	6 00 AM		
180	Lv OELWEIN	2.00 AM	3.20 PM	M 7.00 AM		
185	Lv STANLEY		F 3.31 PM	F 7.11 AM		
190	Lv AURORA		F 3.37 PM	F 7.17 AM		
195	Lv LAMONT		F 3.46 PM	7.25 AM		
200	Lv DUNDEE			F 7.32 AM		
205	Lv THORPE			F 7.38 AM		
210	Lv ONEIDA		4 09 PM	7.48 AM		
218	Lv MANCHESTER		2.00 PM	7 15 AM		
218	Ar MANCHESTER		† 5.45 PM	8 10 AM		
214	Lv ALMORAL			F 7.54 AM		
223	Lv DYERSVILLE	N 2 59 AM	4.27 PM	8.06 AM		
229	Lv FARLEY			F 8.16 AM		
233	Lv KIDDER			F 8.23 AM		
237	Lv GRAF			F 8.31 AM		
245	Lv DURANGO			F 8.45 AM		
253	Lv DUBUQUE	4.00 AM	5.25 PM	9.05 AM		2.15 PM
267	Lv GALENA JUNCTION			9.29 AM		2.39 PM
274	Lv RODDEN					F 2.56 PM
279	Lv NORTH HANOVER					3 02 PM
282	Lv ELIZABETH		6.17 PM	9.57 AM		3 10 PM
287	Lv WOODBINE					3 20 PM
294	Lv STOCKTON	5.17 AM	6.42 PM	10.22 AM		3 38 PM
301	Lv KENT					3 48 PM
305	Lv PEARL CITY			H 10.36 AM		3.58 PM
311	Lv BOLTON					F 4 07 PM
318	Lv SOUTH FREEPORT	N 5 48 AM	H 7.15 PM	10.55 AM		4 20 PM
324	Lv GERMAN VALLEY				8 DAILY	4 30 PM
329	Lv EGAN					F 4 37 PM
331	Lv MYRTLE					F 4 42 PM
337	Lv BYRON	D 6.18 AM	H 7.40 PM	11.20 AM	6.45 AM	4 55 PM
342	Lv STILLMAN VALLEY			F 11.28 AM	6.58 AM	5 03 PM
346	Lv HOLCOMB				7.00 AM	5 13 PM
350	Lv LINDENWOOD				7.05 AM	5 19 PM
355	Lv ESMOND				7.14 AM	5 27 PM
361	Lv CLARE				7.22 AM	5 35 PM
374	Ar DE KALB					
368	Lv SYCAMORE	7.10 AM	8.38 PM	12.15 PM	7.41 AM	5 52 PM
374	Lv RICHARDSON				7.55 AM	6 00 PM
377	Lv VIRGIL				8.03 AM	F 6 04 PM
380	Lv LILY LAKE				8.13 AM	6 10 PM
384	Lv WASCO				8.25 AM	6 17 PM
389	Lv ST. CHARLES	T 7.40 AM	T 9.05 PM	12.43 PM	8.37 AM	6 27 PM
394	Lv INGALTON				8.48 AM	F 6 34 PM
399	Lv GRETNA				9.05 AM	F 6 43 PM
402	Lv N. GLEN ELLYN				9.09 AM	F 6 47 PM
404	Lv LOMBARD				9.22 AM	F 6 52 PM
408	Lv SOUTH ELMHURST				9.30 AM	F 7 01 PM
411	Lv BELLEWOOD				F 9.36 AM	
413	Lv MAYWOOD				F 9.38 AM	7 12 PM
415	Ar FOREST HOME				F 9.40 AM	F 7 15 PM
420	Ar CHICAGO	8.45 AM	10.00 PM	1.40 PM	10.40 AM	7 40 PM

D Dining Car attached. F Stops only on signal. M Stops for meals. † Except Sunday. E Stops to receive passengers for points beyond Oelwein at which train stops. N Stops to discharge passengers from beyond Oelwein. H Stops to discharge passengers from Dubuque and beyond or to receive passengers for Chicago. T Stops to discharge passengers from Dubuque and beyond. TRAINS NOS. 2, 4 and 6 are solid through trains Minneapolis to Chicago. For equipment see page 8.

14

This schedule of passenger trains operating between Chicago and Minneapolis–St. Paul was published in the 1906 timetable. There were five westbound trains and four eastbound. Railroads use odd numbers to designate trains headed west and even numbers east. (Author's collection.)

Shown here are the front and back covers of the September 3, 1921, passenger timetable. CGW replaced the maple leaf trademark in June 1910 with a circular emblem containing ears of corn and a new slogan: the Corn Belt Route. CGW chose the new trademark because it served the Corn Belt, an agricultural region in the Midwest where corn acreage once exceeded that of any other crop. (Author's collection.)

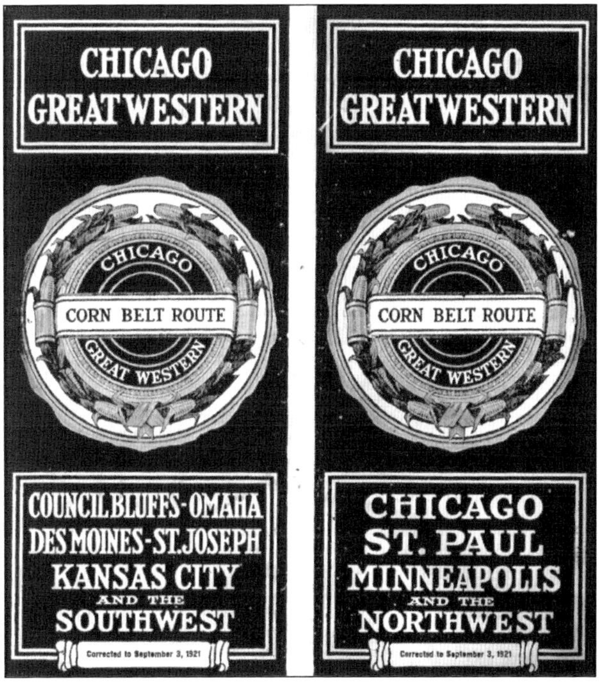

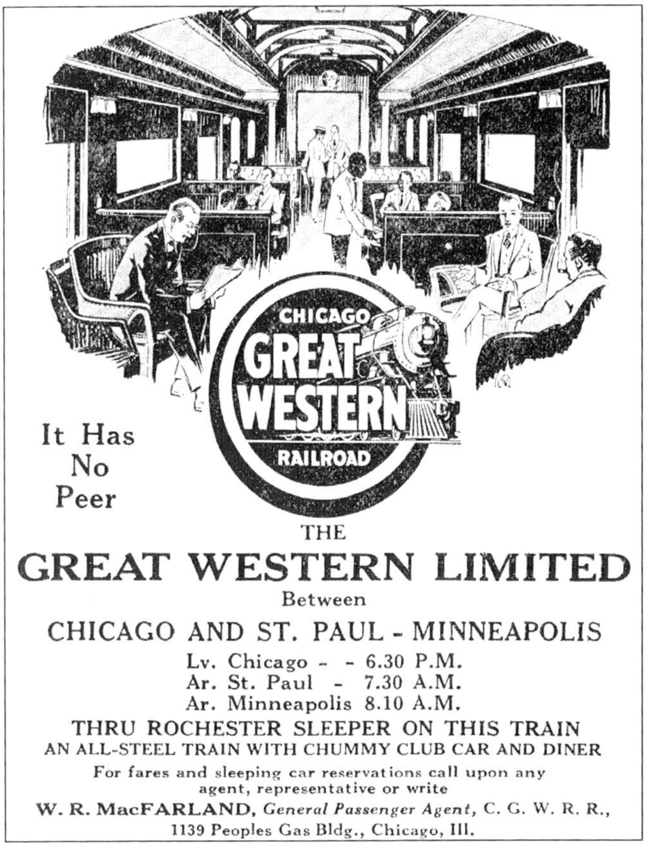

Advertisements on passenger service during the 1920s and 1930s displayed a different emblem without the Corn Belt Route slogan. The design featured the company name with Great Western emphasized in uppercase letters inside a circle with a steam locomotive depicted as traveling at high speed. The new logo was prominently displayed in this 1921 advertisement. (Author's collection.)

Chicago, Dubuque—Rochester, St.Paul, Minneapolis

Read Down — For complete local schedules between Oelwein and St. Paul see Tables 1 and 5 — Read Up

31 DAILY	3 DAILY	5 DAILY	1 DAILY	Mls	TABLE 6	2 DAILY	6 DAILY	4 DAILY	32 DAILY
		Great Western Special	Great Western Limited			Great Western Limited	Chicago Special		
PM	AM	PM	PM			AM	AM	PM	AM
2 45	7 30	11 00	6 30	0	Lv....**Chicago**....Ar	8 40	7 30	7 55	11 00
3 15	7 55	11 25	6 55	10	Lv...Forest Park...Lv	8 13	m & i	7 17	9 55
3 20	7 58	a	b	12	Lv....Maywood....Lv	g	m & o	h	9 51
f 3 23	f 8 01	......	....	13	Lv....Bellewood....Lv	g	m	......	f 9 47
f 3 30	f 8 07	a	b	17	Lv....Elmhurst....Lv	g	m & o	h	f 9 41
3 38	f 8 13	......	....	21	Lv....Lombard....Lv	g	m & o	......	9 34
3 43	f 8 16	......	....	23	Lv.North Glen EllynLv	g	m	......	9 27
3 53	f 8 20	......	....	26	Lv.....Gretna.....Lv	g	m	......	9 20
4 10	f 8 30	......	....	31	Lv....Ingalton....Lv	g	m	......	9 00
4 24	8 42	12 05	7 35	36	Lv...**St. Charles**...Lv	7 37	m	6 32	8 42
f 4 26	f	......	....	37	Lv....Fox River....Lv	g	m	......	f 8 36
4 40	8 52	a & d	....	41	Lv......Wasco......Lv	g	m	f 6 20	8 31
4 51	9 01	a & d	....	46	Lv....Lily Lake....Lv	g	m	f 6 13	8 19
4 58	f 9 06	a & d	....	49	Lv......Virgil......Lv	g	m	f 6 08	8 08
5 10	9 11	a & d	....	51	Lv....Richardson....Lv	g	m	f 6 03	7 57
5 25	9 24	12 43	8 14	57	Lv...**Sycamore**...Lv	7 05	5 54	5 51	7 36
Electric	line bet	ween Sy	camore	and	.......DeKalb.......	DeKalb	See page	39	......
5 37	f 9 33	......	b	62	Lv....Wilkinson....Lv	g	m	......	7 22
5 43	9 37	a	b	64	Lv......Clare......Lv	g	m	f 5 32	7 18
5 54	9 45	a	b	70	Lv.....Esmond.....Lv	g	m	f 5 22	7 09
6 05	9 53	a	b	75	Lv...Lindenwood...Lv	g	m	f 5 13	7 01
6 12	9 59	a	b	78	Lv....Holcomb....Lv	g	m	5 05	6 56
6 20	10 08	a	b	83	Lv.Stillman Valley.Lv	g	m	4 54	6 48
6 28	10 17	1 35	9 04	88	Lv.....**Byron**.....Lv	6 17	m	4 45	6 40
PM	10 29	......	b	94	Lv.....Myrtle.....Lv	g	m	f 4 29	AM
	10 36	a	b	97	Lv......Egan......Lv	g	m	f 4 19	
......	10 46	a	b	101	Lv.....Meekin.....Lv	g	m	4 10	......
......	10 58	2 06	9 37	107	Lv..**So. Freeport**..Lv	f 5 47	m & o	3 58	......
......	gg	gg	gg	...	......Freeport......	gg	gg	gg	......
......	11 10	......	b	114	Lv.....Bolton.....Lv	g	m	f 3 43	......
......	11 25	f 2 27	f 9 58	120	Lv...Pearl City...Lv	g	m	3 32	......
......	11 38	a	b	125	Lv.....Kent.....Lv	g	m	f 3 19	......
......	11 56	2 55	10 25	131	Lv...**Stockton**...Lv	5 03	m	3 00	......
......	12 08	a	b	139	Lv....Woodbine....Lv	g	m	2 47	......
......	12 18	3 17	10 45	143	Lv....Elizabeth....Lv	f 4 40	m	2 36	......
......	12 27	a	b	147	Lv.North Hanover.Lv	g	m	2 25	......
......	† 1 00	......	......	...	Ar.....Hanover.....Lv	......	......	† 1 40	......
......	12 33	......	b	150	Lv.....Rodden.....Lv	g	m	f 2 17	......
......	f12 39	......	b	152	Lv.....Winston.....Lv	g	m	......	......
......	f12 43	......	b	154	Lv......Rice......Lv	g	m	......	......
......	f12 46	......	b	155	Lv......Aiken......Lv	g	m	f 2 04	......
......	12 50	f 3 41	f11 11	158	Lv...Galena Junct...Lv	g	m	1 59	......
......	1 13	4 05	11 35	172	Ar....**Dubuque**....Lv	3 50	2 52	1 34	......
......	1 19	4 13	11 40	172	Lv....**Dubuque**....Ar	3 45	2 47	1 27	......
......	1 37	h & k	b	180	Lv....Durango....Lv	g	m	f 1 08	......
......	f 1 42	......	b	183	Lv......Budd......Lv	g	m	f 1 02	......
......	1 52	h & k	b	188	Lv......Graf......Lv	g	m	f12 52	......
......	f 2 00	......	b	192	Lv.....Kidder.....Lv	g	m	f12 41	......
......	2 13	h & k	b	196	Lv.....Farley.....Lv	g	m	f12 33	......
......	2 23	5 16	f12 38	203	Lv....Dyersville....Lv	j	m & e	12 23	......
......	f 2 31	h & k	b	208	Lv...Petersburg...Lv	g	m	f12 13	......
......	f 2 35	......	b	211	Lv.....Almoral.....Lv	g	m	f12 08	......
......	2 42	5 38	b	215	Lv.....**Oneida**.....Lv	g	m	12 01	......
......	† 3 10	......	......	223	Ar...Manchester...Lv	......	......	†11 30	......
......	......	......	......	223	Lv...Manchester...Ar	......	......	......	......
......	2 50	h & k	b	220	Lv.....Thorpe.....Lv	g	m	f11 50	......
......	2 58	h & k	b	225	Lv.....Dundee.....Lv	g	m	11 41	......
......	3 06	6 03	b c d q	230	Lv.....Lamont.....Lv	g	m o e v	11 31	......
......	3 17	6 12	b	235	Lv.....Aurora.....Lv	g	m	11 22	......
......	3 27	6 21	b	240	Lv.....Stanley.....Lv	g	m	11 12	......
......	3 40	6 35	1 45	246	Ar..**Oelwein 1, 9**..Lv	1 45	12 50	11 00	......
......	PM	6 55	2 00	246	Lv....**Oelwein**....Ar	1 30	AM	AM	......
......		7 09	......	254	Lv...Westgate 1...Lv	......			
......	......	7 22	2 24	261	Lv..Sumner 1, 4..Lv	12 56			
......	......	7 40	......	271	Lv Fredericksburg 1 Lv	......			
......	......	f 7 50	......	276	Lv.....Boyd 1.....Lv	......			
......	......	7 58	2 52	280	Lv New Hampton 1 Lv	12 28			
......	......	f 8 06	......	285	Lv....Devon 1....Lv	......			
......	......	8 15	......	291	Lv...Alta Vista 1...Lv	......			
......	......	8 22	3 16	294	Lv.....Elma 1.....Lv	f12 07			
......	......	f 8 32	......	300	Lv.....Acme 1.....Lv	......			
......	......	8 42	......	305	Lv...Riceville 1...Lv	f11 50			
......	......	8 53	3 42	310	Ar..**McIntire 1, 5**..Lv	11 35			
......	......	†11 05	6 30	359	Ar...**Rochester**...Lv	9 20			
......	......	9 54	4 33	344	Ar...Hayfield 1, 7...Lv	10 37			
......	......	10 15	5 00	353	Ar..**Dodge Center**..Lv	10 17			
......	......	10 48	5 44	372	Ar....Kenyon....Lv	9 46			
......	......	11 47	6 15	392	Ar **Randolph 1, 2, 5** Lv	9 11			
......	......	12 45	j & n	420	Ar...So. St. Paul...Lv	l			
......	......	1 00	7 30	425	Ar....**St. Paul**....Lv	8 10			
......	......	1 40	8 10	435	Ar..**Minneapolis**..Lv	7 40			
		PM	AM			PM			

ON YOUR NEXT TRIP BETWEEN **Chicago** AND **St. Paul-Minneapolis** USE THE **"Great Western Limited"**

Fast and comfortable-You'll feel like at home

The passenger schedule from the 1921 timetable shows four trains in each direction between Chicago and Minneapolis–St. Paul. CGW began to experience a decline in passenger business starting in 1920 due to the use of automobiles. The company was especially susceptible to loss of business to the automobile because the distance between terminals was short enough to be easily traveled by car in a day or two. (Author's collection.)

CGW responded to the decline in passenger business by offering travelers convenient and fast schedules, special amenities aboard trains, and modernized equipment. This advertisement from 1921 proclaimed transit time between Minneapolis–St. Paul was shortened by two hours due to eliminating 27 stops. (Author's collection.)

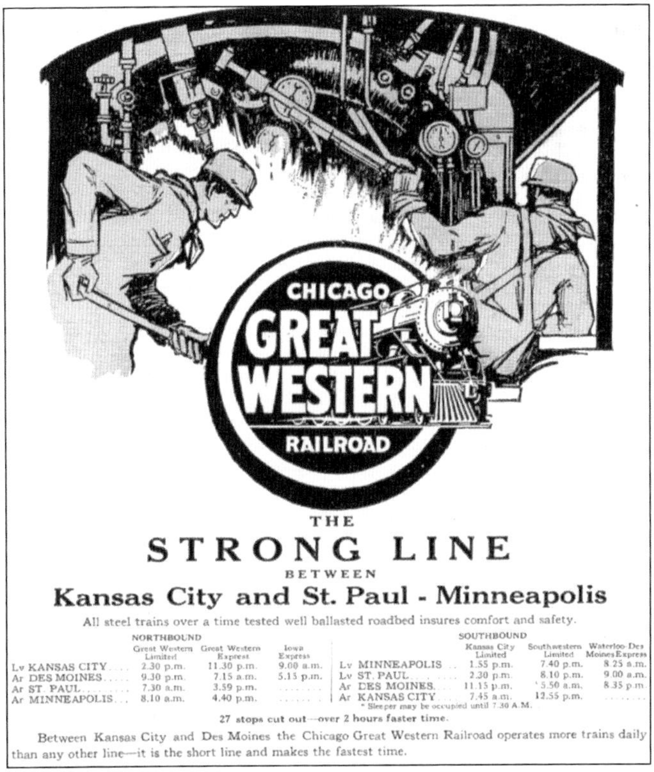

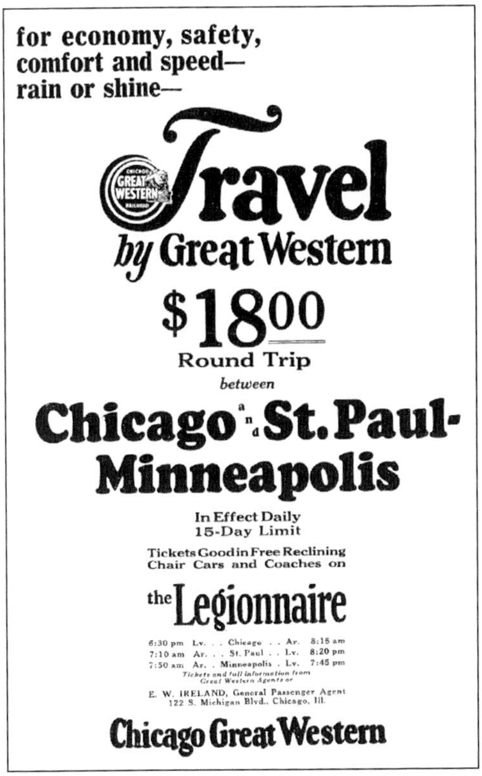

CGW held a nationwide contest in 1924 to rename the Great Western Limited, and it selected the Legionnaire, submitted by four people (each received a prize of $50). The name was chosen to honor the men who served in the armed forces during World War I. The Legionnaire was officially inaugurated on January 16, 1925. CGW publicized the luxury train with phrases such as "You'll find luxurious comfort and warm-blooded hospitality built right into this popular train." This advertisement was published in 1929. (Author's collection.)

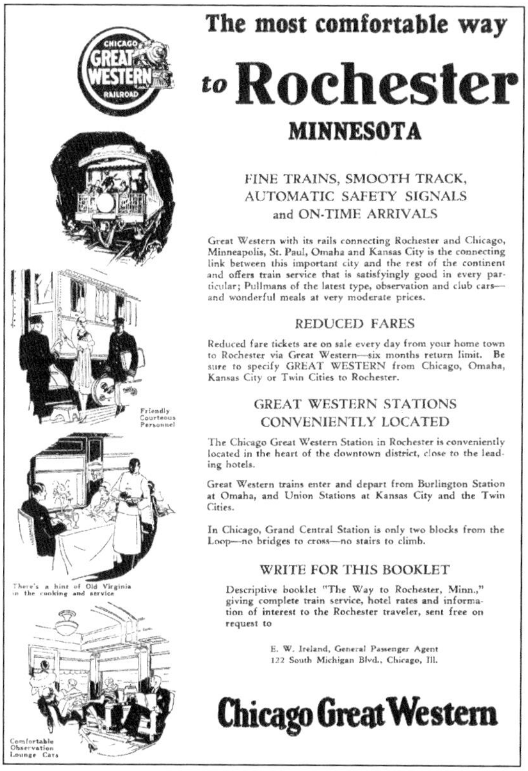

Rochester, Minnesota, was an important source of passenger business partly due to the world-famous Mayo Clinic. CGW attracted travelers to Rochester by offering trains that provided various amenities for their comfort and dining service that featured "a hint of Old Virginia in the cooking." Famous CGW passenger trains that served Rochester included the *Red Bird* and the *Blue Bird*, which provided service from and to Minneapolis–St. Paul. (Author's collection.)

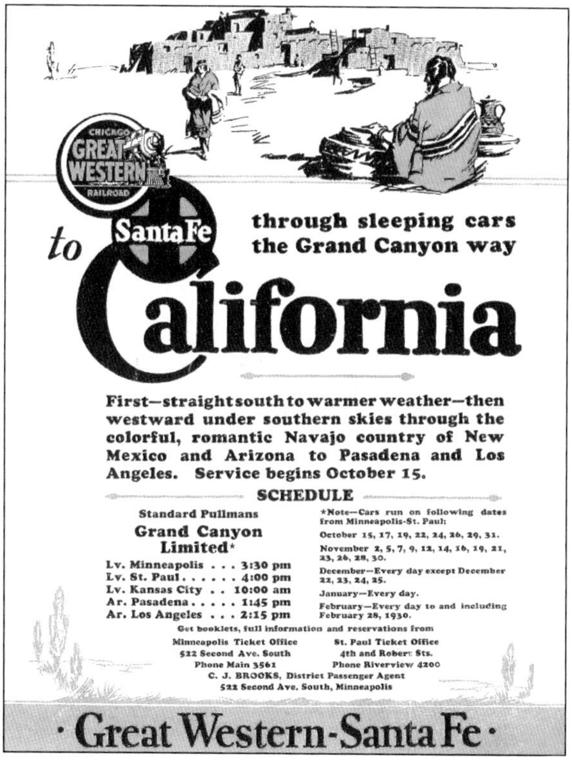

CGW also offered service outside of its territory through connections with other railroads and a combined rail and air service. This 1929 advertisement provided information and a schedule for sleeping car service from Minneapolis–St. Paul to Los Angeles through connections with the Atchison, Topeka and Santa Fe Railroad. (Author's collection.)

Shown here are the front and back covers of the May 1, 1936, passenger timetable. CGW revised the Corn Belt Route trademark during the 1930s to present a modern, austere appearance. (Author's collection.)

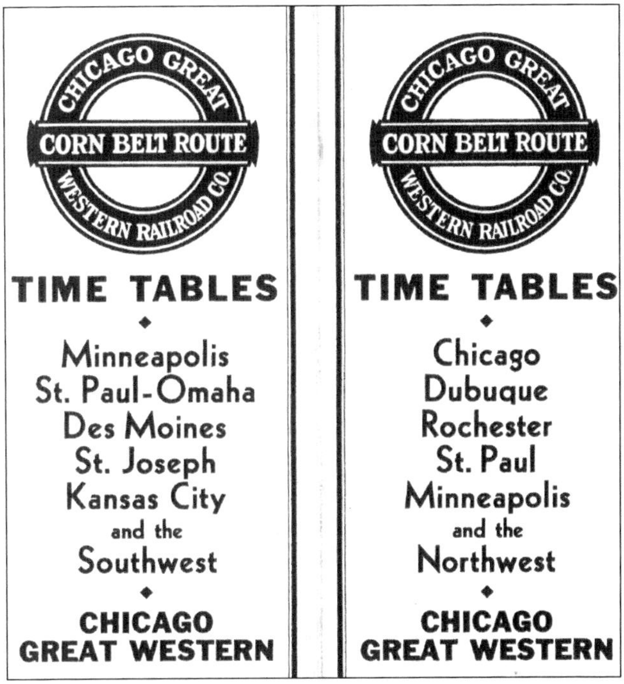

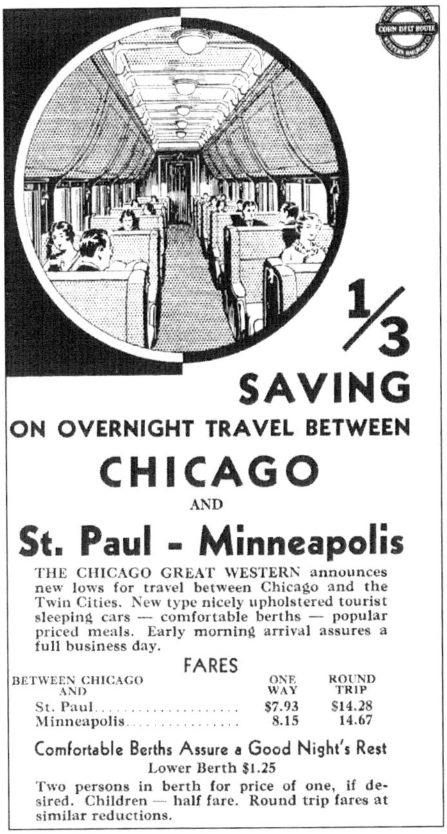

Although CGW was in receivership when this advertisement was published in 1936, the company reduced fares between Chicago and Minneapolis–St. Paul in an effort to increase business. (Author's collection.)

Chicago, Dubuque—Rochester, St. Paul, Minneapolis

(For complete local schedules Oelwein and St. Paul, see Tables 1 and 3)

Read Down					Read Up
3 DAILY EX. SAT (MOTOR)	1-21 DAILY THE MINNESOTAN	MLS.	TABLE 2	26-2 DAILY THE MINNESOTAN	4 DAILY EX. SUN. MOTOR
PM	PM		*Central Time*	AM	PM
‡11 30	7 30	0	Lv **Chicago** Ar	8 30	† 7 30
11 55	7 52	10	Lv Forest Park Lv	8 08	6 55
......	q	12	Lv Maywood Lv	m	f 6 50
......	q	13	Lv Bellewood Lv	m	......
12 07	q	17	Lv Elmhurst Lv	m	6 38
f12 11	q	19	Lv Villa Park Lv	m	f 6 33
f12 16	q	21	Lv Lombard Lv	m	......
f12 25	q	26	Lv Gretna Lv	m	f 6 20
f12 33	q	31	Lv Ingalton Lv	m	......
12 45	8 28	36	Lv **St. Charles** Lv	7 32	6 01
......	q	37	Lv Fox River Lv	m	......
f12 56	q	41	Lv Wasco Lv	m	f 5 44
f 1 06	q	46	Lv Lily Lake Lv	m	f 5 37
f 1 10	q	49	Lv Virgil Lv	m	f 5 30
f 1 14	q	51	Lv Richardson Lv	m	f 5 20
1 31	8 58	57	Lv **Sycamore** Lv	7 01	5 11
c	c	...	DeKalb	c	c
f 1 41	q	62	Lv Wilkinson Lv	m	......
1 48	q	64	Lv Clare Lv	m	f 4 55
1 59	q	70	Lv Esmond Lv	m	f 4 44
f 2 09	q	75	Lv Lindenwood Lv	m	f 4 35
f 2 16	f 9 27	78	Lv Holcomb Lv	m	4 29
f 2 25	q	83	Lv Stillman Valley Lv	m	4 20
2 35	9 41	88	Lv **Byron** Lv	6 17	4 12
f 2 45	q	94	Lv Myrtle Lv	m	f 4 03
f 2 52	q	97	Lv Egan Lv	m	3 57
f 3 02	q	101	Lv German Valley Lv	m	3 49
f 3 12	f10 04	107	Lv **So. Freeport** Lv	f 5 51	3 40
n	n	...	Freeport	n	n
f 3 25	q	114	Lv Bolton Lv	m	f 3 28
f 3 35	f10 21	120	Lv Pearl City Lv	f 5 36	3 20
f 3 45	q	125	Lv Kent Lv	m	3 11
4 00	10 43	131	Lv **Stockton** Lv	5 20	3 00
f 4 16	q	139	Lv Woodbine Lv	m	2 47
4 26	f11 00	143	Lv Elizabeth Lv	f 4 52	2 38
4 34	q	147	Lv North Hanover Lv	m	2 30
f 4 40	q	150	Lv Rodden Lv	m	2 25
f 4 48	q	152	Lv Winston Lv	m	......
f 4 53	q	154	Lv Rice Lv	m	......
f 4 56	q	155	Lv Aiken Lv	m	f 2 12
f 5 02	q	158	Lv Galena Junction Lv	m	2 08
5 35	11 48	172	Ar **Dubuque** Lv	4 05	1 45
5 35	11 48	172	Lv **Dubuque** Ar	4 05	1 45
f 5 55	q	180	Lv Durango Lv	m	f 1 24
f 6 01	q	183	Lv Budd Lv	m	f 1 19
f 6 12	q	188	Lv Graf Lv	m	f 1 10
f 6 21	q	192	Lv Kidder Lv	m	f 1 03
f 6 34	q	196	Lv Farley Lv	m	f12 55
6 47	f12 52	203	Lv Dyersville Lv	f 3 06	12 44
f 6 57	q	208	Lv Petersburg Lv	m	f12 36
f 7 04	q	211	Lv Almoral Lv	m	f12 30
7 15	f 1 10	215	Lv **Oneida** Lv	m	12 23
† 9 00	......	223	Ar Manchester Lv	......	†11 55
......	......	223	Lv Manchester Ar	......	†12 50
f 7 27	q	220	Lv Thorpe Lv	m	f12 15
f 7 38	q	225	Lv Dundee Lv	m	12 07
7 50	f 1 34	230	Lv Lamont Lv	m	11 59
8 00	q	235	Lv Aurora Lv	m	11 50
8 10	q	240	Lv Stanley Lv	m	11 41
8 30	2 00	246	Ar **Oelwein 1, 6** Lv	2 05	†11 30
AM	2 15	246	Lv **Oelwein** Ar	2 00	AM
Runs to Clarion see table 6	s	254	Lv Westgate Lv	f 1 46	From Kansas City; see tables 1 and 5.
	2 46	261	Lv **Sumner 8** Lv	1 35	
	s	271	Lv Fredericksburg Lv	f 1 19	
	3 20	280	Lv New Hampton Lv	1 05	
	s	291	Lv Alta Vista Lv	f12 49	
	s	294	Lv Elma Lv	12 44	
	s	305	Lv Riceville Lv	f12 28	
	4 08	310	Ar **McIntire 1, 3** Lv	12 20	
	# 7 00	359	Ar **Rochester 3** Lv	■10 00	
	5 10	344	Lv **Hayfield 1, 4** Lv	11 20	
......	5 28	353	Lv **Dodge Center** Lv	10 52	......
......	a-s	362	Lv West Concord Lv	l-r	......
......	5 58	372	Lv Kenyon Lv	10 22	......
......	s	378	Lv Nerstrand Lv	r	......
......	s	384	Lv Dennison Lv	r	......
......	kk-s	392	Lv **Randolph 1, 3, 7** Lv	9 50	......
......	s	420	Lv South St. Paul Lv	9 05	......
......	7 30	425	Ar **St. Paul** Lv	8 55	......
......	8 10	435	Ar **Minneapolis** Lv	8 20	......
	AM			PM	

This schedule for passenger trains between Chicago and Minneapolis–St. Paul was published in the 1936 timetable. The number of trains has been significantly reduced to two each way. Six years previously, in March 1930, the Legionnaire was renamed the Minnesotan. Note that local trains Nos. 3 and 4 were assigned motorcars, which were the mail-express-passenger coaches powered by gasoline engines. (Author's collection.)

CGW published this eye-catching advertisement to promote patronage between Chicago and Des Moines, Iowa. The train was named the Chicago Special, and it featured a dining car, coaches, and sleeping cars. (Author's collection.)

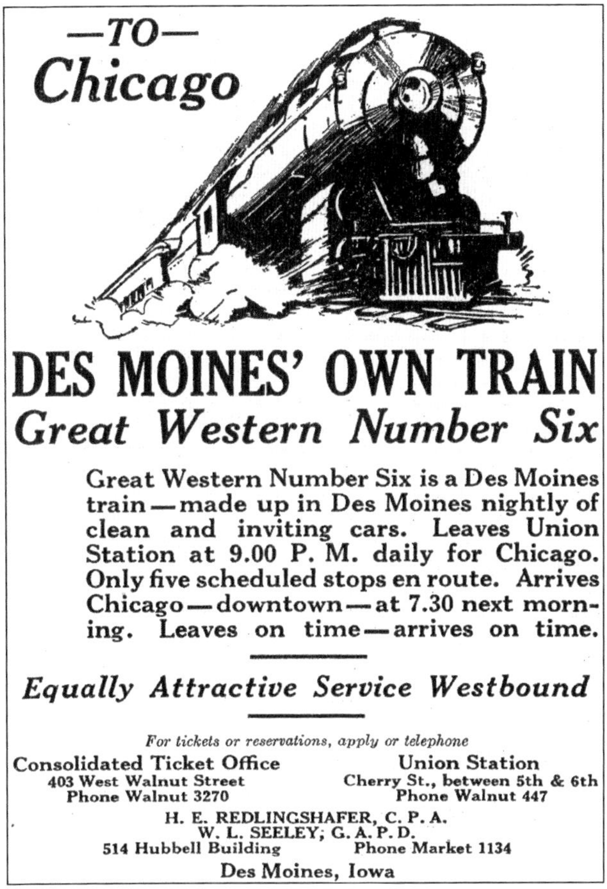

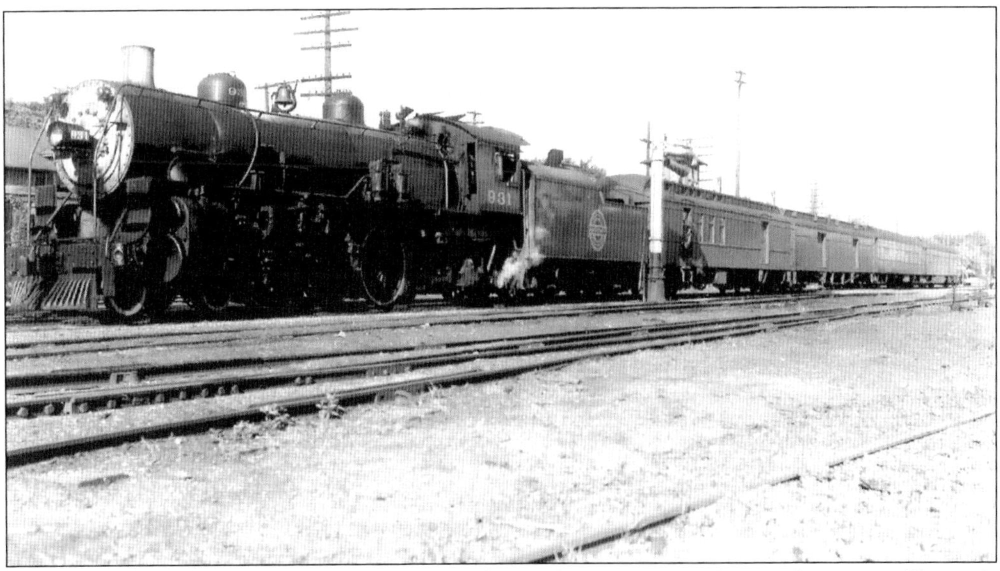

The Minnesotan is eastbound at Sycamore, Illinois. (Joiner History Room, Sycamore, Illinois.)

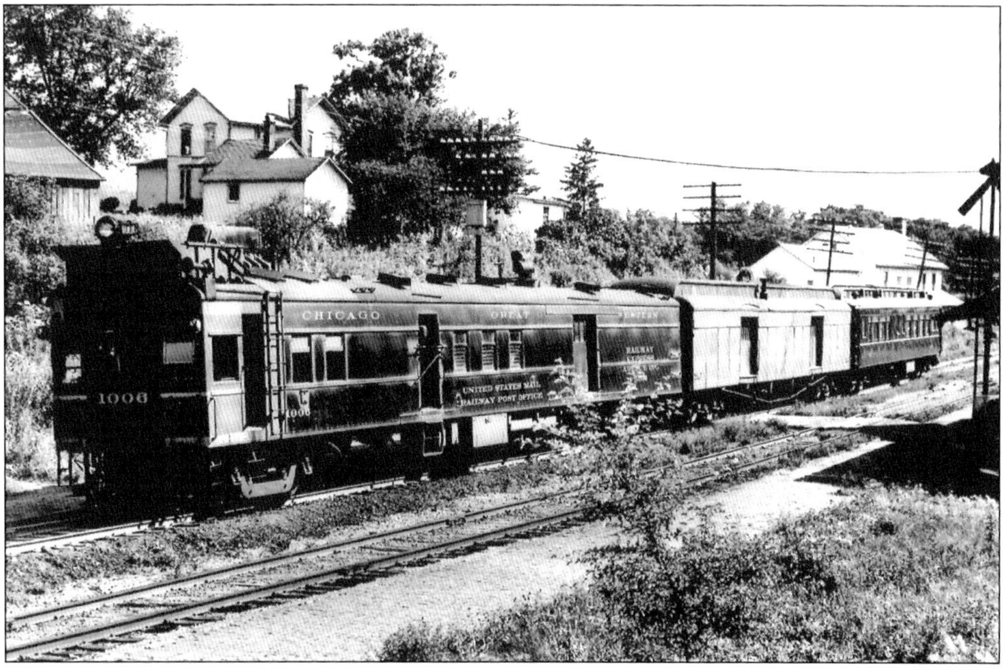

Motorcar No. M-1006, with baggage car and coach, passes through Elizabeth, Illinois. The train is one of the daily locals that ran between Chicago and Oelwein. (Joiner History Room, Sycamore, Illinois.)

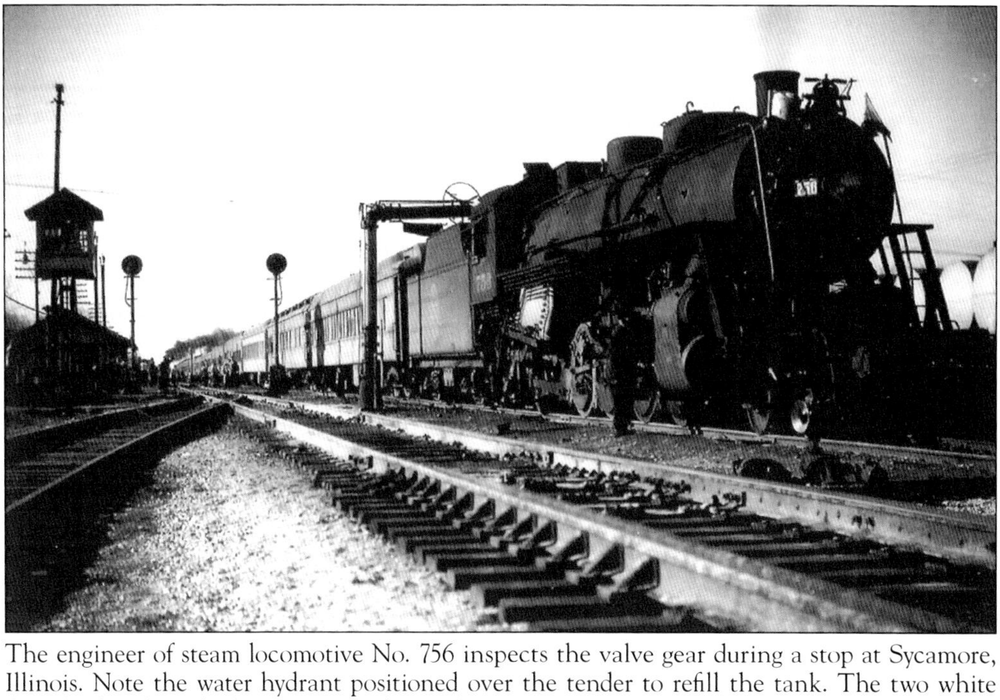

The engineer of steam locomotive No. 756 inspects the valve gear during a stop at Sycamore, Illinois. Note the water hydrant positioned over the tender to refill the tank. The two white flags displayed on the locomotive indicate that it was an extra passenger train not operating by timetable schedule. Although headed east, the extra was on the westbound track to clear the train approaching from the rear. (Joiner History Room, Sycamore, Illinois.)

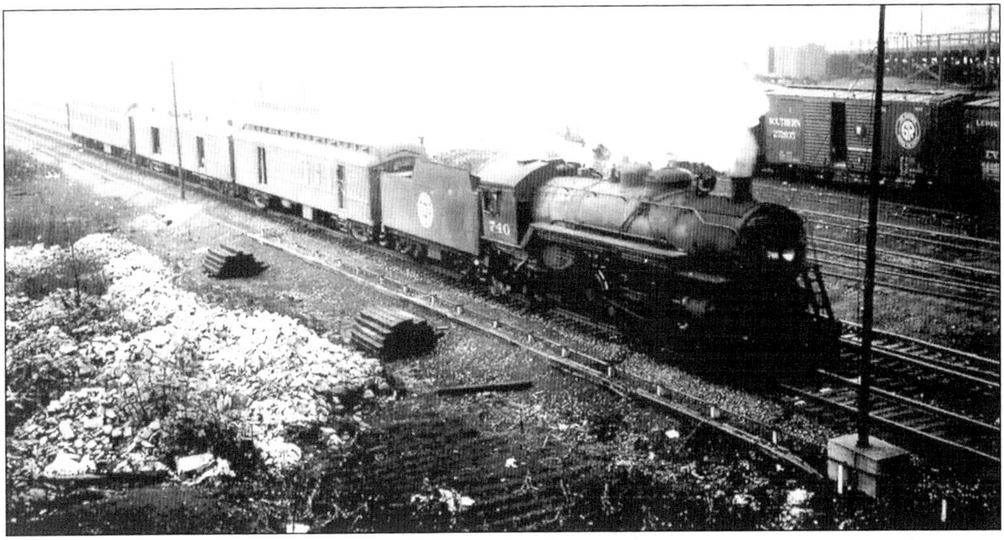

During World War II, CGW experienced a substantial increase in passenger business, which quickly declined again after the war ended. During the first nine months of 1948, the company sustained a loss of $750,575 from its passenger services. It began an intensive effort to discontinue passenger trains, and more than half of passenger train miles, along with all parlor, buffet, and sleeping car service, were eliminated by 1953. This photograph of the Minnesotan arriving at Chicago in 1949 equipped with a single coach clearly shows the train was lightly patronized by this time. The Minnesotan was discontinued on May 10, 1949. (Joiner History Room, Sycamore, Illinois.)

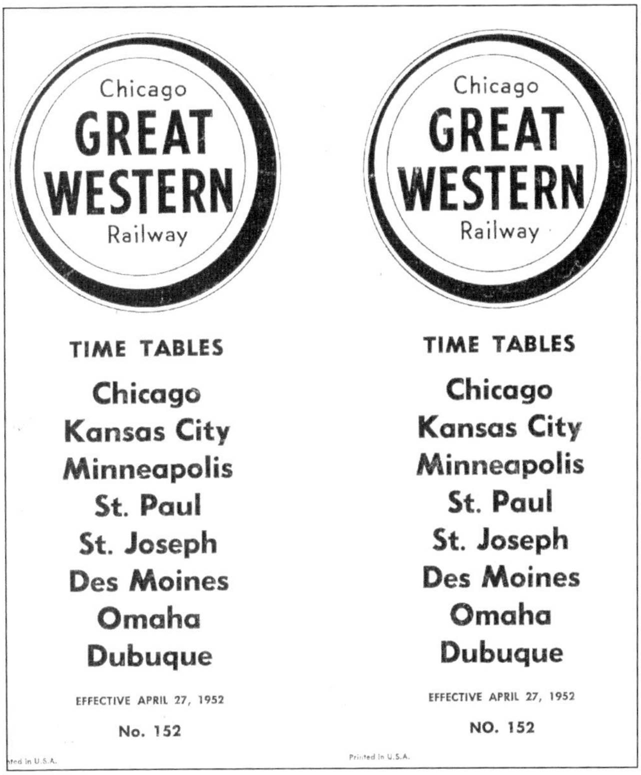

Chicago GREAT WESTERN Railway

TIME TABLES

Chicago
Kansas City
Minneapolis
St. Paul
St. Joseph
Des Moines
Omaha
Dubuque

EFFECTIVE APRIL 27, 1952

No. 152

Printed in U.S.A.

Chicago GREAT WESTERN Railway

TIME TABLES

Chicago
Kansas City
Minneapolis
St. Paul
St. Joseph
Des Moines
Omaha
Dubuque

EFFECTIVE APRIL 27, 1952

NO. 152

Printed in U.S.A.

Shown here are the front and back covers of the April 27, 1952, passenger timetable. CGW replaced the Corn Belt Route trademark in 1950 with the logo shown. It has been referred to as the "Lucky Strike" emblem after a similar circular trademark used by a popular brand of cigarettes. (Author's collection.)

Local Schedules

Chicago, Dubuque, Oelwein

Read Down | **Read Up**

7 Daily	Mls	TABLE 3			8 Daily
		Central Time (Grand Central Station)			
PM					AM
4 30	0	Lv	**Chicago**	Ar	11 00
4 55	10	Lv	Forest Park	Lv	10 30
4 58	12	Lv	Maywood	Lv	10 27
......	13	Lv	Bellwood	Lv	......
5 07	17	Lv	Elmhurst	Lv	f10 17
......	19	Lv	Villa Park	Lv	......
......	21	Lv	Lombard	Lv	......
f **5 24**	26	Lv	Gretna	Lv	*f* 9 58
f **5 32**	31	Lv	Ingalton	Lv	*f* 9 49
5 43	36	Lv	**St. Charles**	Lv	9 40
5 52	41	Lv	Wasco	Lv	9 27
6 00	46	Lv	Lily Lake	Lv	9 19
6 05	49	Lv	Virgil	Lv	9 13
6 24	57	Lv	Sycamore	Lv	9 00
			De Kalb		
6 36	64	Lv	Clare	Lv	8 39
6 46	70	Lv	Esmond	Lv	8 28
6 55	75	Lv	Lindenwood	Lv	8 17
7 02	78	Lv	Holcomb	Lv	8 10
......	83	Lv	Stillman Valley	Lv	......
7 22	88	Lv	**Byron**	Lv	7 50
f **7 32**	94	Lv	Myrtle	Lv	*f* 7 39
......	97	Lv	Egan	Lv	......
7 44	101	Lv	German Valley	Lv	7 25
f **7 52**	107	Lv	**So. Freeport**	Lv	*f* 7 15
......	114	Lv	Bolton	Lv	......
8 11	120	Lv	Pearl City	Lv	6 55
......	125	Lv	Kent	Lv	......
8 34	131	Lv	**Stockton**	Lv	6 35
......	139	Lv	Woodbine	Lv	......
8 55	143	Lv	Elizabeth	Lv	6 00
9 02	147	Lv	North Hanover	Lv	5 50
......	154	Lv	Rice	Lv	......
f **9 18**	155	Lv	Aiken	Lv	*f* 5.30
f **9 23**	158	Lv	Galena Junction	Lv	5 25
9 51	172	Lv	**Dubuque**	Lv	5 05
f **9 59**	174	Lv	Fair Ground	Lv	4 50
......	180	Lv	Durango	Lv	......
10 25	188	Lv	Graf	Lv	4 23
f **10 41**	196	Lv	Farley	Lv	*f* 4 07
10 55	203	Lv	Dyersville	Lv	3 55
11 05	208	Lv	Petersburg	Lv	3 42
f **11 10**	211	Lv	Almoral	Lv	*f* 3 37
11 19	215	Lv	**Oneida**	Lv	3 30
......	220	Lv	Thorpe	Lv	......
......	225	Lv	Dundee	Lv	......
11 46	230	Lv	Lamont	Lv	2 59
11 55	235	Lv	Aurora	Lv	2 50
......	240	Lv	Stanley	Lv	......
12 15	246	Ar	**Oelwein 1, 2.**	Lv	2 30

The 1952 timetable for Chicago listed only two local trains between Chicago and Oelwein. The number of passenger trains between Chicago and Oelwein was reduced from four to two in 1949 after ridership dropped to an average of 14 passengers per trip westbound and less than eight eastbound. The last two trains were kept in service for carrying U.S. mail. (Author's collection.)

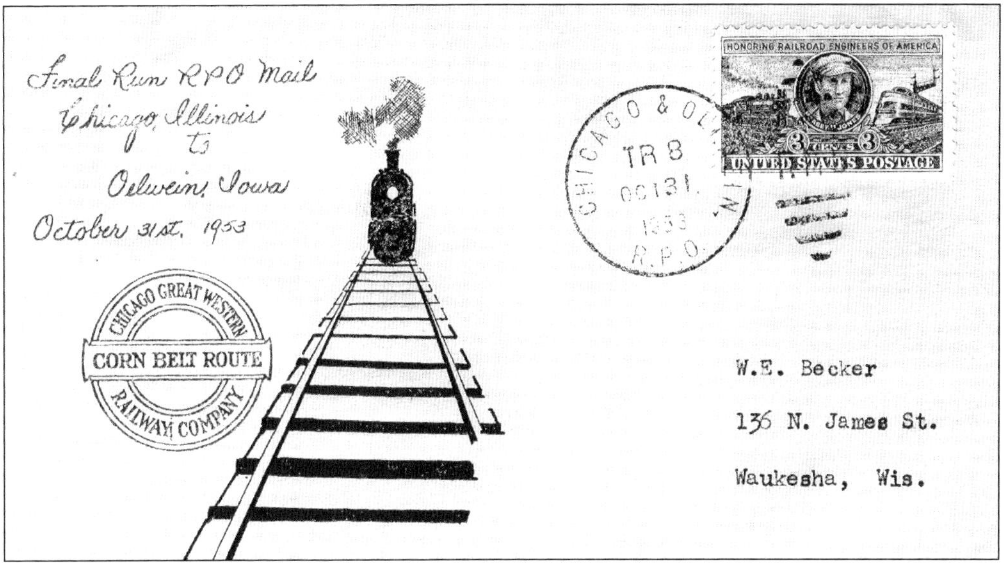

A severe blow to the final passenger trains between Chicago and Oelwein occurred in 1953, when CGW lost its mail contract. This postal cover was issued to commemorate the last run of the railway post office (RPO) car that year. (Author's collection.)

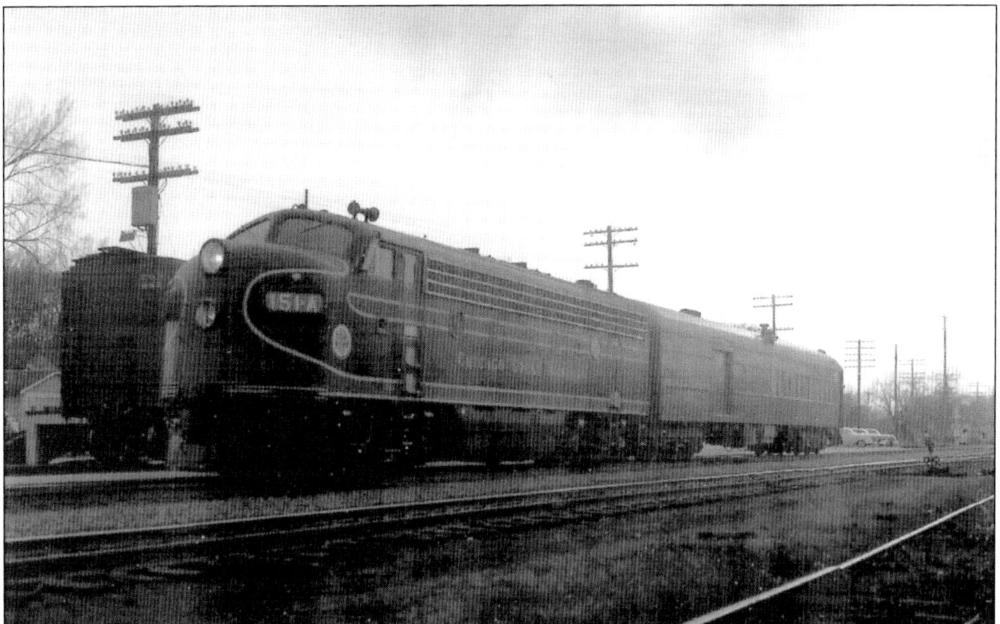

This gloomy photograph shows the last run of the RPO car in October 1953. (Joiner History Room, Sycamore, Illinois.)

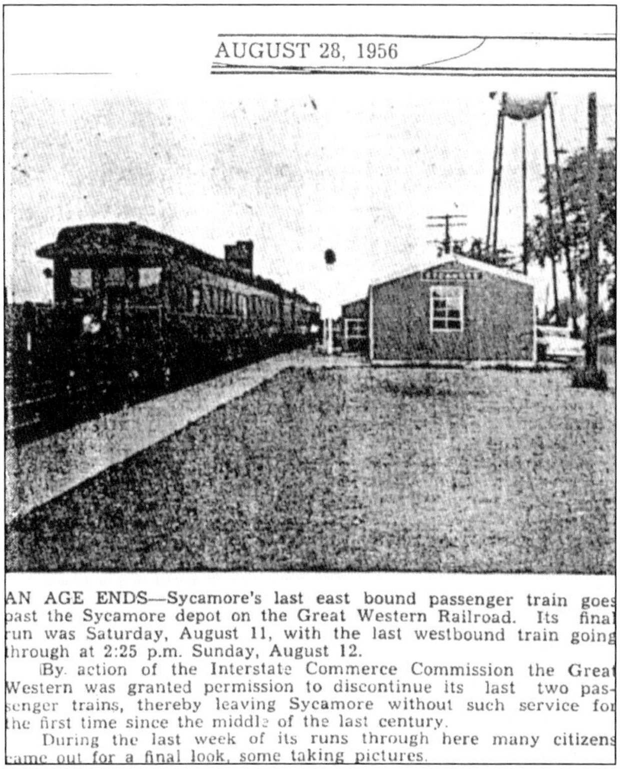

AUGUST 28, 1956

AN AGE ENDS—Sycamore's last east bound passenger train goes past the Sycamore depot on the Great Western Railroad. Its final run was Saturday, August 11, with the last westbound train going through at 2:25 p.m. Sunday, August 12.

By action of the Interstate Commerce Commission the Great Western was granted permission to discontinue its last two passenger trains, thereby leaving Sycamore without such service for the first time since the middle of the last century.

During the last week of its runs through here many citizens came out for a final look, some taking pictures.

CGW continued to operate the locals between Chicago and Oelwein after the loss of the mail contract. However, during a six-month period from 1955 to 1956, the trains averaged two riders per trip. The loss from providing this service during 1955 totaled $170,000. CGW filed a petition with the ICC in 1956 to end passenger service between Chicago and Oelwein, and the company quickly received approval. This old clipping from a Sycamore newspaper reported on the last runs in August 1956. (Joiner History Room, Sycamore, Illinois.)

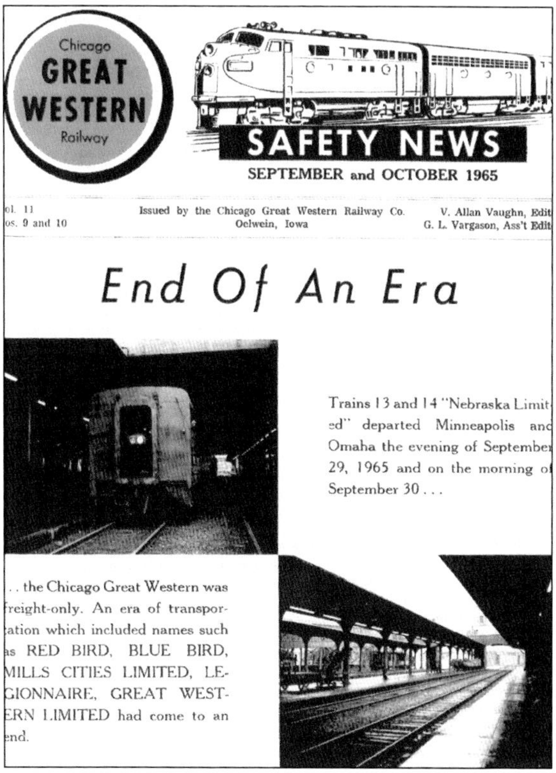

Chicago GREAT WESTERN Railway

SAFETY NEWS

SEPTEMBER and OCTOBER 1965

ol. 11
os. 9 and 10

Issued by the Chicago Great Western Railway Co.
Oelwein, Iowa

V. Allan Vaughn, Edit
G. L. Vargason, Ass't Edit

End Of An Era

Trains 13 and 14 "Nebraska Limited" departed Minneapolis and Omaha the evening of September 29, 1965 and on the morning of September 30 . . .

. . the Chicago Great Western was freight-only. An era of transportation which included names such as RED BIRD, BLUE BIRD, MILLS CITIES LIMITED, LEGIONNAIRE, GREAT WESTERN LIMITED had come to an end.

By 1965, CGW was operating passenger trains only between Minneapolis–St. Paul and Omaha. Decreasing revenues and increasing expenses forced the company to end this service in September 1965. *Safety News* featured a brief article on this historic event when CGW became a "freight only" railroad. (Author's collection.)

Five

Chicago Great Western in Illinois

B. & O. C. T. OUTBOUND

Distance from Chicago	Time Table No. 160 November 20, 1949 STATIONS DEPART	Passing siding capacity in 45 foot cars	FIRST CLASS 301 Soo Line No. 1 DAILY	10 B. & O. No. 10 DAILY	26 B.& O. No. 26 DAILY	608 C. & O. No. 8 DAILY	6 B. & O. No. 6 DAILY	403 C. G. W. No. 3 DAILY	317 Soo Line No. 17 DAILY	246 B. & O. No. 246 DAILY	8 B. & O. No. 8 DAILY	602 C. & O. No. 2 DAILY Except Saturday	32 B. & O. No. 32 DAILY
			A. M.	A. M.	P. M.	P. M.	P. M.	P. M.	P. M.	P. M.	P. M.	P. M.	P. M.
0.0	**Chicago**		1.15	11.10	4.00	**4.20** 6	**4.30** 608-403	**4.35** 6	5.50	8.45	11.00	11.15	11.30
	1.0												
1.0	**16th Street**												
	Chgo.Riv.Brg. 0.8												
1.8	**Halsted Street**		1.23	11.13	4.03	4.23	4.33	4.38	5.53	8.48	11.03	11.18	11.33
	0.5												
2.3	**Throop Street**		1.25	11.14	4.04	4.24	4.34	4.39	5.54	8.50	11.04	11.19	11.34
	0.9												
3.2	**Robey Yard**												
	0.5												
3.7	**Western Ave. Jct** C. & N. W.		1.28	11.16	4.06	4.26	4.36	4.41	5.56	8.52	11.06	11.21	11.36
	0.5												
4.2	**Rockwell St.**												
	C.N.W.-Pa.Co. 0.4												
4.6	**Sacramento Ave**		1.31					4.44	5.59				
	0.8												
5.4	**St. Louis Ave**												
	0.4												
5.8	**Springfield Ave**												
	0.8												
6.6	**Forty-Fifth Ave**												
	0.3												
6.9	**Forty-Eighth Ave**		1.35					4.47	6.03				
	1.2												
8.1	**Central Ave**		1.37					4.49	6.05				
	2.4												
10.5	**Chgo. Grt. West. Jct**		1.40					4.55	6.10				
	CA&E 0.5												

CGW did not own its right-of-way in Chicago. Instead, it used the tracks of the Baltimore and Ohio Chicago Terminal Railroad (B&OCT). The track connection, named Chicago Great Western Junction, was located in Forest Park. CGW train crews were governed by B&OCT train orders, rules, and special instructions when operating on that railroad. This portion of B&OCT employee timetable No. 160, effective November 20, 1949, shows mileage and stations between Chicago Great Western Junction and Grand Central Station. (Author's collection.)

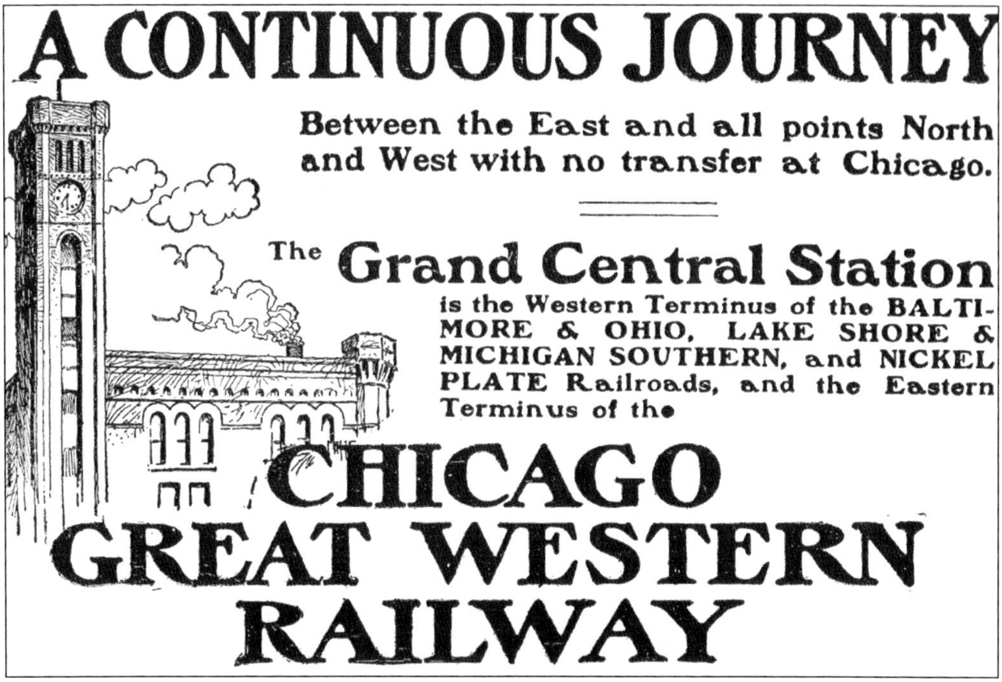

CGW used a temporary depot at Fifth Avenue (Wells Street) and Polk Street in Chicago when it inaugurated passenger service in Illinois on July 31, 1887. It continued to use this facility until April 1, 1892, when it moved operations one block north to Grand Central Station. This advertisement was published in 1902. (Author's collection.)

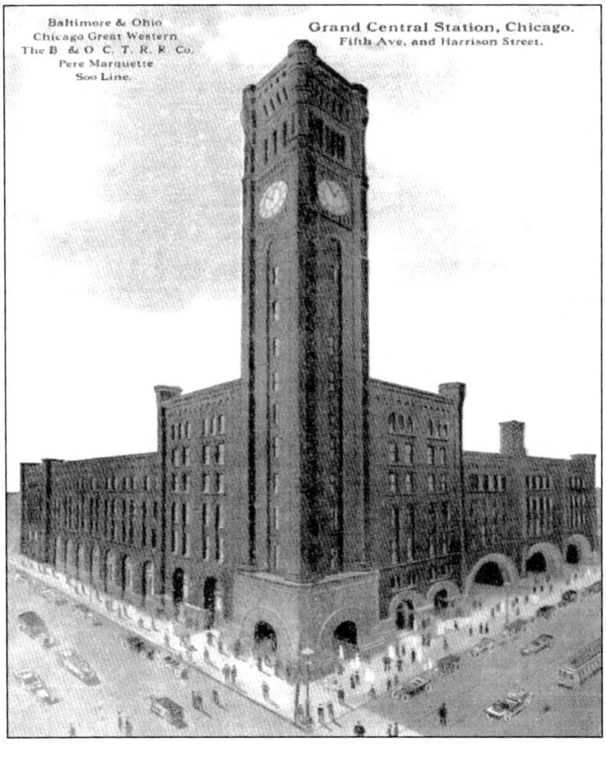

This postcard view shows the famous Grand Central clock tower at the corner of Fifth Avenue (left) and Harrison Street (right). The tower height was 273 feet, and it contained a bell, inscribed, "I ring for all," that rang on the hour. Different railroad companies owned Grand Central over the years after the formal opening on December 8, 1890, but CGW was always a tenant. (Author's collection.)

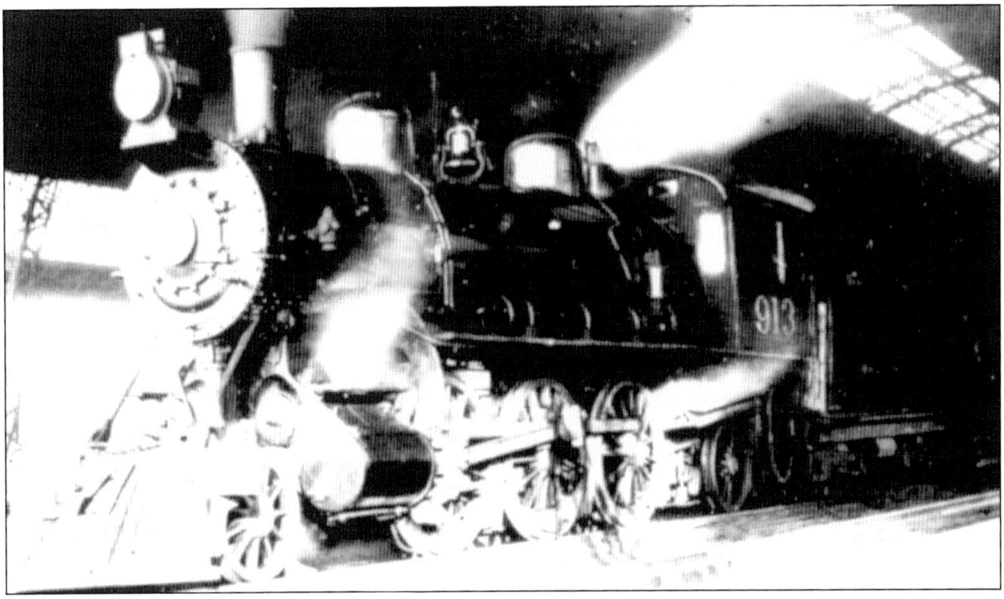

Steam locomotive No. 913 was photographed in the Grand Central train shed at the head end of a passenger train. Solon Spencer Beman, architect, and Willis S. Jones, chief engineer of the Wisconsin Central Railroad, which owned the facility, designed what was called a "balloon shed," supported entirely by arches without intermediate supports. It was the second-largest balloon shed in the country after the New York Grand Central Station. (Joiner History Room, Sycamore, Illinois.)

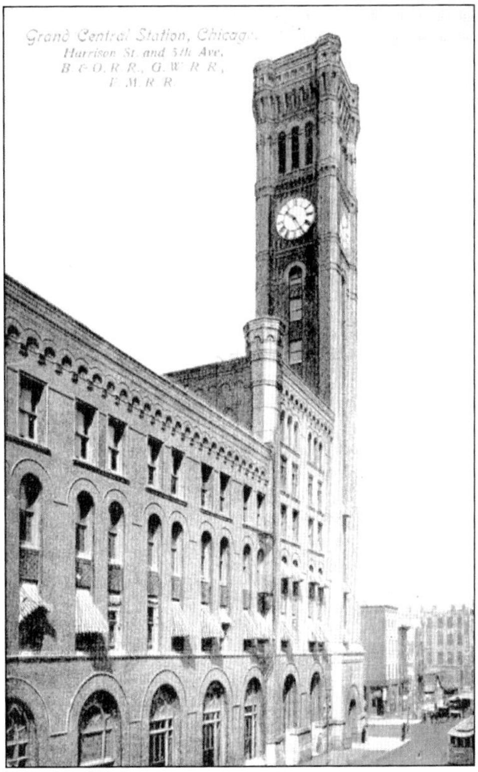

This 1909 postcard scene shows the east side of Grand Central along Fifth Avenue. CGW passenger trains arrived and departed Grand Central continuously until the company ended passenger service in Illinois in August 1956. The station complex included the CGW Harrison Street freight house, located between Grand Central and the Chicago River. (Author's collection.)

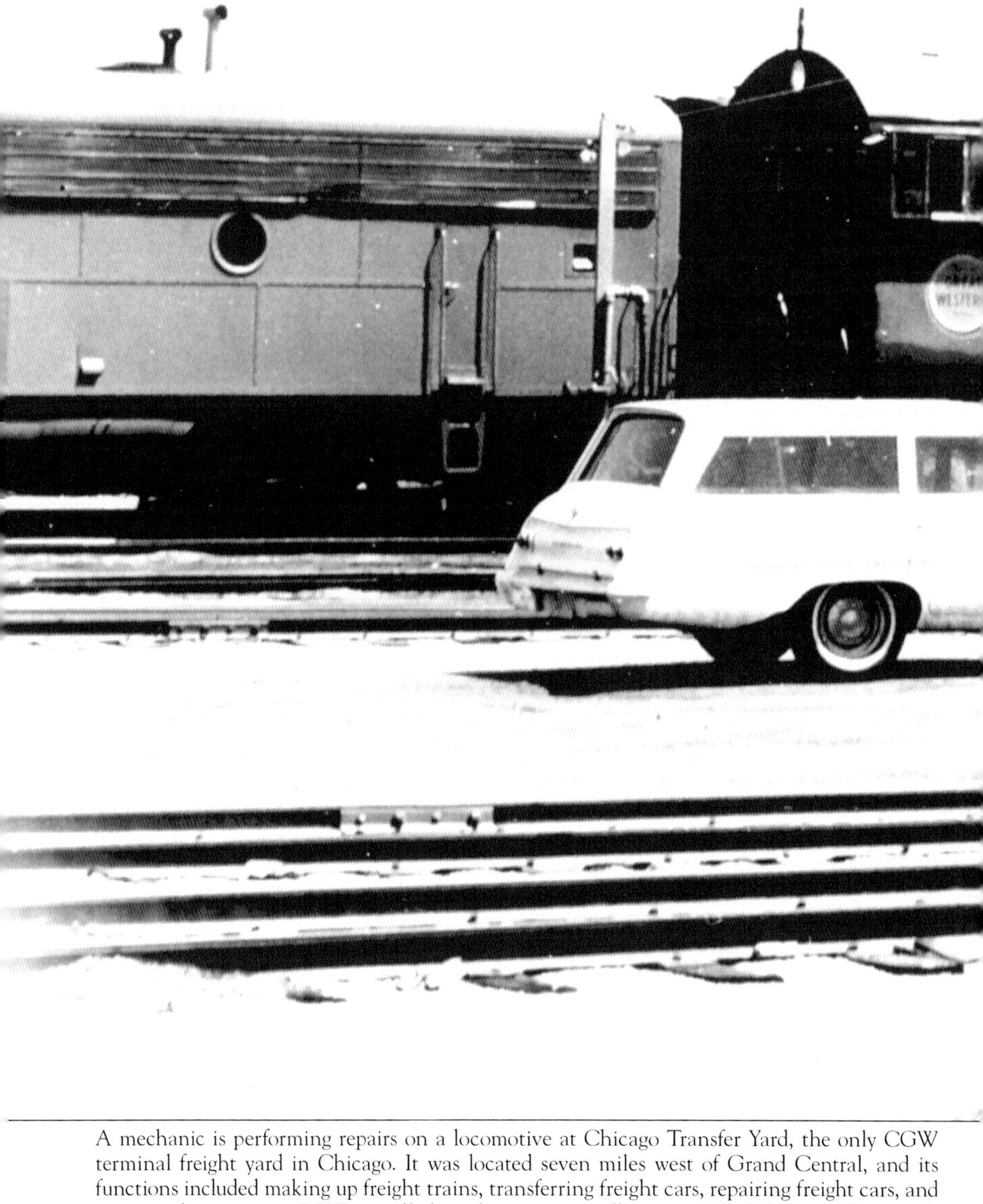

A mechanic is performing repairs on a locomotive at Chicago Transfer Yard, the only CGW terminal freight yard in Chicago. It was located seven miles west of Grand Central, and its functions included making up freight trains, transferring freight cars, repairing freight cars, and servicing locomotives. CGW initially leased space at roundhouses on Twelfth Street (Roosevelt

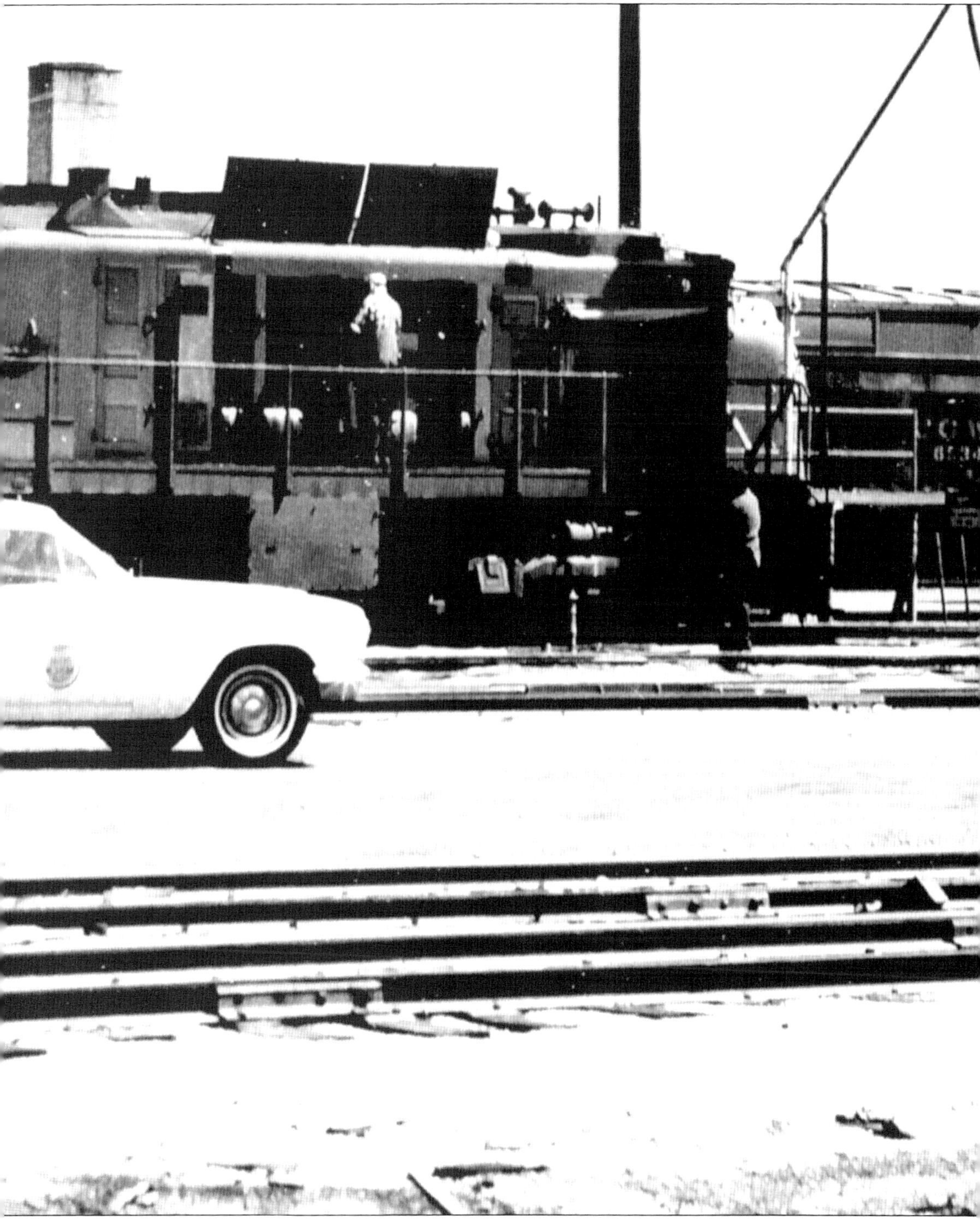

Road) and Robey Street for servicing passenger and freight locomotives, respectively. Later the company built its own roundhouse for freight engines at Forty-sixth Street (Kenyon Avenue) just east of Chicago Transfer. Passenger power was then serviced at Robey Street. (Joseph Piersen.)

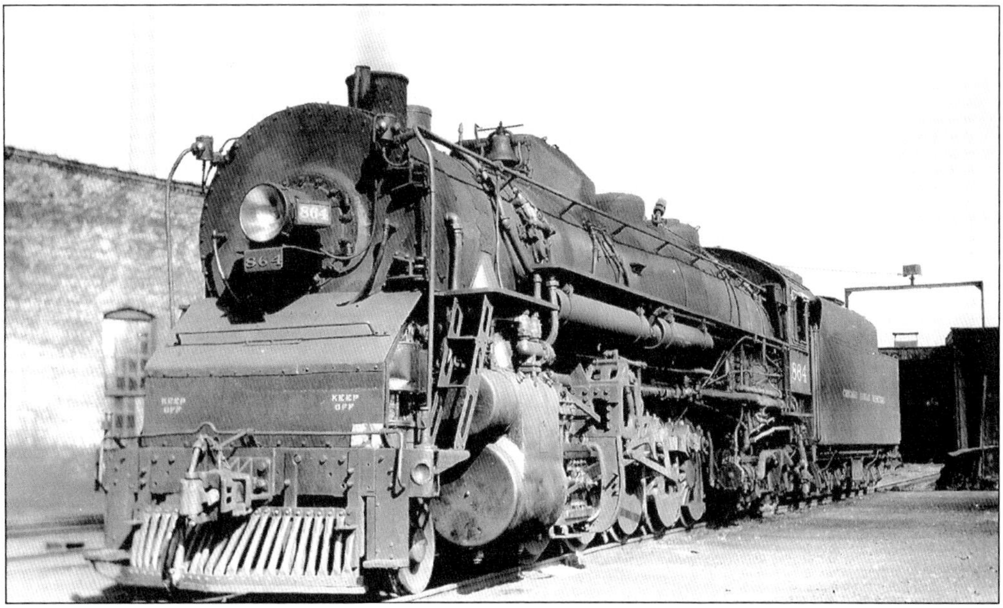

Steam locomotive No. 864 was photographed at the Forty-sixth Street roundhouse (background). Note the turntable behind the engine. Forty-sixth Street included a 100-ton capacity coal tipple and a 50,000-gallon water tank. (Author's collection.)

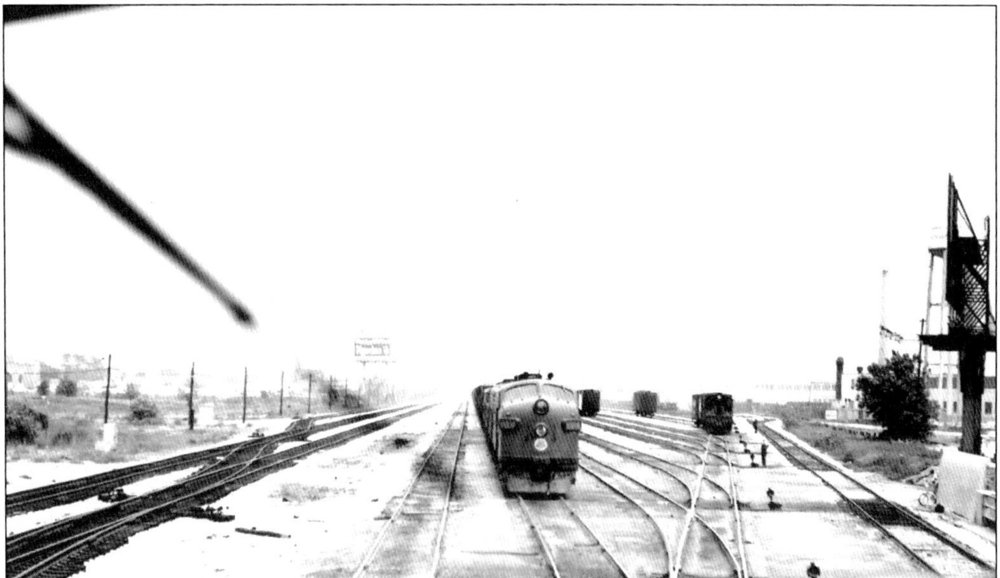

This photograph was taken from the cab of diesel engine No. 108-C as it arrived at Chicago Transfer Yard with a freight train on June 12, 1967. The yard was situated on leased property and was much smaller when M&NW began operations in Illinois in 1887. CGW expanded the size of the yard to increase capacity in 1900 and 1901 by purchasing land to the south. Chicago Transfer Yard was located north of Twelfth Street (Roosevelt Road) between Forty-eighth Street (Cicero Avenue) and Central Avenue, almost one mile in length. By 1907, it consisted of an eastbound yard between Forty-eighth Street and Fifty-second Street (Laramie Avenue) and a westbound yard between Fifty-second Street and Central Avenue. (Joseph Piersen.)

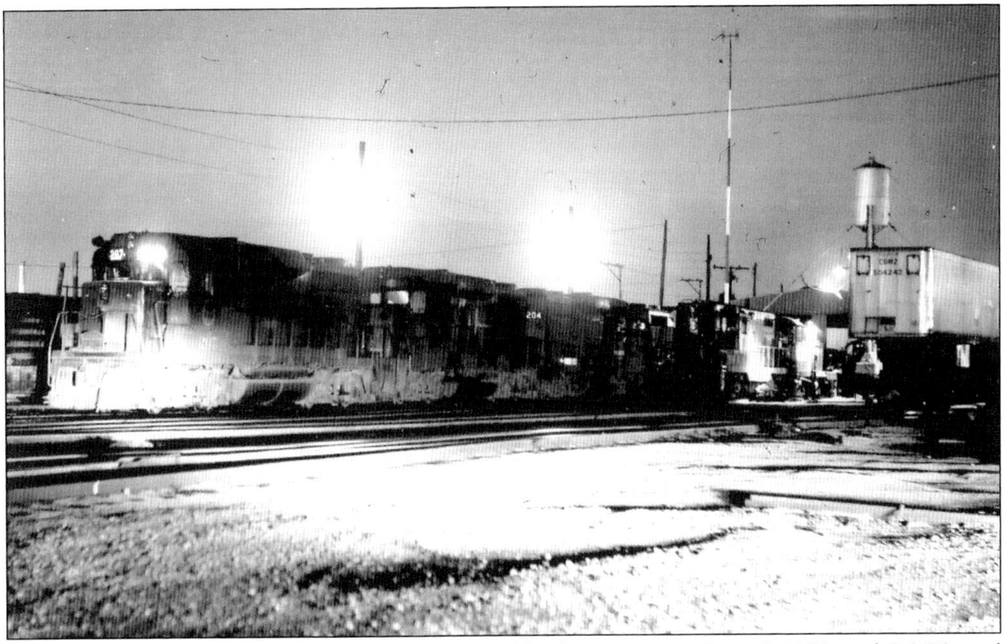

The Forty-sixth Street roundhouse was destroyed by fire on September 15, 1955, and CGW used a temporary facility until it built a new engine house in 1962 as part of a major reconstruction of Chicago Transfer Yard. This photograph shows the new locomotive servicing area at 12:30 a.m. on August 13, 1966. (Joseph Piersen.)

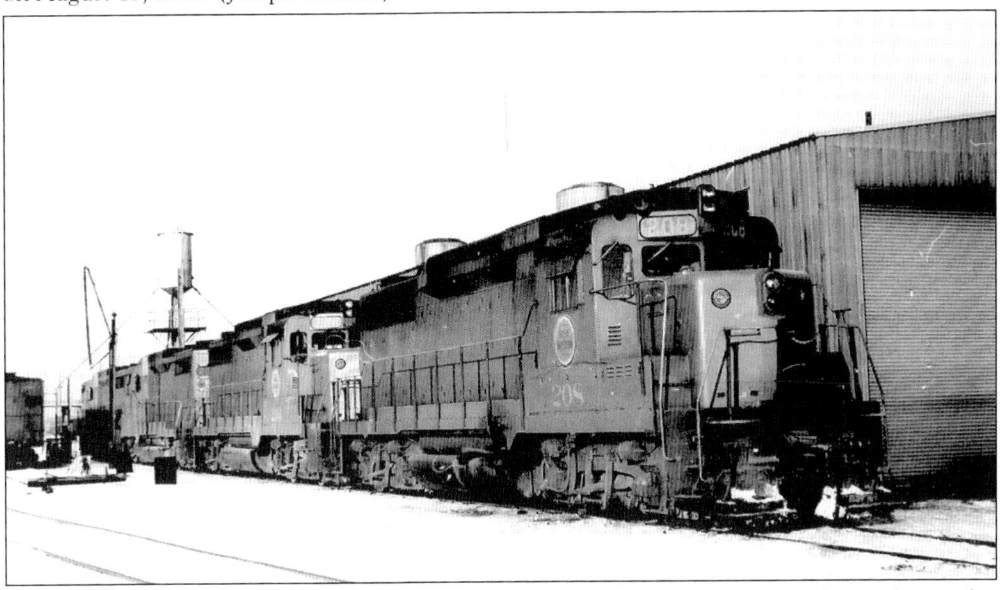

GP-30 locomotives are at the engine house on a winter day in the 1960s. The yard was also called Forty-eighth Street Yard, but Chicago Transfer Yard was an appropriate description. Arriving freight trains were broken apart at this facility, and cars were then classified either for interchange or delivery to local industries by the daily wayfreight. Most of the cars that were to be transferred to other railroads were interchanged with the Belt Railway, which provided intermediate switching service between carriers. The process worked in reverse for assembling outbound freight trains destined for the main yard at Oelwein. (Author's collection.)

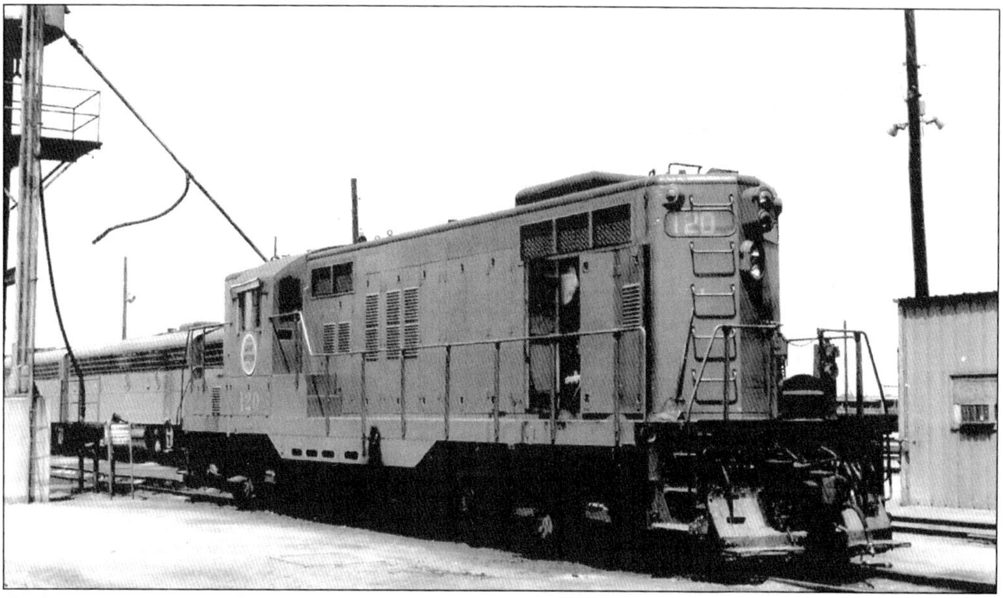

GP-7 No. 120 was undergoing servicing at Chicago Transfer Yard when this photograph was taken in May 1967. CGW rebuilt and modernized the yard over a four-year period from 1959 to 1963. The company laid new track and constructed new freight car and locomotive repair facilities, a yard office, a pump house, a toolhouse, a sanding plant, fueling facilities, and a new "piggyback" ramp. (Author's collection.)

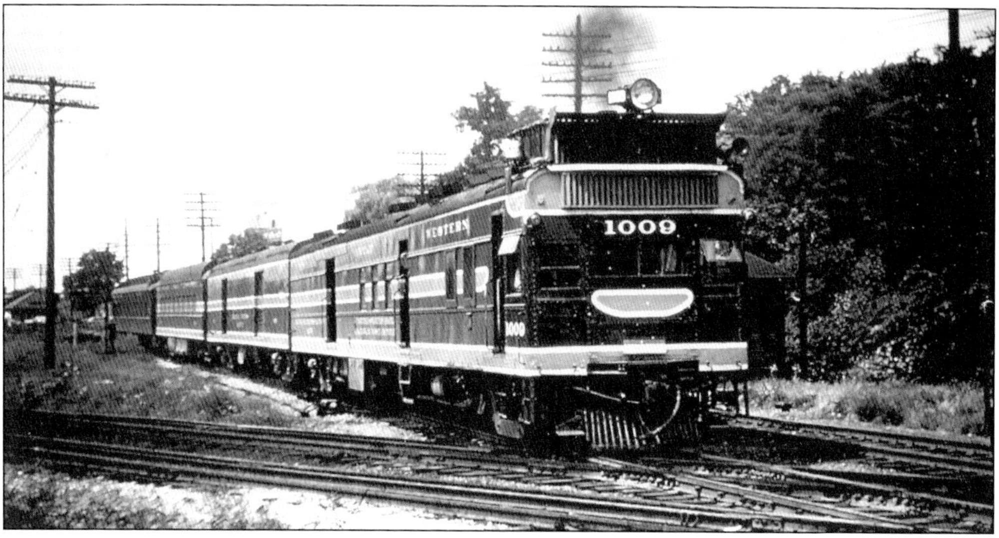

Forest Park was located three miles west of Chicago Transfer Yard. It was originally named Forest Home, and CGW constructed a depot here between 1912 and 1913. CGW trains crossed Des Plaines Avenue, streetcar tracks, and the Chicago, Aurora and Elgin Railroad (CA&E) at grade. A manned interlocking plant controlled train movements. Chicago Great Western Junction was located between Des Plaines Avenue and the CA&E crossing. The area was extensively changed between 1954 and 1960, when the Congress Street Expressway was constructed. This photograph shows CGW railcar M-1009 headed eastbound at the CA&E crossing in 1949, with the CGW depot in the background. Forest Park station was closed on May 19 of that year. (Author's collection.)

CHICAGO DISTRICT — CHICAGO TO OELWEIN

WESTBOUND SECOND CLASS 91 Manifest Freight Depart Daily	143 Manifest Freight Depart Daily		Miles between stations	TIME TABLE No. 9 Effective January 20, 1957	Distance from Chicago.	Station Numbers.	Office Calls.	HOURS OF TELEGRAPH SERVICE Monday Thru Friday	Saturdays, Sundays, Holidays
		PH		CHICAGO (B.&O.C.T. Rules gov.; Two Main Tracks)	0.0	425			
11.00 PM	12.01 PM [192]	PH-R	7.3	CHICAGO TRANSFER	7.3	417	JR	6.00 AM to 2.00 PM 8.30 PM to 4.30 AM	6.00 AM to 2.00 PM 8.30 PM to 4.30 AM
11.45 PM	12.15	PH	3.0	C. G. W. Jct. FOREST PARK	10.3	415	KC	Continuous	Continuous
		PH	1.3	MAYWOOD	11.6	414			
12.45 AM [90]	12.25	PH-R	1.5	BELLWOOD	13.1	412	BQ	7.00 AM to 3.00 PM 9.00 PM to 5.00 AM	7.00 AM to 3.00 PM 9.00 PM to 5.00 AM
1.00	12.40	PH	3.7	ELMHURST	16.8	409	PR	7.00 AM to 11.30 AM 12.30 PM to 4.00 PM	
			0.4	End of Two Main Tracks. I. C. R. R. Crossing	17.2				
1.20	1.00	PH	8.4	GRETNA (Automatic Block Signals)	25.6	400	GA	7.00 AM to 12 Noon 1.00 PM to 4.00 PM	
1.30	1.30	PH-R	5.1	INGALTON	30.7	395	NI	6.15 AM to 11.30 AM 12.30 PM to 3.15 PM	6.15 AM to 11.30 AM 12.30 PM to 3.15 PM
1.40	1.40	PH	6.2	ST. CHARLES	35.9	390	SB	7.00 AM to 12 Noon 1.00 PM to 4.00 PM	
1.50	1.50	PH	5.5	WASCO	41.4	384	WO	8.00 AM to 12 Noon 1.00 PM to 5.00 PM	
2.00	2.00	PH	4.2	LILY LAKE	45.6	380			
2.05	2.06	PH	3.0	VIRGIL	48.6	377	VX	8.00 AM to 12 Noon 1.00 PM to 5.00 PM	
2.20	2.20	PH-R	8.0	SYCAMORE	56.6	369	DX	8.00 AM to 12 Noon 1.00 PM to 5.00 PM	(Saturday Only) 8.00 AM to 12 Noon 1.00 PM to 5.00 PM
		PH	5.3	C. M. St. P. & P. Crossing	61.9				
2.45	2.35	PH	2.2	CLARE	64.1	361	KU	8.00 AM to 12 Noon 1.00 PM to 5.00 PM	
2.55	2.45	PH	5.7	ESMOND	69.8	355	UY	8.45 PM to 12.30 AM 1.30 AM to 5.45 AM	
3.05	2.55	PH	6.1	LINDENWOOD	74.9	350	WD	8.00 AM to 12 Noon 1.00 PM to 5.00 PM	
3.15	3.02	PH	3.5	C. B. & Q. Crossing HOLCOMB	78.4	347			
3.35	3.20	PH-R	9.4	BYRON	87.8	337	BY	8.00 AM to 12 Noon 1.00 PM to 5.00 PM	
				C. M. St. P. & P. Crossing	88.3				
3.50	3.33	PH	6.0	MYRTLE	93.8	332			
4.05	3.45	PH	7.1	GERMAN VALLEY	100.9	325	GY	8.00 AM to 12 Noon 1.00 PM to 5.00 PM	
4.15	4.15	PH	5.8	SOUTH FREEPORT	106.7	319	DA	8.00 AM to 12 Noon 1.00 PM to 5.00 PM	
4.45	4.50	PH	13.3	PEARL CITY	120.0	306	BG	8.00 AM to 12 Noon 1.00 PM to 5.00 PM	
5.05	5.10	PH	9.0	End of Two Main Tracks. EAST STOCKTON (Two Main Tracks)	129.0				
5.10	6.00	PH-R	2.1	STOCKTON	131.1	294	NS	6.00 AM to 2.00 PM 8.30 PM to 4.30 AM	6.00 AM to 2.00 PM 8.30 PM to 4.30 AM
5.15	6.30	PH	0.4	GOLDEN End of Two Main Tracks.	131.5				
		PH	11.8	ELIZABETH	143.3	282	ZA	8.00 AM to 12 Noon 1.00 PM to 5.00 PM	
5.45 [92]	7.00 [90]	PH	3.3	NORTH HANOVER	146.6	279	AF	8.00 AM to 12 Noon 1.00 PM to 5.00 PM	
6.10	7.20	PH	8.8	AIKEN End of Two Main Tracks.	155.4	260			
6.15	7.25	PH	2.2	GALENA JCT. (C.B.& Q. Rules gov.; Two Main Tracks) End of Two Main Tracks.	157.6	268	RQ	Continuous	Continuous
		PH	0.5	PORTAGE	158.1				
		PH	12.8	EAST CABIN (I. C. R. R. Rules govern)	170.9		CB	Continuous	Continuous
			0.4	C. B. & Q. Crossings	171.3				
6.45	7.55	PH	0.6	DUBUQUE JCT.	171.9		JC	Continuous	Continuous
		PH	0.2	C. M. St. P. & P. Crossing DUBUQUE	172.1	253			
7.01	8.10	PH-R	2.1	FAIR GROUND End of Two Main Tracks.	174.2	251	RZ	5.00 AM to 1.00 PM 4.00 PM to 12 Mid.	(Except Holidays) 5.00 AM to 1.00 PM 4.00 PM to 12 Mid.
7.30	8.40	PH	13.7	GRAF	187.9	237			
7.55	9.00	PH	8.1	FARLEY	196.0	229			
8.05	9.15	PH	6.5	DYERSVILLE	202.5	223	DY	8.00 AM to 12 Noon 1.00 PM to 5.00 PM	
8.20	9.35	PH	8.1	ALMORAL	210.6	215			
		PH	4.6	C. M. St. P. & P. Crossing	215.2	210			
8.50	10.25	PH	15.2	LAMONT	230.4	195	DJ	8.00 AM to 12 Noon 1.00 PM to 5.00 PM	
		PH	4.8	AURORA	235.2	190	OU	8.00 AM to 12 Noon 1.00 PM to 5.00 PM	
9.10	10.55	PH	7.3	FELTON (Two Main Tracks) End of Two Main Tracks.	242.5				
			2.7	C. R. I. & P. Crossing	245.2				
9.20 AM	11.01 PM	PH-R-Ry	0.6	OELWEIN	245.8	180	WI	Continuous	Continuous
Arrive Daily	Arrive Daily			245.8					
10 20	11 00			Time on District					

Eastbound trains are superior to westbound trains of the same class. Rule 71.

This is the westbound schedule of CGW Eastern Division employee timetable No. 9, effective January 20, 1957. The reader may find it useful to locate stations and facilities as this book continue westward. (Author's collection.)

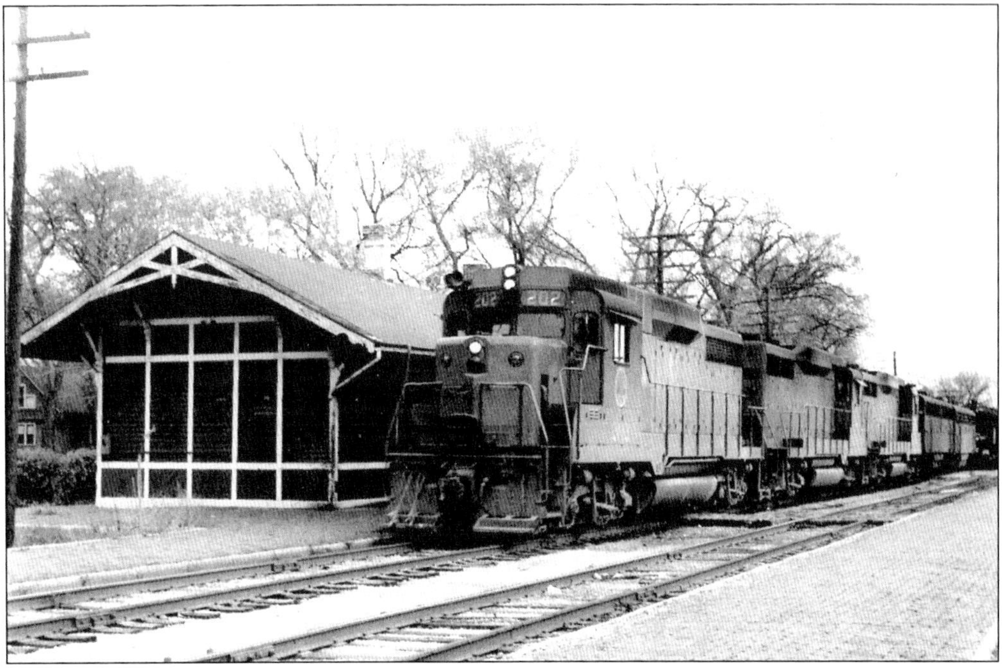

A westbound CGW freight train passes the Maywood depot, one mile west of Chicago Great Western Junction. M&NW opened a station here in 1887. The railroad received a substantial amount of business from American Can Company at Maywood, and it constructed the Seventeenth Avenue Yard to accommodate shipments. American Can signed a contract with CGW and Chicago Junction Railway (Indiana Harbor Belt Railroad or IHB) in 1897 to build a long spur track from the company's factory located one mile north of the CGW. Maywood station was closed on August 29, 1958. (Joseph Piersen.)

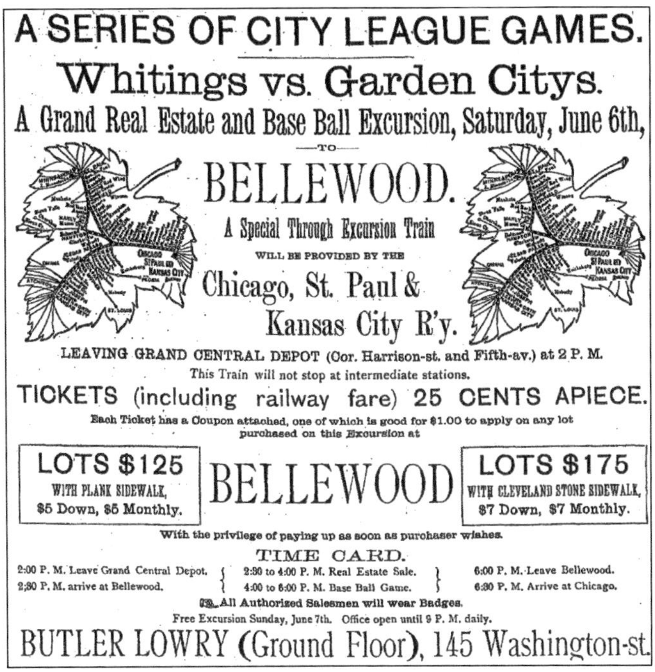
A SERIES OF CITY LEAGUE GAMES.

Whitings vs. Garden Citys.

A Grand Real Estate and Base Ball Excursion, Saturday, June 6th,

—TO—

BELLEWOOD.

A Special Through Excursion Train

WILL BE PROVIDED BY THE

Chicago, St. Paul & Kansas City R'y.

LEAVING GRAND CENTRAL DEPOT (Cor. Harrison-st. and Fifth-av.) at 2 P. M.

This Train will not stop at intermediate stations.

TICKETS (including railway fare) 25 CENTS APIECE.

Each Ticket has a Coupon attached, one of which is good for $1.00 to apply on any lot purchased on this Excursion at

LOTS $125 WITH PLANK SIDEWALK, $5 Down, $5 Monthly.

BELLEWOOD

LOTS $175 WITH CLEVELAND STONE SIDEWALK, $7 Down, $7 Monthly.

With the privilege of paying up as soon as purchaser wishes.

TIME CARD.

2:00 P. M. Leave Grand Central Depot.
2:30 P. M. arrive at Bellewood.
2:30 to 4:00 P. M. Real Estate Sale.
4:00 to 6:00 P. M. Base Ball Game.
6:00 P. M. Leave Bellewood.
6:30 P. M. Arrive at Chicago.

All Authorized Salesmen will wear Badges.

Free Excursion Sunday, June 7th. Office open until 9 P. M. daily.

BUTLER LOWRY (Ground Floor), 145 Washington-st.

Real estate developers established the first subdivisions in Bellwood during the 1890s, and baseball games were held to attract customers. CStP&KC provided excursion service, as shown in this *Chicago Tribune* newspaper advertisement from 1891. Note the early spelling of the subdivision name. The railroad constructed a depot at Bellwood in 1891, which was slightly more than a mile west of Maywood station. (Chicago Tribune.)

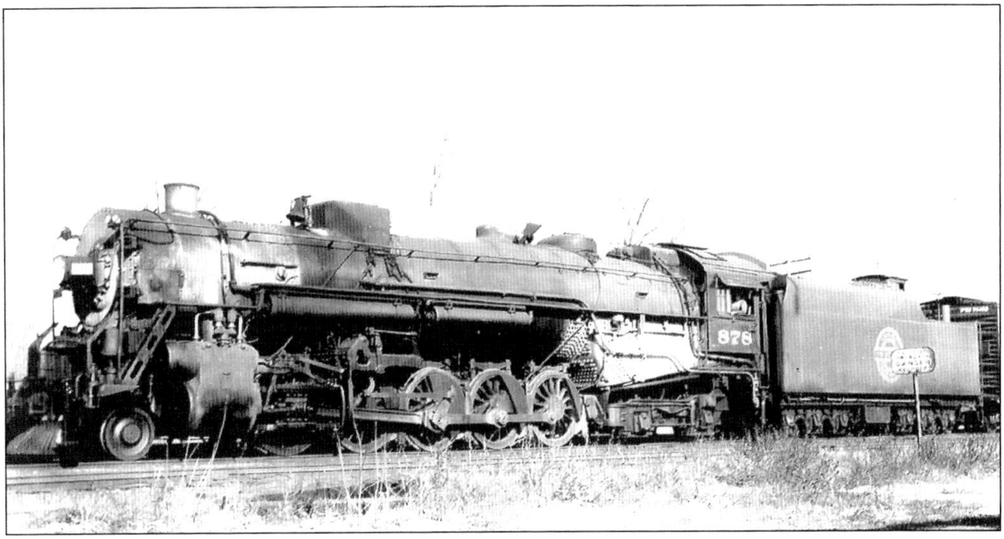

A predecessor company of the IHB signed an agreement in 1897 with CGW that allowed the Chicago, Hammond and Western Railroad (CH&W) to cross CGW at grade at Bellwood. The contract also included provisions on constructing an interchange track. This junction became one of the most important on the CGW because most of the eastbound perishable traffic was interchanged with the IHB at Bellwood. Also, CGW and IHB provided freight service at a stone quarry south of Bellwood. CGW steam locomotive No. 878, at the head end of a freight train, was photographed at Bellwood on November 12, 1937. (Author's collection.)

24. CLOSE CLEARANCES:

CHICAGO	Viaducts and trolley wires over various foreign line tracks in Chicago terminals used by C.G.W. trains, transfers and yard engines will not clear man on top or side of car.
BELLWOOD	IHB railway bridge will not clear man on top or side of car.
GALENA JCT.	Bridge over Galena River will not clear man on top or side of car.
MARSHALLTOWN	Guard against close clearances between main track and siding between First and Second Avenue. Between South track and adjacent tracks serving coal and oil companies.
TALMAGE	C.B.&Q. overhead bridge will not clear man on top or side of car.
CONCEPTION	Wabash overhead bridge will not clear man on top or side of car.

Special instructions were published in the 1957 employee timetable regarding close clearances at Bellwood. During 1930 and 1931, IHB elevated its tracks through the area, which then crossed over CGW. A wooden ramp was constructed from the elevated IHB main line to the interchange track at ground level. On March 11, 1949, the ramp, heavily coated with creosote, was destroyed by fire. It was rebuilt and returned to service on July 15, 1949. (Author's collection.)

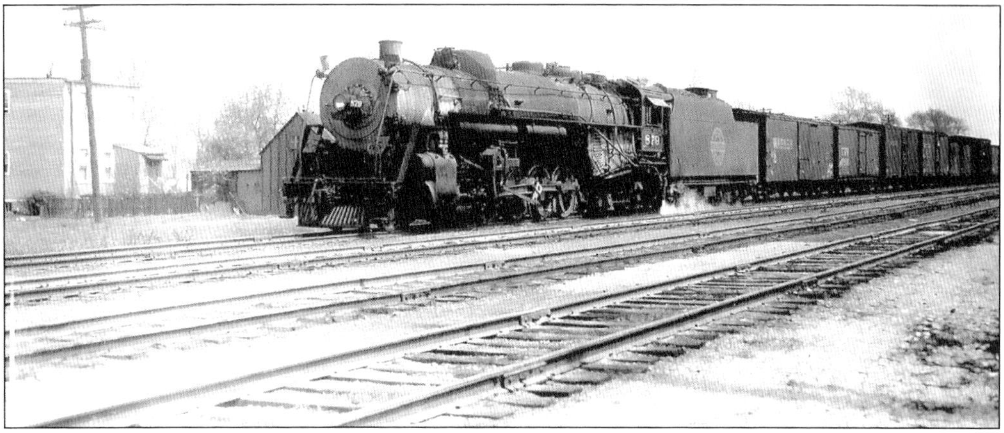

A westbound CGW freight train powered by steam locomotive No. 879 is passing IHB interchange tracks at Bellwood in 1941. The volume of interchange business was substantial, and in 1965, CGW reported that it interchanged an average of 110 cars per day with the IHB at Bellwood. (Author's collection.)

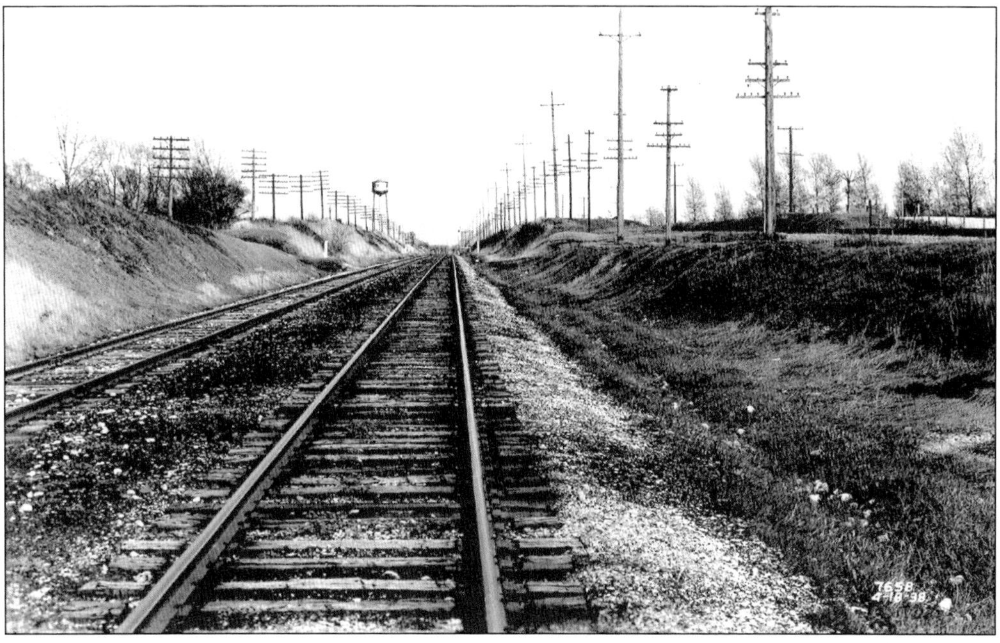

The CGW main line in DuPage County near Elmhurst, four miles west of Bellwood, is shown on April 18, 1938, in a view facing east. CGW followed a policy of constructing a second main track for a distance of at least 10 miles out of important terminals to relieve congestion. It double-tracked the main line between Forest Park and Elmhurst in 1910. (M. D. McCarter Collection, negative No. N47658.)

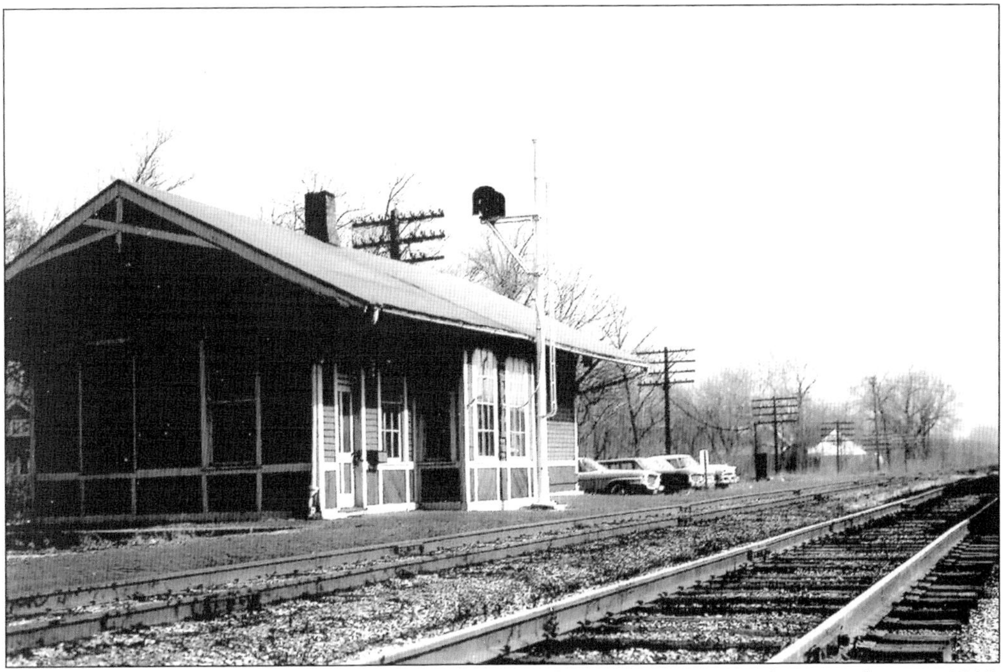

Elmhurst station was first named South Elmhurst when M&NW started service here in 1887. The depot was constructed at that time and remained in service until the merger in 1968. Other facilities at Elmhurst included a water tank originally supplied from an artesian well 1,700 feet deep (the tank was later connected to the city water main). The depot and station grounds were purchased by the City of Elmhurst and developed into a public park called Wild Meadows Trace. This photograph was taken in 1961. (Joiner History Room, Sycamore, Illinois.)

Elmhurst, Ill.			
Alexander Lumber Co.	Coal-Building Material	C&NW	No
Bade, Edward, & Sons	Paper Products	C&NW	No
Building Supply Co.	Building Material	Team Track	
Davis Fuel Co.	Coal-Fuel	IC	Yes
Dramm Greenhouses, Inc.	Florist-Coal	IC	Yes
DuPage Feed & Supply Co.	Feed	Team Track	
Elmhurst-Chicago Stone Co.	Stone-Sand-Gravel	C&NW	No
Elmhurst College	Coal	Team Track	
Hammerschmidt & Franzen Co.	Lumber-Millwork	C&NW	No
Peoples Coal & Material Co.	Coal-Building Material	CGW	Yes
Standard Oil Co.	Petroleum Products	IC	Yes
Sturtevant, P. A., Co.	Manufacturing	Team Track	
Swanson Feed & Hardware	Feed-Poultry Supplies	Team Track	

CGW served few industries at Elmhurst. The company had an interchange here with the Illinois Central Railroad (IC), which crossed CGW at grade. (Author's collection.)

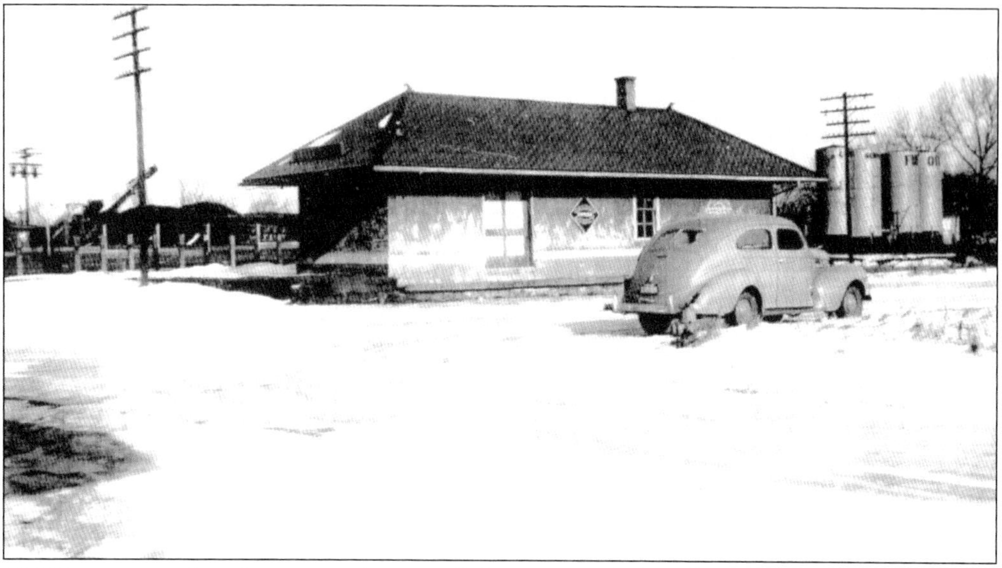

CGW constructed a siding one mile west of Elmhurst in 1910 to deliver construction materials for a new subdivision called Villa Park. In 1914, Villa Park was incorporated as the village of Ardmore. The name was changed to the village of Villa Park in 1917, partly because CGW tariffs referred to the community by this name. CGW constructed the Villa Park depot in 1926. It was closed on October 19, 1958, and sold to the community for use as a skaters' shelter at the village ice rink. The building is still owned by the village, and on May 14, 2001, Villa Park received a historic preservation plaque to recognize its efforts restoring the depot. (James L. Rueber.)

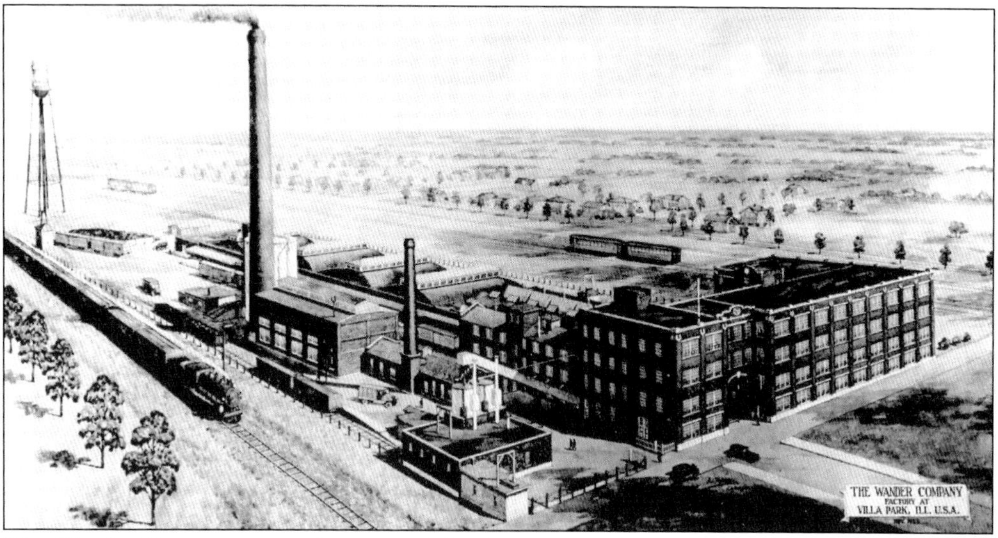

The Wander Company, manufacturers of Ovaltine, opened its only plant in the United States at Villa Park in 1917. CGW published an article on the facility in its company magazine, *The Maize*, and reported Wander was expected to ship and receive 200 carloads annually. Volume became substantial over the years, and CGW was handling between 500 and 600 carloads a year by 1961. This drawing of the plant was made in 1928, and it features a speeding westbound CGW freight train (left). (Villa Park Historical Society.)

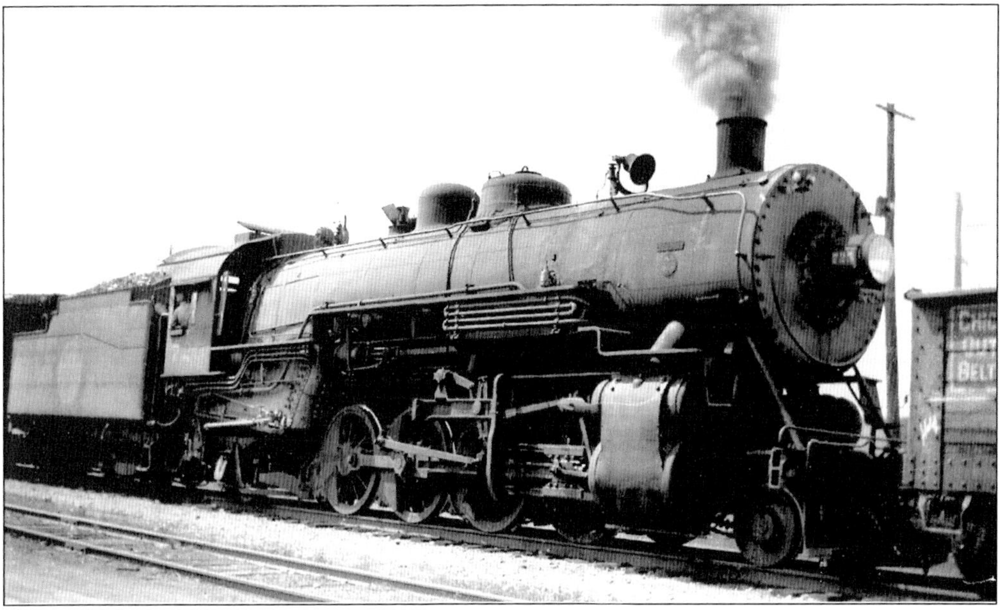

Steam locomotive No. 725 was photographed switching freight cars at Villa Park in June 1934. (M. D. McCarter Collection, negative No. N31066.)

Villa Park, Ill.			
General Lumber Corp.	Lumber	Team Track	
Hines, Edward, Lumber Co.	Lumber	CGW	No
Pioneer Garden Paint & Pet Supply	Salt	Team Track	
Villa Park Coal & Material Co.	Coal	CGW	No
Wander Co., The	Beverage Preparation-Chemists	CGW-CA&E	No

This is a list of rail shippers at Villa Park. (Author's collection.)

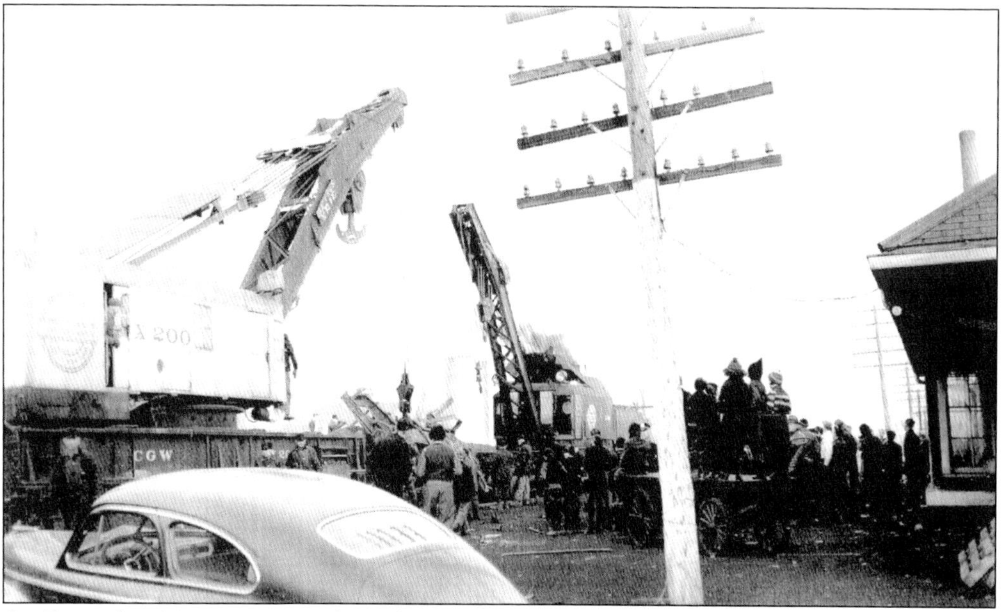

On December 28, 1941, an eastbound CGW freight train derailed due to a broken axle while passing through Villa Park. Bacon, cuts of meat, soap, and grease were scattered about the depot as eight boxcars left the rails and broke open. Within minutes, motorists and bystanders were carrying away as much as they could! (James L. Rueber.)

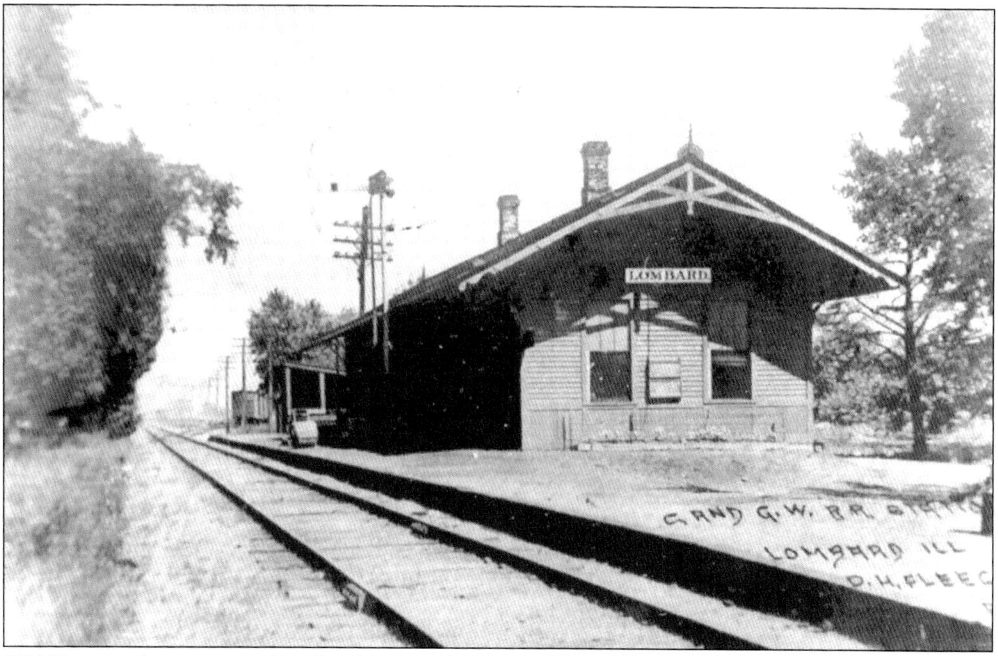

CGW opened a station at Lombard, two miles west of the Villa Park depot, in 1887. It was closed on July 21, 1931, and company records show the railroad razed the structure in October 1957 because it "was old and beyond repair." (Lombard Historical Society.)

Lombard, Ill.			
Alexander Lumber Co.	Coal-Building Material	CGW	No
Du Page Community Builders, Inc.	Cement Blocks	Team Track	
Hammerschmidt Lumber & Fuel Co.	Coal-Building Material	C&NW	No
Lombard Floral Co., The	Flowers-Coal	CGW	No
Lombard Lumber Co.	Lumber-Building Material	Team Track	
Pure Oil Co.	Petroleum Products	CA&E	No
Westmore Supply Co.	Coal-Building Material	CA&E	No

Lombard industries were served by CGW. (Author's collection.)

SIDINGS AND SPURS BETWEEN STATIONS

	STATION NO.	MILE POST	CAR CAPACITY	CONNECTED
Villa Park	407	18.5	20	Both ends
Lombard	405	20.9	20	Both ends
North Glen Ellyn	402	23.3	3	West end
Campbell's Spur	394	29.7	15	East end
Fox River	388	37.3	97	Both ends
Five Points	365	59.3	15	East end
Stillman Valley	342	83.4	24	Both ends
Egan	329	96.7	27	Both ends
Bolton	311	114.3	25	East end
Kent	301	124.9	20	East end
Woodbine	287	138.6	21	Both ends
Rice	271	153.6	10	Both ends
Aiken Spur		155.1	9	East end
Durango	245	180.1	25	East end
Petersburg	217	207.5	32	Both Ends
Oneida	210	215.2	37	East end
Thorpe	220	220.2	5	East end
Dundee	200	225.3	15	West end
Stanley	185	239.7	28	Both Ends
DeKalb	7374	On branch 6 miles south of Sycamore Yard		

M&NW followed a policy of establishing local stations approximately every five miles while constructing its line through Illinois between 1886 and 1887. Some stations consisted of a depot and siding; others were only a platform or shed for shipping milk. Stations that were seldom patronized were eventually closed and the sidings left in place as passing tracks. The old station name remained in use, however, to identify the siding location. This list, published in the 1957 employee timetable, includes long-abandoned stations, such as North Glen Ellyn, which closed April 12, 1920. (Author's collection.)

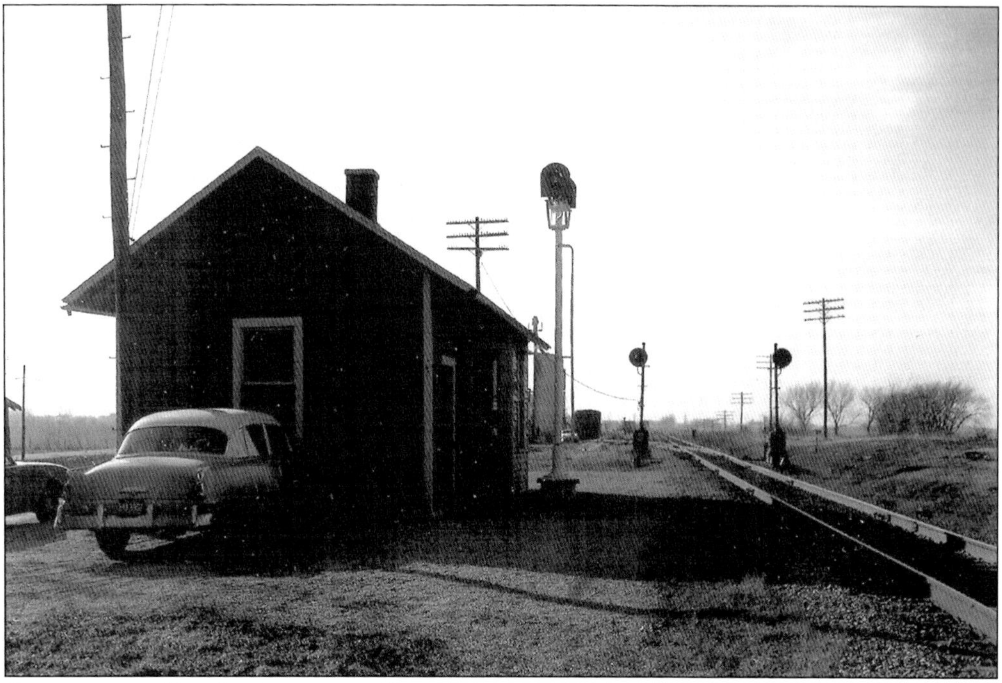

Gretna, west of Lombard, was a small rural community when the M&NW started service here in 1887. Subdivisions were established in this area during the late 1950s, and the community was incorporated as the village of Carol Stream in 1959. CGW renamed the station accordingly in 1962. It remained in use by the railroad after the 1968 merger, and C&NW eventually sold the depot to the village. The structure was dismantled and reassembled at Armstrong Park, where it is now Gretna Station Museum. (Joiner History Room, Sycamore, Illinois.)

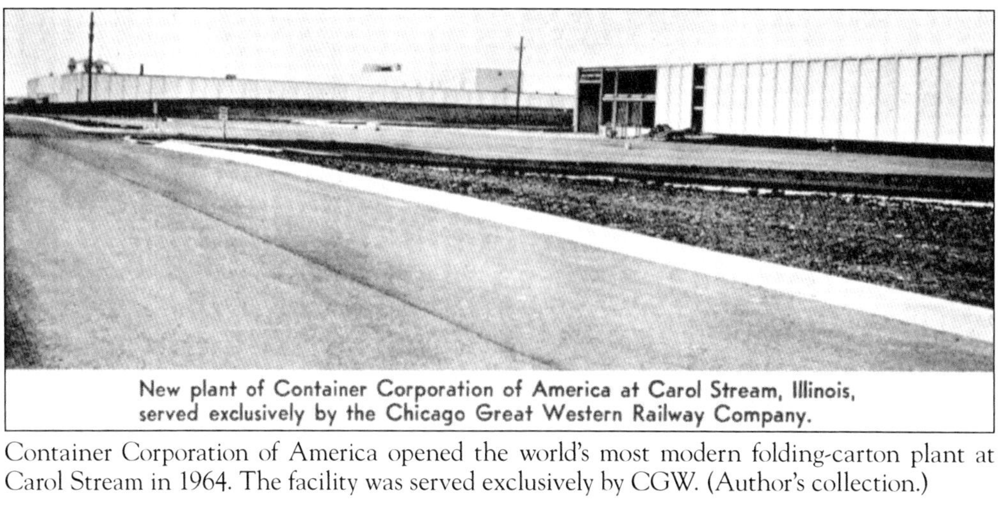

Container Corporation of America opened the world's most modern folding-carton plant at Carol Stream in 1964. The facility was served exclusively by CGW. (Author's collection.)

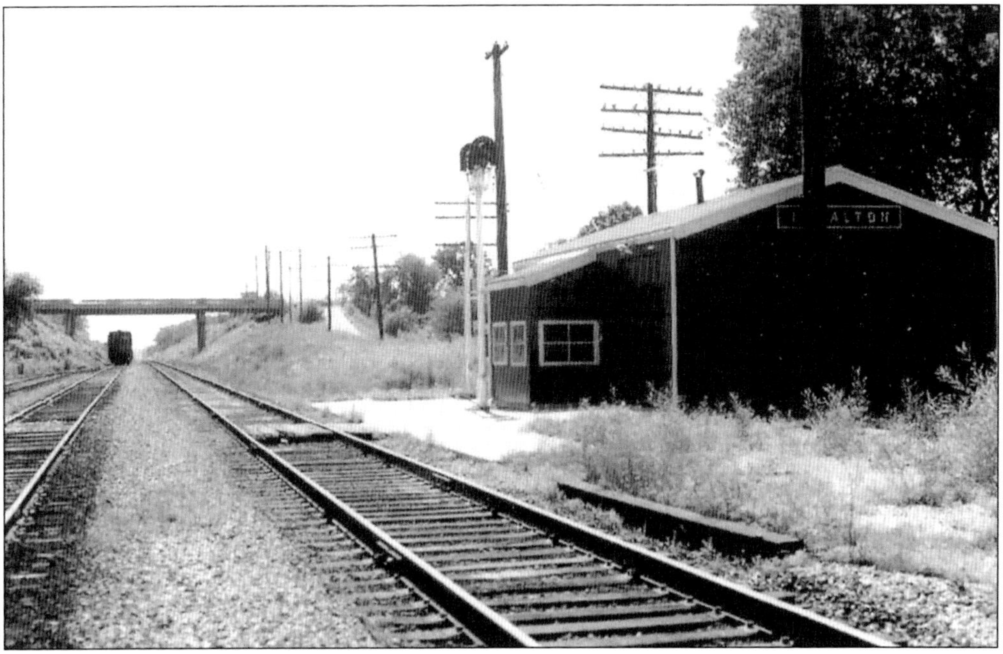

M&NW constructed a depot, stockyard, and milk platform at Ingalton in the spring of 1887 on land donated by Theodore Schramer, a local farmer. The town of Ingalton developed around the depot, and it eventually consisted of a general store, blacksmith shop, and post office. It eventually became a ghost town after the post office closed in 1934. The first Ingalton depot was replaced with this Armco Steel structure in 1951. (Joiner History Room, Sycamore, Illinois.)

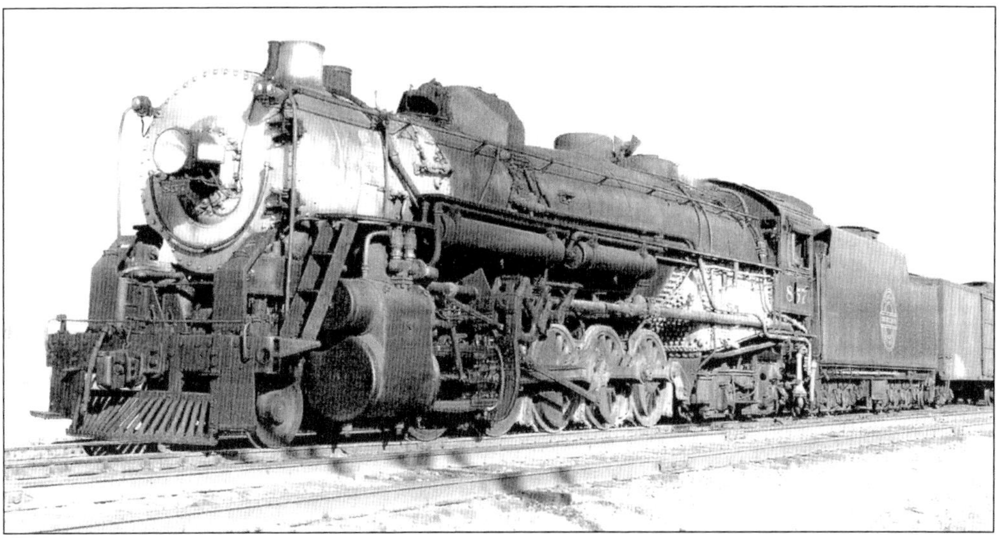

CGW had an interchange connection with the Elgin Joliet and Eastern Railroad (EJ&E) at Ingalton and a small freight yard with a wye track. Oversize shipments were interchanged here because EJ&E had ample clearance around the congested Chicago Switching District. The station continued in use after the 1968 merger, and the depot was not dismantled until the early 1980s. CGW steam locomotive No. 857 was photographed at Ingalton in September 1937. (James L. Rueber.)

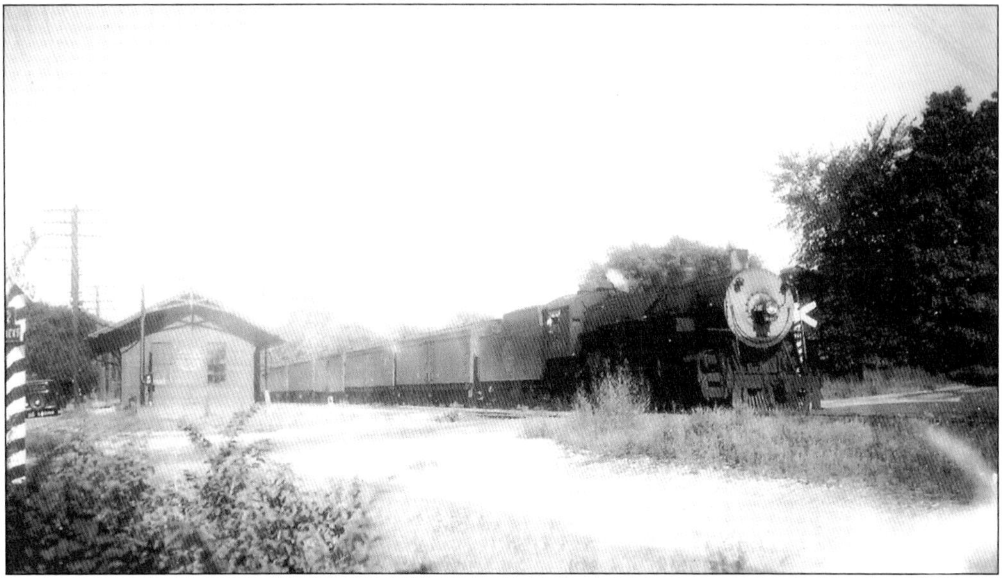

An eastbound freight train is rushing past the depot at St. Charles, six miles west of Ingalton. M&NW began service at St. Charles in 1887, and the station developed into a complex of rail facilities, including a water tank, a milk shed, a supervisor's office, section hands' bunkhouses, toolsheds, and a signal maintainer's shed. CGW also owned the St. Charles Hotel and Park Company, incorporated in April 1889 to develop a summer resort hotel and picnic grounds along the west bank of the Fox River. The hotel was never built, some of the property was later platted for residences, and most of the land was sold in 1912 to St. Charles Township for continued use as a public park. The St. Charles Hotel and Park Company was dissolved on April 20, 1927. (Joiner History Room, Sycamore, Illinois.)

St. Charles, Ill.

Chronicle Publishing Co., Inc.	Newsprint	Team Track	
Cities Service Oil Co.	Petroleum Products	CGW	No
Colonial Ice Cream, Inc.	Salt	Team Track	
Du Kane Corp.	Electrical Supplies	Team Track	
Fox Valley Box Co., Inc.	Paper Boxes	CGW	No
Gerdau Co.	Furniture	Team Track	
Hawley Products Co.	Paper Products	CGW	No
Hines, Edward, Lumber Co.	Building Supplies	CGW	No
Howell Co., Inc., The	Furniture	C&NW	No
Joshel, M. A., & Bros., Inc.	Lumber-Cement-Fuel	CGW	No
Kane Distributing Co.	Beverages	C&NW	No
Lindahl, S. C., Co.	Feeds	C&NW	No
McCormack Oil Co.	Petroleum Products	CGW	No
Moline Malleable Iron Co.	Castings	CGW	No
Owens Illinois Glass Co.	Plastic Products	C&NW	No
Parkers Builders Supplies	Fuel-Lumber	CGW	No
Roto Color, Inc.	Printers	CGW	No
St. Charles, City of	Coal-Salt	Team Track	
St. Charles Lumber & Fuel Co.	Fuel-Building Supplies	C&NW	No
St. Charles Manufacturing Co.	Cabinets	CGW	No

CGW served many shippers at St. Charles. Some of these businesses were located along a dangerous spur called the "hole track." It was constructed in 1891 and descended on a steep, curving grade from the elevated Fox River Bridge approach. CGW switchers "ran away" several times while descending the spur and ended up on Main Street at the end of track. The spur was removed during the early 1960s. (Author's collection.)

St. Charles, Ill.—Concluded			
Standard Oil Co.	Petroleum Products	CGW	No
State School for Boys	Supplies-Coal	C&NW	No
Stover Water Softener Co.	Water Softeners	CGW	No
United States Printing & Lithograph Co.	Printers	CGW	No

Associates of the CGW promoted a manufacturing district on the west side of St. Charles in 1893. Several industries located here as well as a spur track that ran north three quarters of a mile to reach a stone quarry purchased by CGW in 1895. The railroad called this area West St. Charles and Fox River at various times, and records indicate a depot was also constructed here. (Author's collection.)

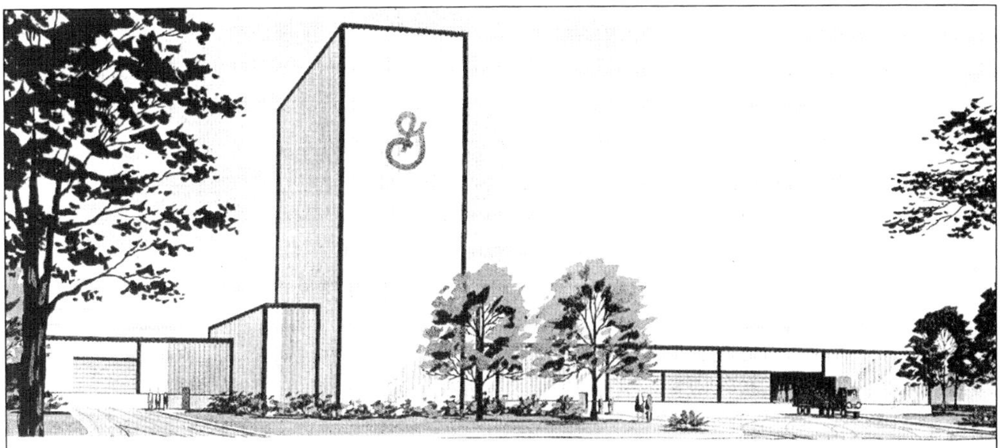

Architect's drawing of new institutional products plant to be built by General Mills, Inc., at St. Charles, Illinois, and to be served exclusively by Chicago Great Western.

General Mills purchased a 13-acre tract in the West St. Charles area from CGW in 1964 for a new institutional products plant. It was built in 1965 and featured a seven-story structure that housed storage bins. Rail shipments were handled exclusively by CGW. (Author's collection.)

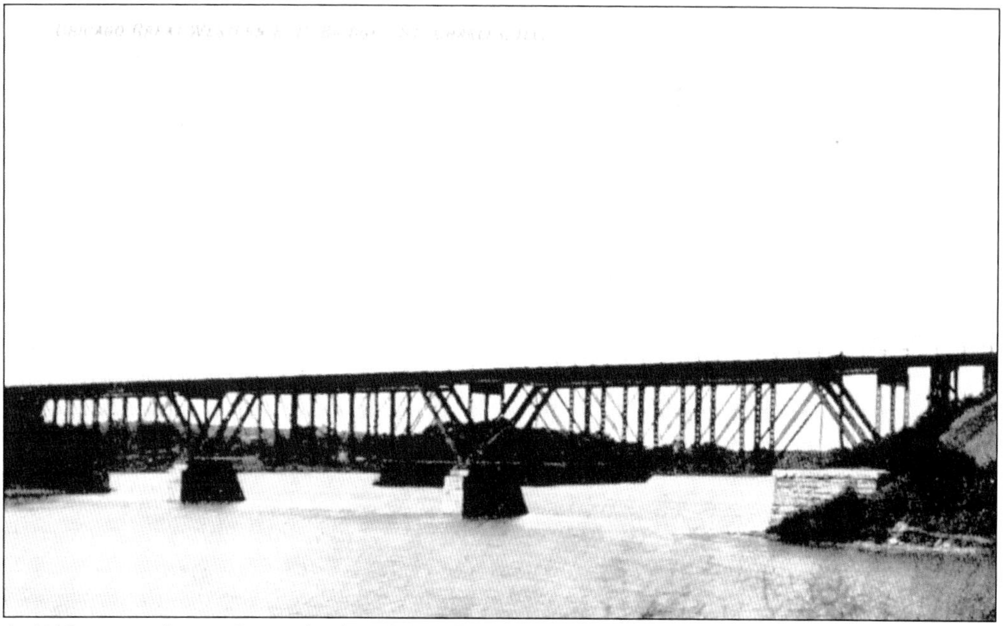

A 1910 postcard view shows the first CGW Fox River Bridge at St. Charles constructed in 1886. A M&NW construction train was the first train to cross the bridge on December 31, 1886. (Author's collection.)

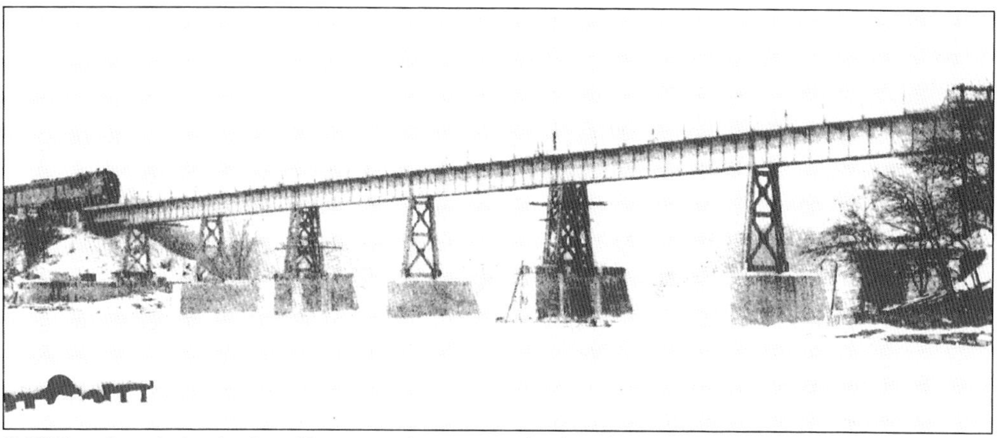

CGW replaced the bridge 70 years after it was built, when the railroad determined it was becoming structurally weak. Work began on August 10, 1956, and a new steel and concrete bridge 477 feet long was completed on January 4, 1957. This photograph shows an eastbound train about to cross the new bridge shortly after it was placed in service. St. Charles remained an open station after the 1968 merger, and the depot was not taken out of service until April 1983. Several organizations tried to raise funds to buy the building but were not successful, and C&NW tore down the structure in 1984. (Author's collection.)

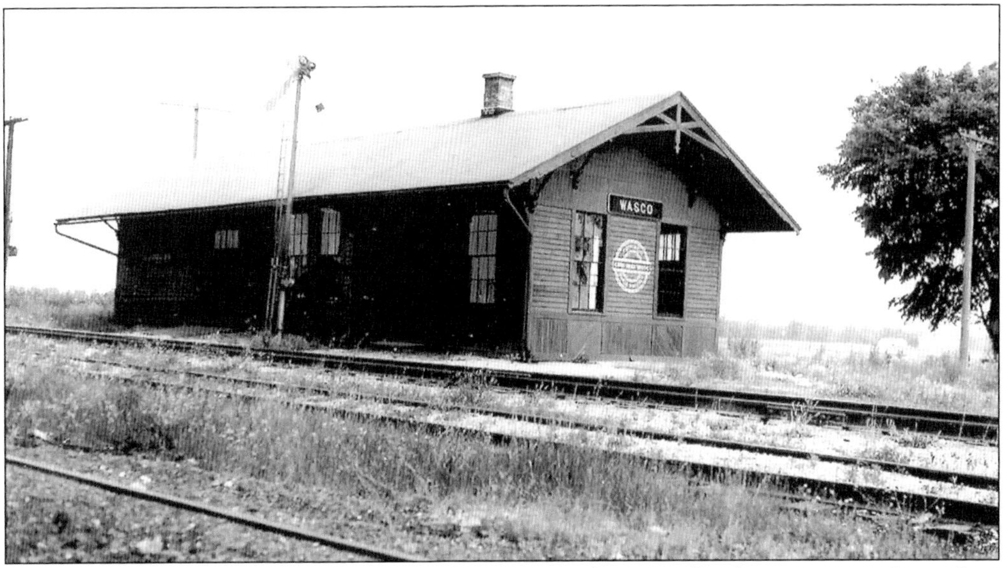

A. B. Stickney, the company founder, reported in 1888 that most local stations were located on farms away from towns and villages. The company anticipated that the few residents in the area would provide sufficient business until a prosperous community developed, which would then depend upon the railroad for all of its transportation needs. This policy resulted in stations such as Wasco, opened in 1887 and closed on October 26, 1959. Wasco was located five miles west of St. Charles. (Joiner History Room, Sycamore, Illinois.)

Dispatchers' telephone also placed in waiting rooms of the following stations. These waiting rooms can be opened by switch key:

Lombard.	Esmond	North Hanover.
N. Glen Ellyn.	Lindenwood.	Aiken.
Gretna.	Stillman Valley.	Budd.
Wasco	Myrtle.	Petersburg.
Virgil.	Meekin.	Almoral.
Richardson.	Bolton.	Dundee.
Clare.	Woodbine.	Lamont.

Remote stations were not manned 24 hours a day, so train crews were provided with these instructions in case they had to contact their dispatcher from a closed depot. The instructions were published in Eastern Division employee timetable No. 22, effective June 4, 1922, for stations in Illinois and Iowa. (Chicago and North Western Historical Society.)

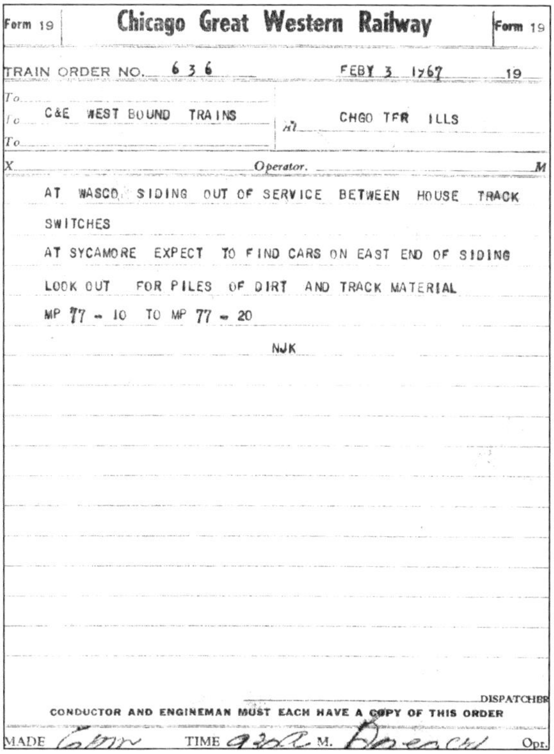

Form 19 **Chicago Great Western Railway** Form 19

TRAIN ORDER NO. 636 FEBY 3 1967 19

To C&E WEST BOUND TRAINS At CHGO TER ILLS

X Operator. M

AT WASCO, SIDING OUT OF SERVICE BETWEEN HOUSE TRACK SWITCHES

AT SYCAMORE EXPECT TO FIND CARS ON EAST END OF SIDING

LOOK OUT FOR PILES OF DIRT AND TRACK MATERIAL MP 77 - 10 TO MP 77 - 20

NJK

DISPATCHER

CONDUCTOR AND ENGINEMAN MUST EACH HAVE A COPY OF THIS ORDER

MADE [illegible] TIME [illegible] M. [illegible] Opr.

CGW used a system of train dispatching called "timetable and train order." Train orders are instructions from the dispatcher communicated to the station operator, who then passes the information on to the engineer and conductor. The operator displays a signal when he has orders for an approaching train. There are two types of orders used. Form 19 is handed to the engineer and conductor, using a hoop, as the train passes. Form 31 requires the engineer to stop the train, and both he and the conductor must sign for the order. This Form 19 order was issued on February 3, 1967, to warn westbound train crews that Wasco siding was out of service and to watch out for obstructions farther west. (Conrad "Pete" Pedersen.)

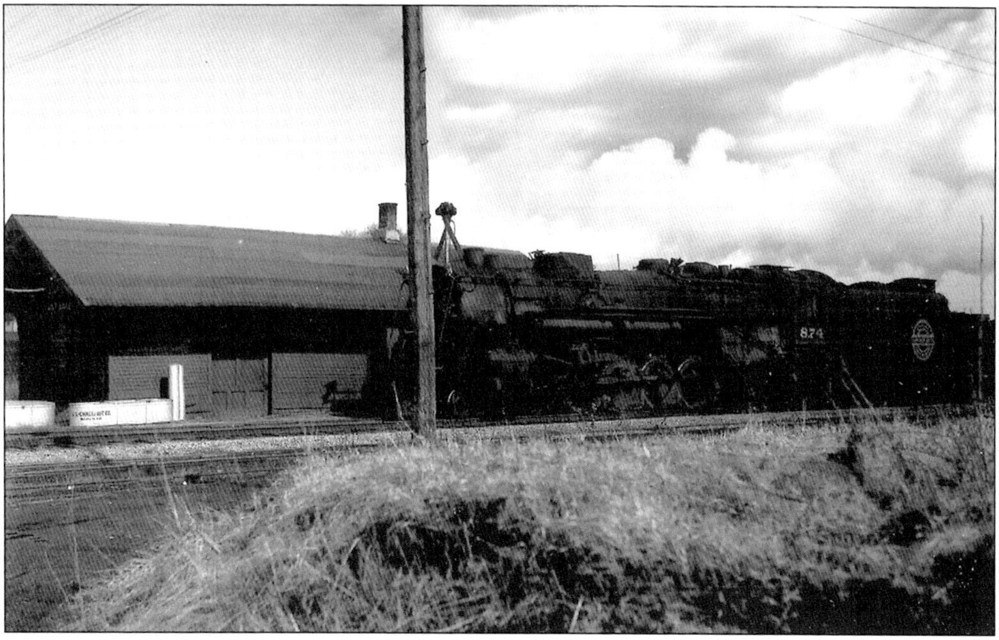

Eastbound locomotive No. 874 with a freight train passes Lily Lake depot in 1943, slightly more than four miles west of Wasco. The first M&NW train order in Illinois was issued May 5, 1887, at Sycamore, instructing work trains to meet at Campton Pit, a stone quarry in Campton Township, east of Lily Lake. A station was opened at Lily Lake in 1887 and remained in service until it closed on December 7, 1951. (Joiner History Room, Sycamore, Illinois.)

(22). **Telephones connected with Dispatchers' office are located at following passing track switches:**

Gretna	West switch.
Ingalton	West switch.
St. Charles	East switch.
Fox River	Middle of Siding
Lily Lake	Extreme west switch.
Sycamore	Extreme east and west switches.
Wilkinson	East switch.
Holcomb	West switch.
Stillman Valley	West switch.
Byron	East and west switches.
South Freeport	East end south passing track. West end north passing track.
Bolton	West switch.
Pearl City	East switch.
Fair Ground	West switch.
Durango	East switch.
Graf	East and west switches.
Kidder	East switch.
Farley	West switch.
Dyersville	East switch.
Oneida	East switch.
Thorpe	West switch.
Lamont	East and west switches.

CGW also installed telephones at sidings for train crews to contact their dispatcher. This list of sidings in Illinois and Iowa, equipped with phones, was published in Eastern Division employee timetable No. 22, effective June 4, 1922. (Chicago and North Western Historical Society.)

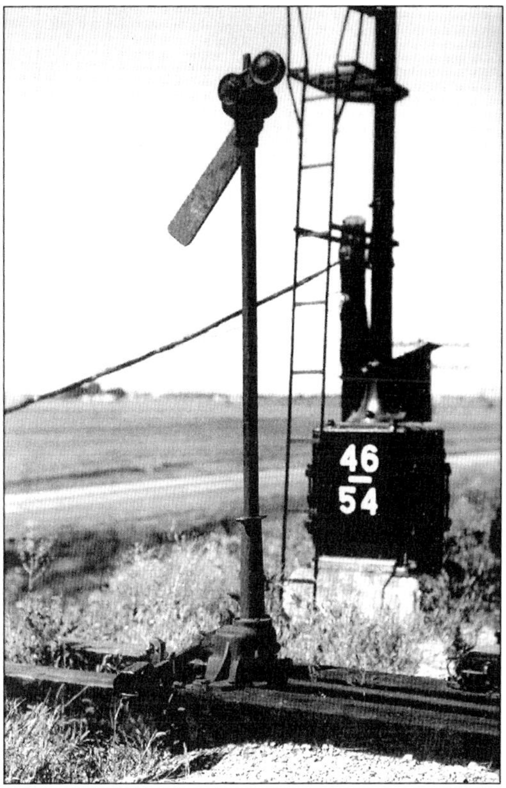

This photograph shows a siding switch with a telephone box mounted on a pole in the background, west of Lily Lake. The numbers on the signal case are mileage from Chicago (top) and the number of the signal (bottom). (Joiner History Room, Sycamore, Illinois.)

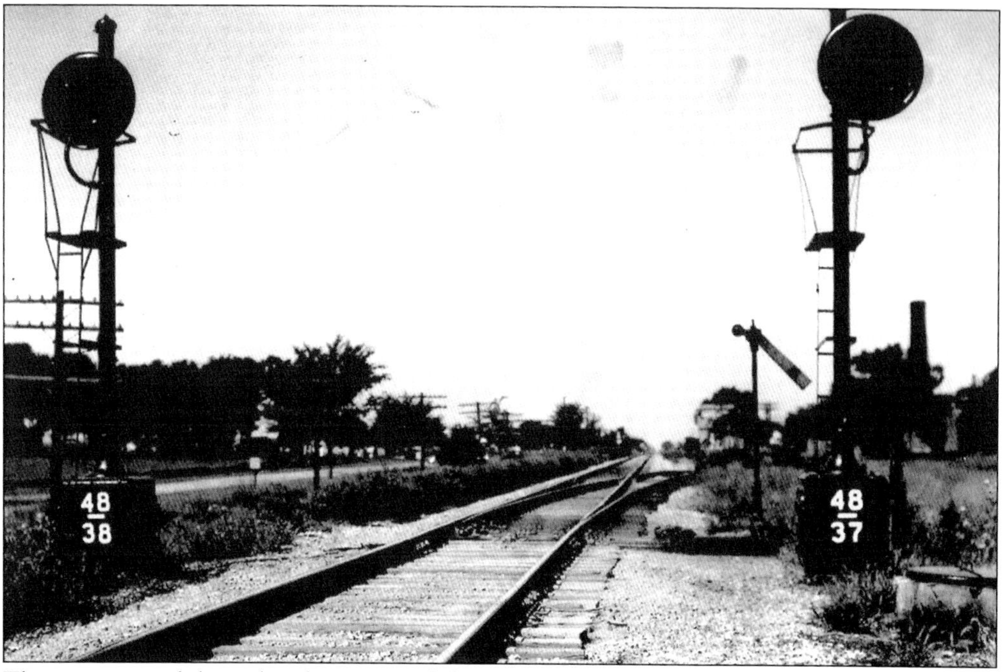

This is a view of the right-of-way east of the Virgil depot, which is in the background to the left. CGW began to install its first automatic signals, semaphore type, between Forest Park and Aiken, Illinois, in April 1910 and completed the work in March 1911. The system was modernized starting in 1942, when CGW replaced the semaphore type with searchlight signals as shown. The upgrade was completed in 1947. (Joiner History Room, Sycamore, Illinois.)

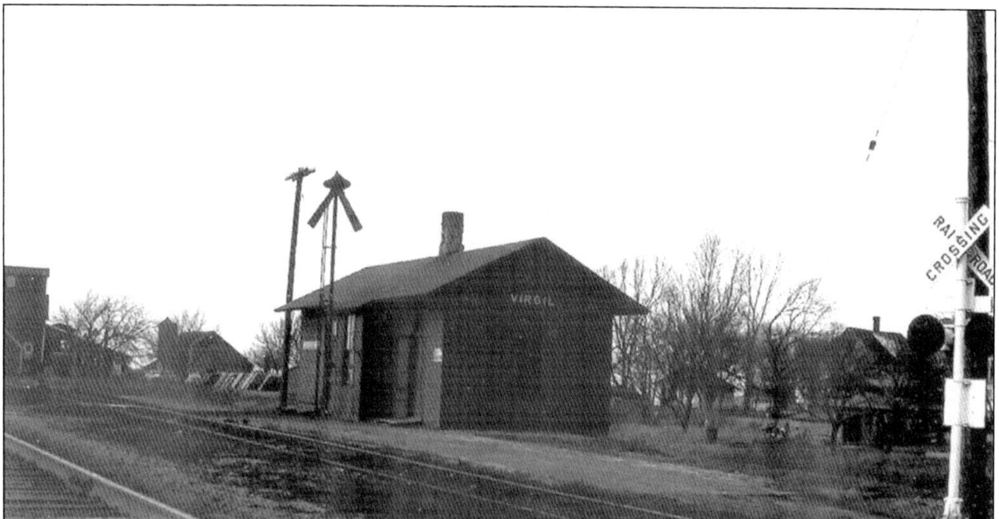

CGW stations in rural Illinois typically consisted of a frame depot, livestock pen, and milk shed. The company also provided housing for the agent if none was available due to the remote location. These conditions applied at Virgil, three miles west of Lily Lake. The first station name was Virgil Center, and CGW reported that it had built a depot there in the company's 1897 annual report. Virgil was closed on February 28, 1962. (Joiner History Room, Sycamore, Illinois.)

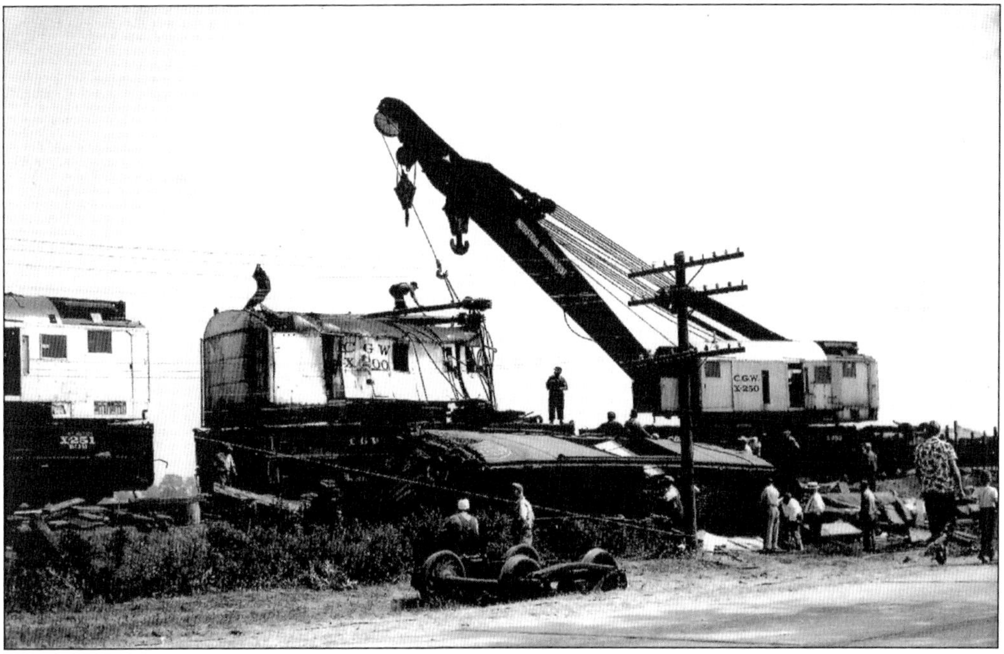

At 5:00 p.m. on Saturday, August 22, 1953, a burned-out journal on a gondola loaded with coal caused a spectacular derailment east of Sycamore. The incident happened as westbound manifest No. 91 was traveling through at a fast rate of speed. Eighteen of 80 cars in the train went off the track and tore up 150 yards of track. While clearing away the wreckage, wrecker No. X200 was damaged and three crewmen injured when the 175-ton crane tipped over while lifting a heavily loaded boxcar. (Joiner History Room, Sycamore, Illinois.)

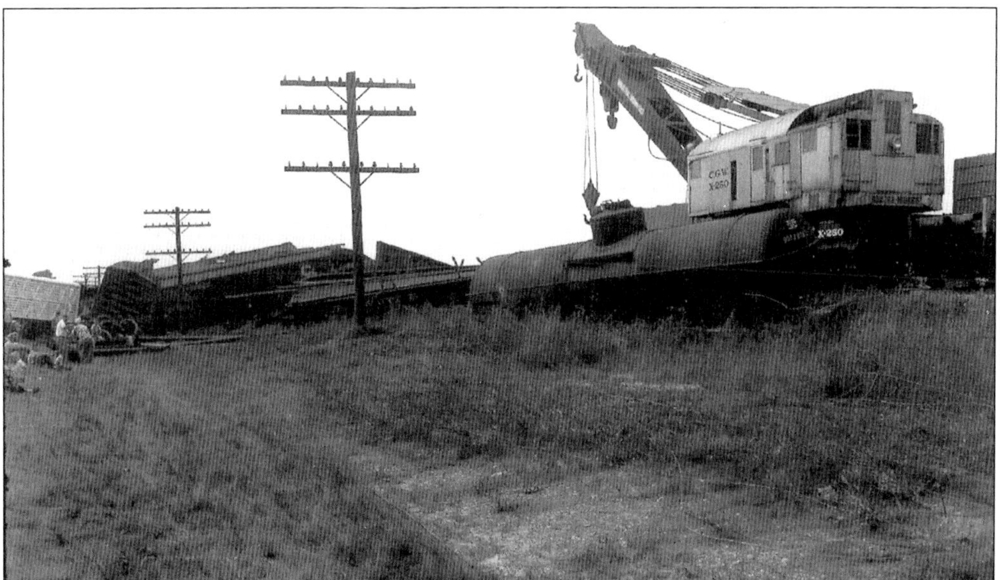

Most of the wreckage was removed by the following Wednesday, August 26. Several destroyed boxcars were set on fire to burn away all wood parts, and remaining metal parts were removed as scrap. (Joiner History Room, Sycamore, Illinois.)

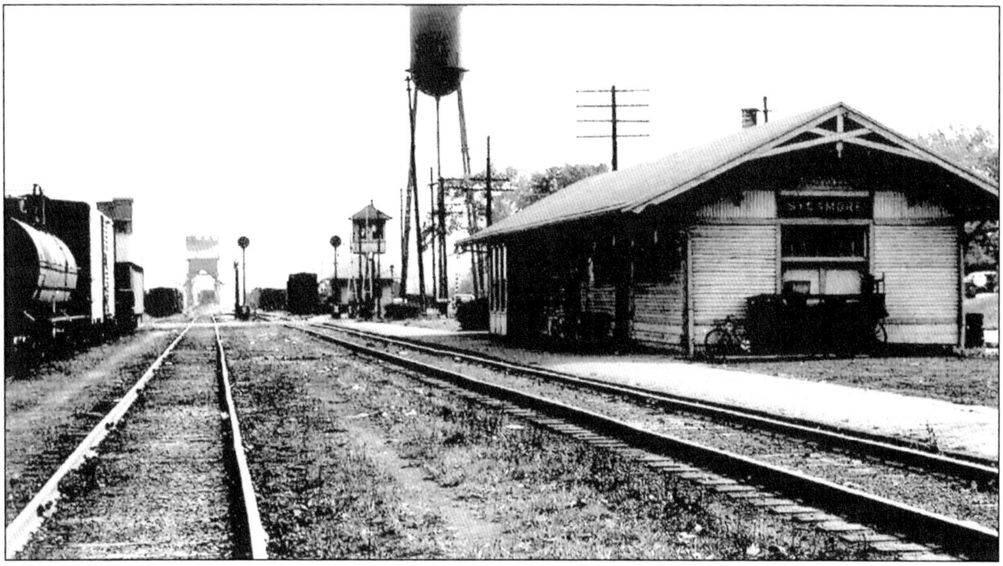

Sycamore, eight miles west of Virgil, was an important and busy junction with facilities to service locomotives, freight yard, and online industries. It was also the site of a grade crossing and interchange with C&NW and a connection with the CGW branch to DeKalb. The railroad constructed a passenger depot here in 1887 (foreground) and a freight house in 1923 (right background). The 1968 merger did not have a major effect on business at Sycamore because C&NW operated its own line to this city from DeKalb. (Joiner History Room, Sycamore, Illinois.)

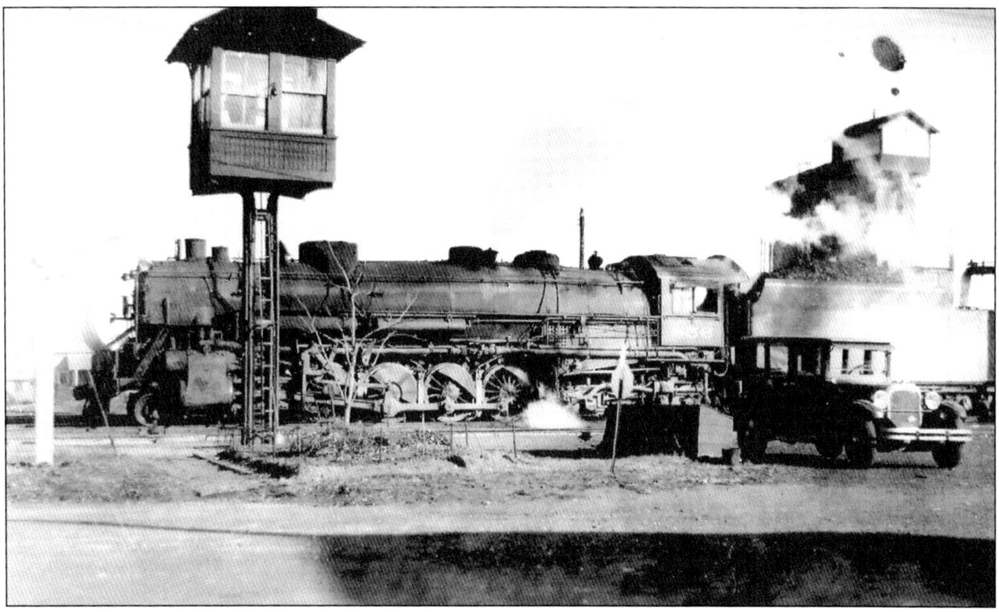

Locomotive No. 856 has stopped at Sycamore to replenish its water supply. Engine-servicing facilities included an engine house for the DeKalb switcher, a coal chute, and a water tank. Note the elevated flagman's shanty. (Joiner History Room, Sycamore, Illinois.)

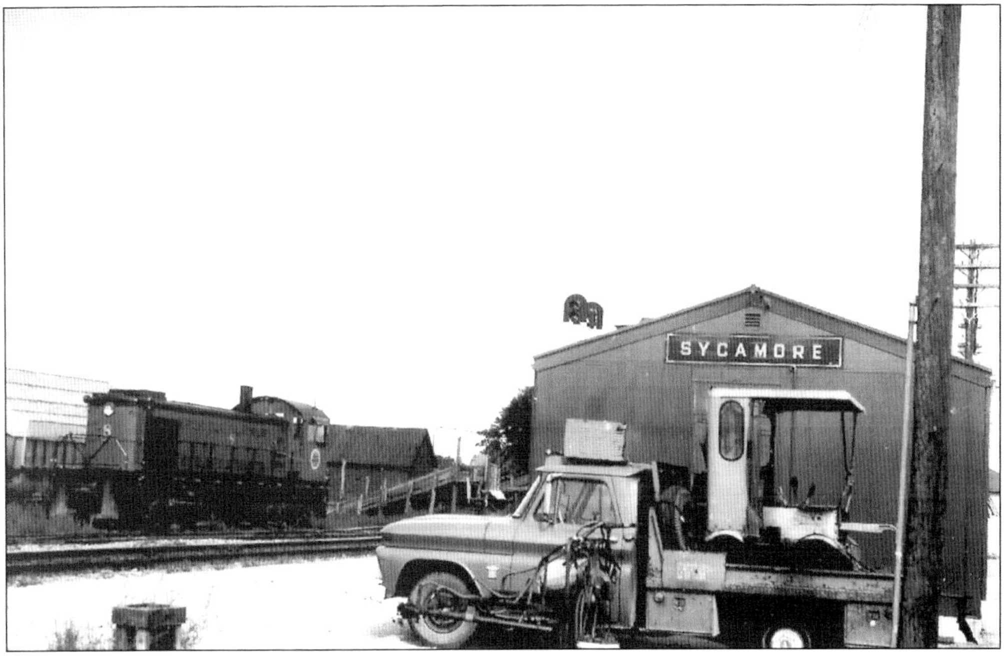

CGW tore down the freight house and replaced it with this Armco Steel depot in 1951. The passenger depot was sold to a resident and moved off-site in March of that year. (Joiner History Room, Sycamore, Illinois.)

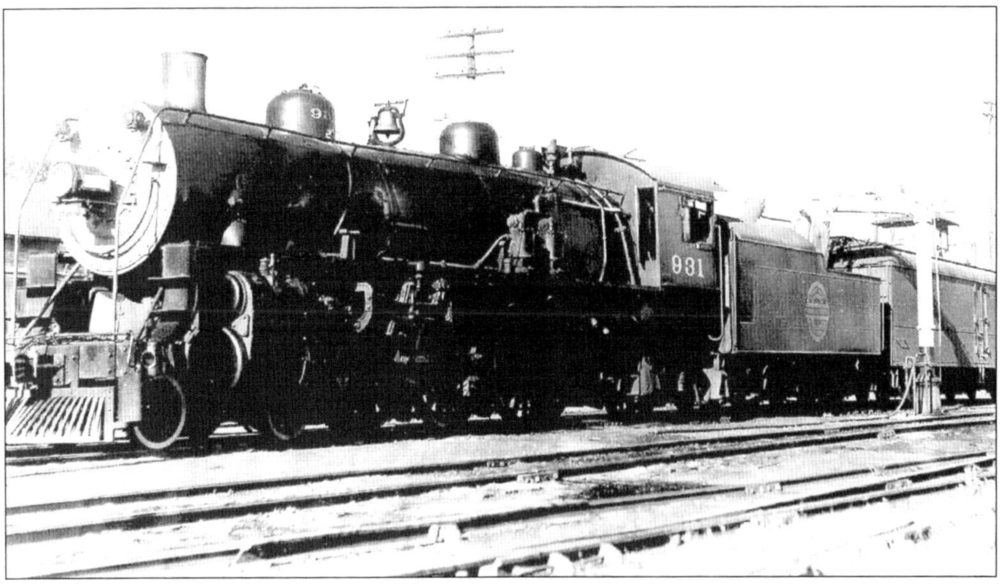

Eastbound locomotive No. 931, with a passenger train, has stopped at Sycamore to top off the tender water tank. O. T. Willard, the first CGW operator at Sycamore, often told the story of a fireman who fell into the tender. The only remark the engineer made when he found the fireman splashing around inside the tank was "John, we have enough water now. No need to get in and stamp it down!" (Joiner History Room, Sycamore, Illinois.)

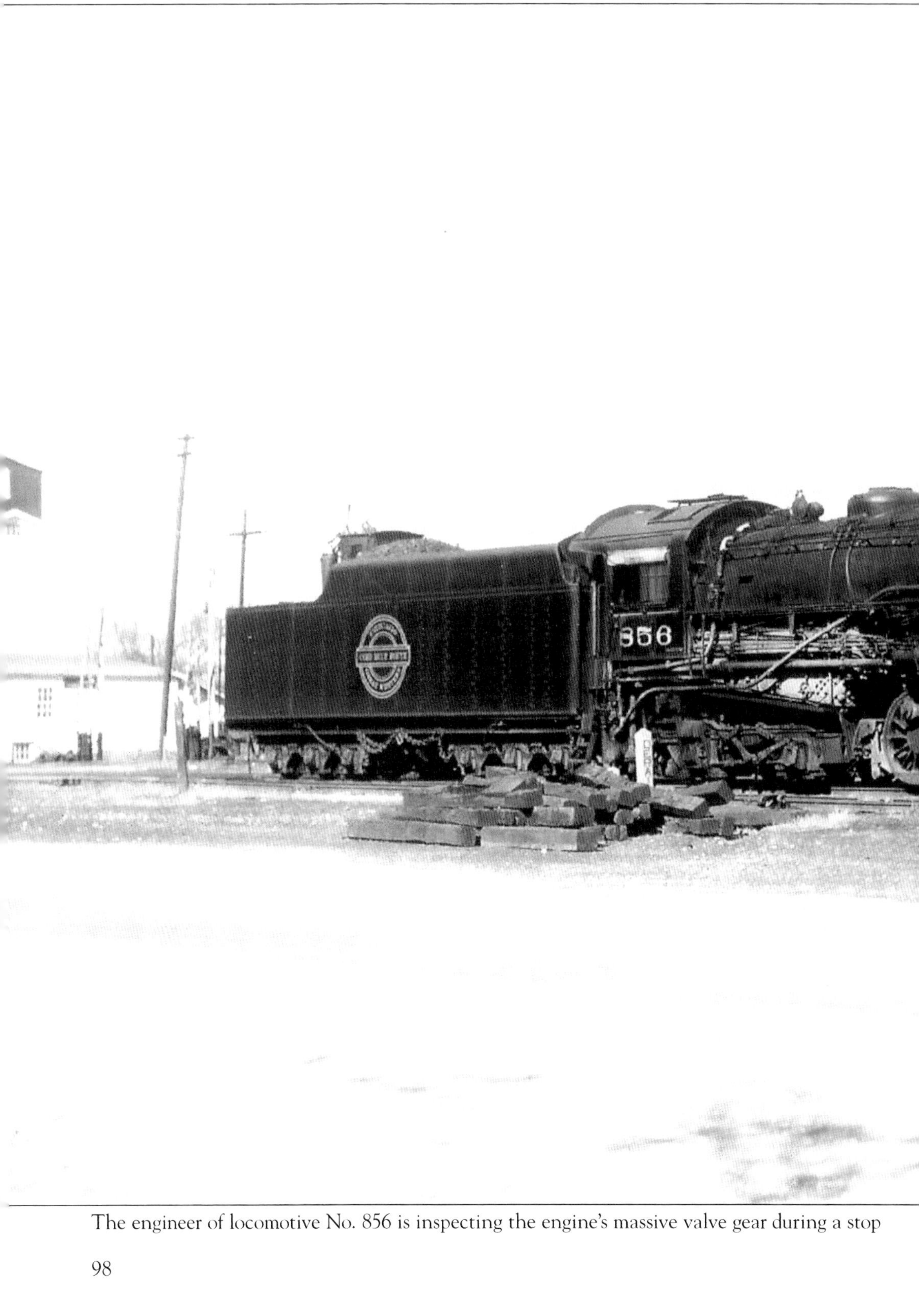

The engineer of locomotive No. 856 is inspecting the engine's massive valve gear during a stop

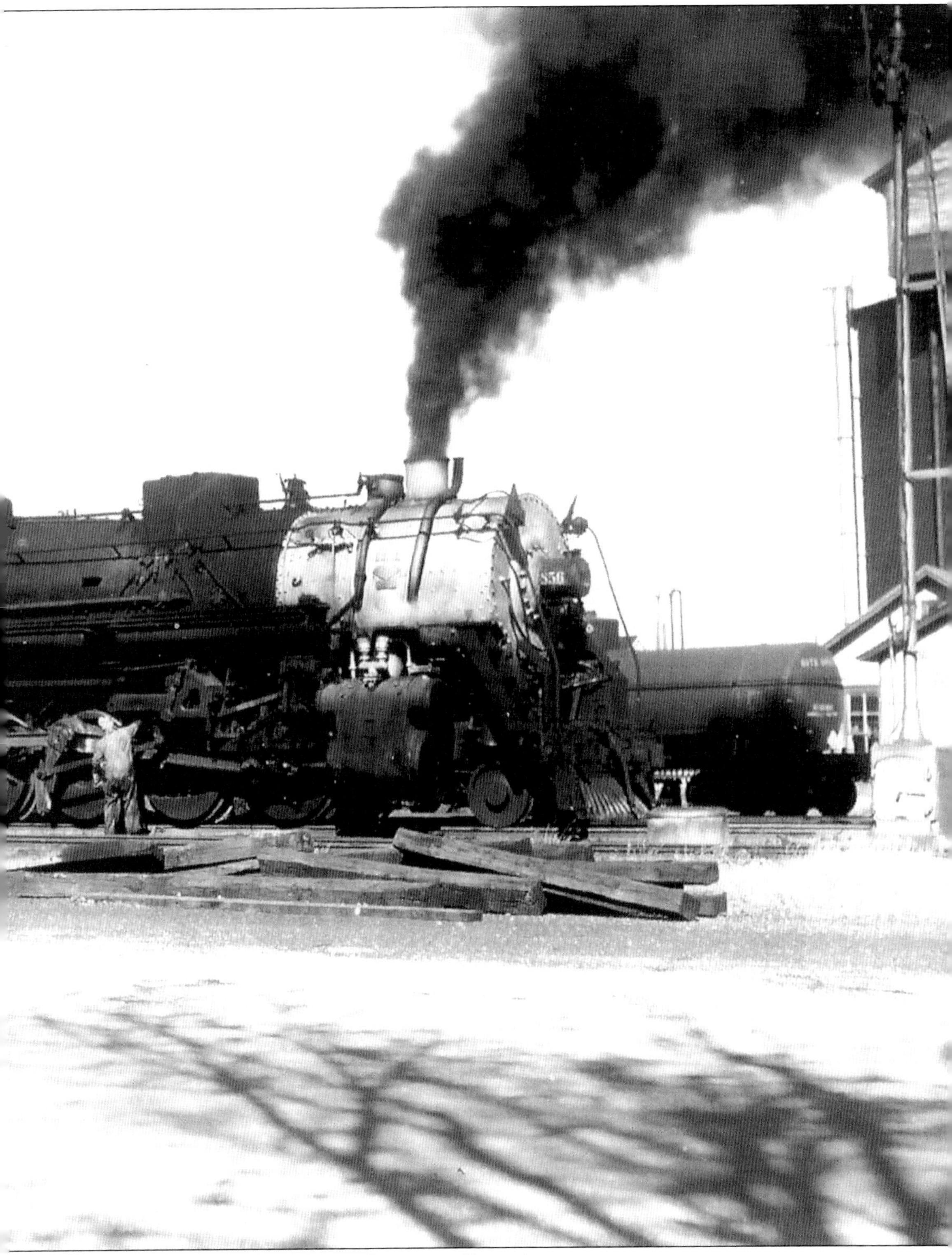

at Sycamore. (Joiner History Room, Sycamore, Illinois.)

Sycamore, Ill.			
Anaconda Wire & Cable Co.	Wire	CGW	Yes
Arison Implement Co.	Implements	Team Track	
Arrow Feed Co.	Feeds	C&NW	No
B B Distributors	Beverages	C&NW	No
D-X Sunray Oil Co.	Petroleum Products	CGW	Yes
Dean Coal & Lumber Yard	Lumber-Fuel	CGW	Yes
DeKalb Agricultural Assn.	Feeds-Cattle	Team Track	
Diamond Wire & Cable Co.	Wire	CGW-C&NW	Yes
Driv Lok Pin Co.	Steel Specialties	C&NW	No
Duplex Products, Inc.	Printing	Team Track	
Farmers Grain & Lumber Co.	Feed-Building Supplies	CGW	Yes
Holcomb Yard	Fuel-Building Supplies	CGW	Yes
Holub Industries, Inc.	Electrical Supplies	Team Track	
Ideal Industries, Inc.	Electrical Supplies	Team Track	
Julep Co.	Syrups	Team Track	
Leader Oil Co.	Petroleum Products	C&NW	No

Anaconda Wire and Cable Company was Sycamore's largest industry, and it had five rail sidings. CGW published an article about the company in the November 1956 issue of *Safety News*. (Author's collection.)

Sycamore, Ill.—Concluded			
Micro Matic Hone Corp.	Specialties	CGW	Yes
Patten, J. V., Co.	Furnaces	CGW	Yes
Quinn Grain Co.	Grain	CGW	No
Socony Mobil Oil Co.	Petroleum Products	CGW	No
Standard Oil Co.	Petroleum Products	CGW	Yes
Stark, Frank	Livestock	C&NW	No
Sycamore, City of	Utilities	Team Track	
Sycamore Feed Yards, Inc.	Sheep	CGW	No
Sycamore Fuel Co.	Scrap Iron	C&NW	Yes
Sycamore Lumber Co.	Fuel-Building Supplies	C&NW	Yes
Sycamore Preserve Works, Inc.	Canners	C&NW	Yes
Sycamore Ready Mix	Concrete	C&NW	No
Turner Brass Works	Brass Goods	C&NW	Yes
Wells Lumber Co.	Building Supplies	Team Track	

Industries continued at Sycamore. Industrial development at this station, such as construction of a siding to wire works in 1893 and harvester works in 1900, was commented upon frequently in CGW annual reports. (Author's collection.)

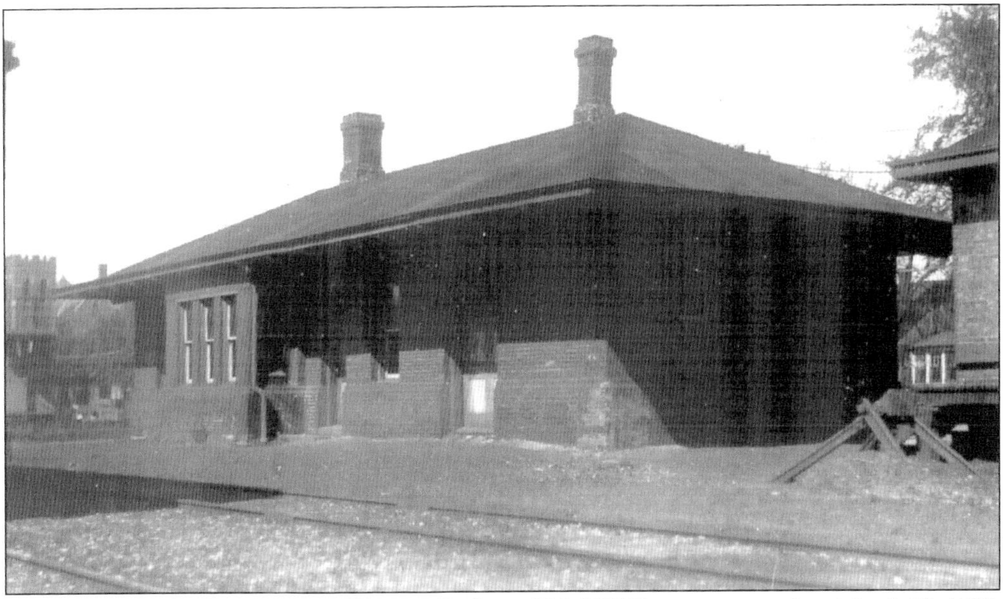

The DeKalb and Chicago Great Western Railway (D&CGW), incorporated on March 23, 1895, constructed a six-mile branch from a connection with CGW at Sycamore south to DeKalb. CGW began operations over the branch in August 1895, and D&CGW was later sold to CGW on December 21, 1911. This old photograph, reproduced from a glass negative, shows the CGW depot at DeKalb. (Joiner History Room, Sycamore, Illinois.)

DeKalb, Ill.			
Builders Lumber & Supply	Building Supplies	C&NW	Yes
California Packing Corp.	Canners	C&NW	Yes
Chesney, John, Co.	Printers	Team Track	
City Fuel & Supply Co.	Fuel	CGW	Yes
Cortland DeKalb Yards	Elevator-Feed-Fuel	C&NW	Yes
Creamery Package Mfg. Co.	Milking Equipment	CMStP&P	Yes
Cyclone Fence Co., Division of United States Steel Corp.	Wire Cloth	CGW-C&NW	Yes
DeKalb Agricultural Assn., Inc.	Seeds	CGW-C&NW	Yes
DeKalb Commercial Body Corp.	Truck Bodies	C&NW	Yes
DeKalb County Grain Co.	Grain-Feed	C&NW	No
DeKalb Daily Chronicle	Newsprint	Team Track	
DeKalb Equipment Co.	Implements	Team Track	
DeKalb Ice Co.	Coal-Ice	C&NW	Yes
DeKalb Iron & Coal Co.	Scrap	CGW-C&NW	Yes
DeKalb Molasses Feed Co.	Feeds	C&NW	Yes
DeKalb Ogle Telephone Co.	Poles	Team Track	
DeKalb Phosphate Service	Rock-Phosphate	CGW	No
DeKalb Toy & Novelties Co.	Toys	Team Track	
Englander Co., Inc.	Bed Springs	CGW-C&NW	Yes
General Electric Co.	Electric Motors	CMStP&P	Yes
Hallgren Lumber & Coal Co., Inc.	Building Supplies	CGW-C&NW	Yes
Halverson Implement Co.	Implements	Team Track	
Heide Implement Co.	Implements	CGW	Yes
Hueber Quitno Farm Equipment	Implements	Team Track	
Hunt Feed Store & Mill	Feeds	CGW	Yes
Illinois State Highway Dept.	Salt	Team Track	
Johnson Concrete Co.	Concrete	C&NW	No
Kahle Oil Co.	Petroleum Products	CGW	No
Kishwaukee Service Co.	Petroleum Products	CGW-CMStP&P	No
McGirr Equipment Co.	Implements	Team Track	
Montgomery Ward & Co.	Merchandise	Team Track	
Nehring Electrical Works	Wire	C&NW	Yes
Newquist Foundry Co.	Castings	C&NW	Yes
Northern Illinois Produce Co.	Fruits-Vegetables	CGW	No
Northern Illinois State College	Coal	Team Track	
Northern Illinois Utilities	Power Plant	CGW	Yes

There were many shippers at DeKalb who routed freight by CGW, so it negotiated an agreement to use the C&NW line between Sycamore and DeKalb to continue service after it decided to abandon the DeKalb Branch. The ICC approved the plan on February 17, 1947. The last train operated over the DeKalb Branch in June of that year, and the rails were lifted in November. (Author's collection.)

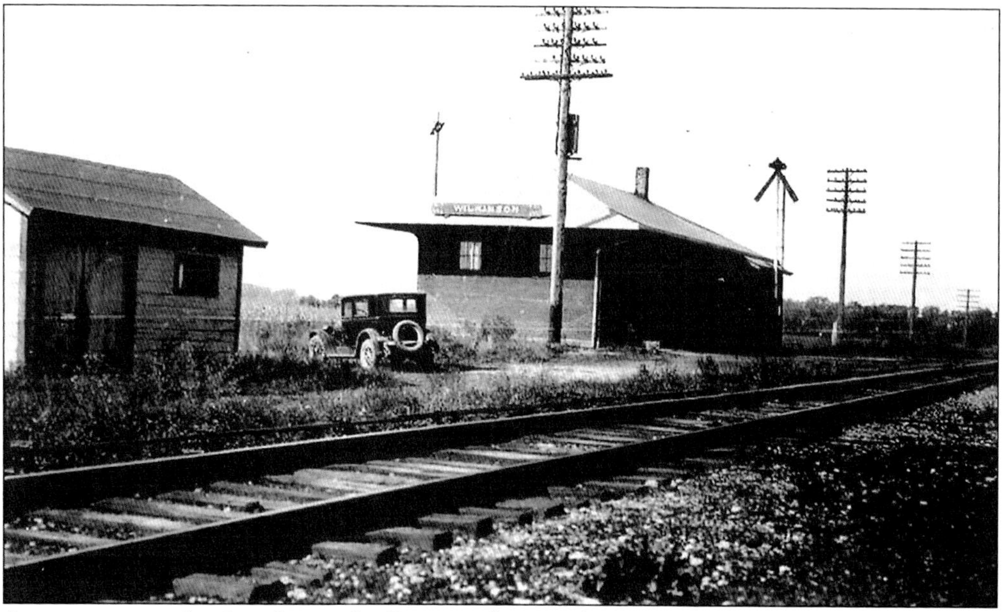

A new junction developed near the R. N. Wilkinson farm, six miles west of Sycamore, when a predecessor company of the Chicago, Milwaukee, St. Paul & Pacific Railroad (CMStP&P) constructed a grade crossing there with CGW in 1905. The station was called Wilkinson, and it included a depot with an interlocking plant. It was closed on June 8, 1935, after an automatic interlocker was installed. (Joiner History Room, Sycamore, Illinois.)

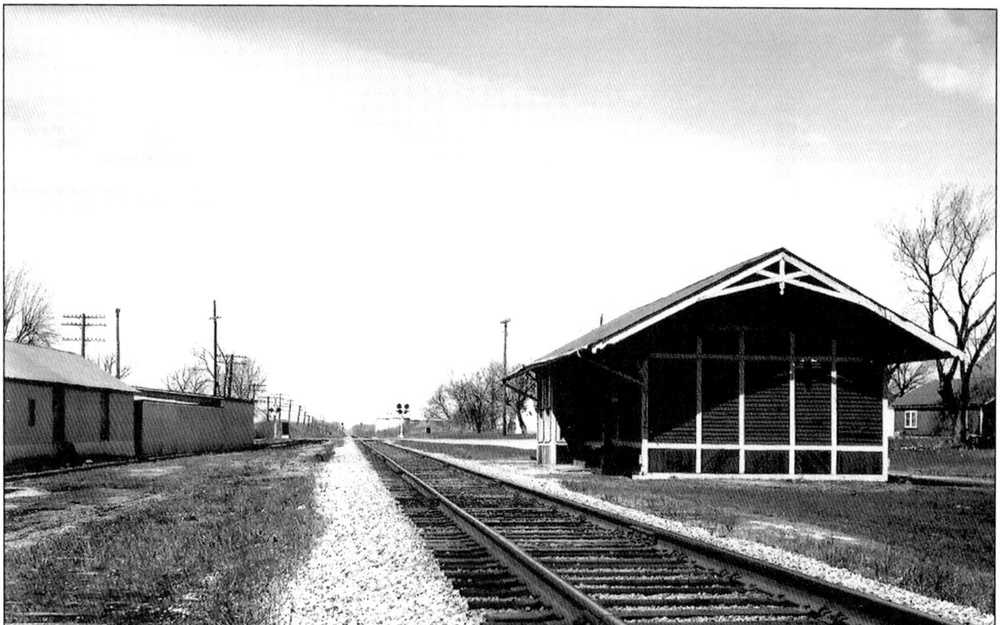

M&NW established a station at Clare, two miles west of Wilkinson in 1887. A local newspaper reported in 1904 that the depot would be closed after CGW opened the nearby facility at Wilkinson. However, Clare remained open until August 29, 1958. (Joiner History Room, Sycamore, Illinois.)

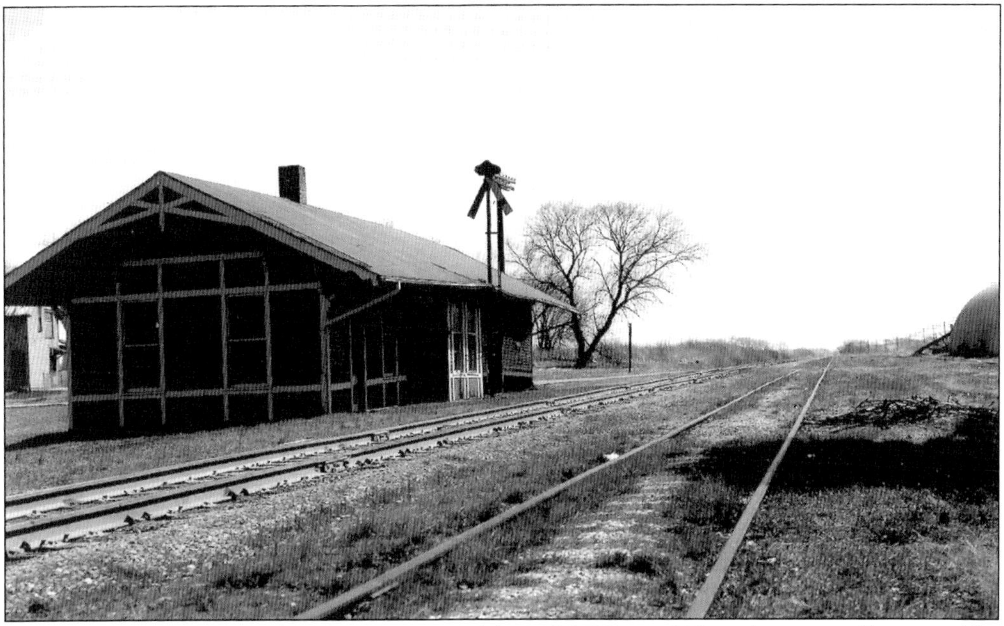

Esmond, five miles west of Clare, was opened by M&NW in 1887, and it was still manned by an agent in 1969. The depot was closed sometime before C&NW abandoned this section of the old CGW in 1981. CGW built a residence for the Esmond agent in 1910 that consisted of two old bunk cars covered with a new roof. The dwelling was dismantled in 1953. (Joiner History Room, Sycamore, Illinois.)

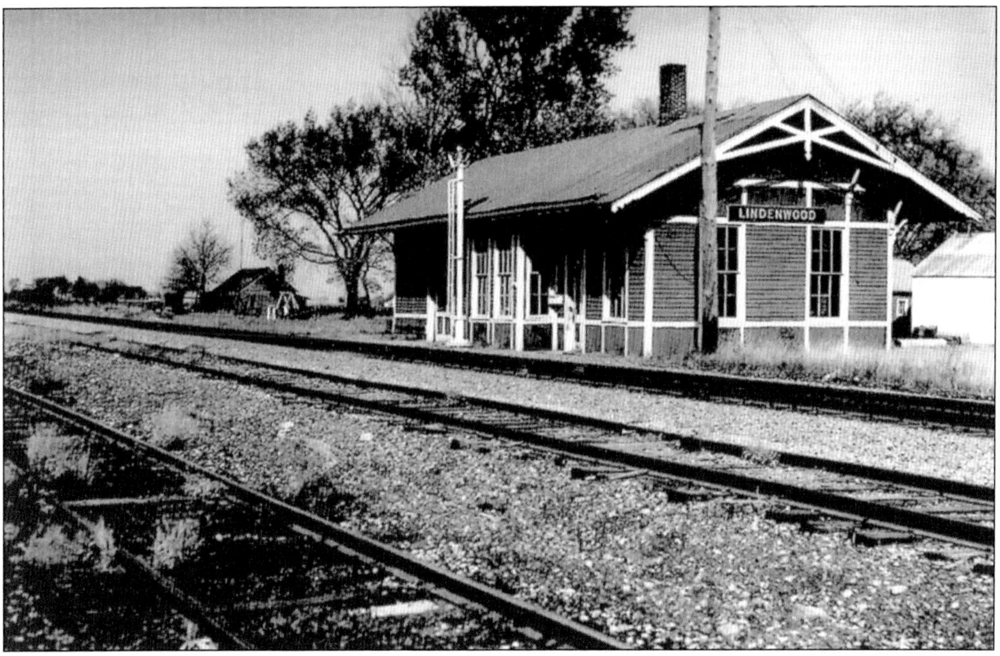

Lindenwood, six miles west of Esmond, was placed in service by M&NW in 1887. Livestock shipments may have been the primary business here during the early years because CGW built an addition to the station sheep shed in 1893. The depot was damaged by fire in 1908, repaired, and remained in service until closed August 27, 1958. (Joiner History Room, Sycamore, Illinois.)

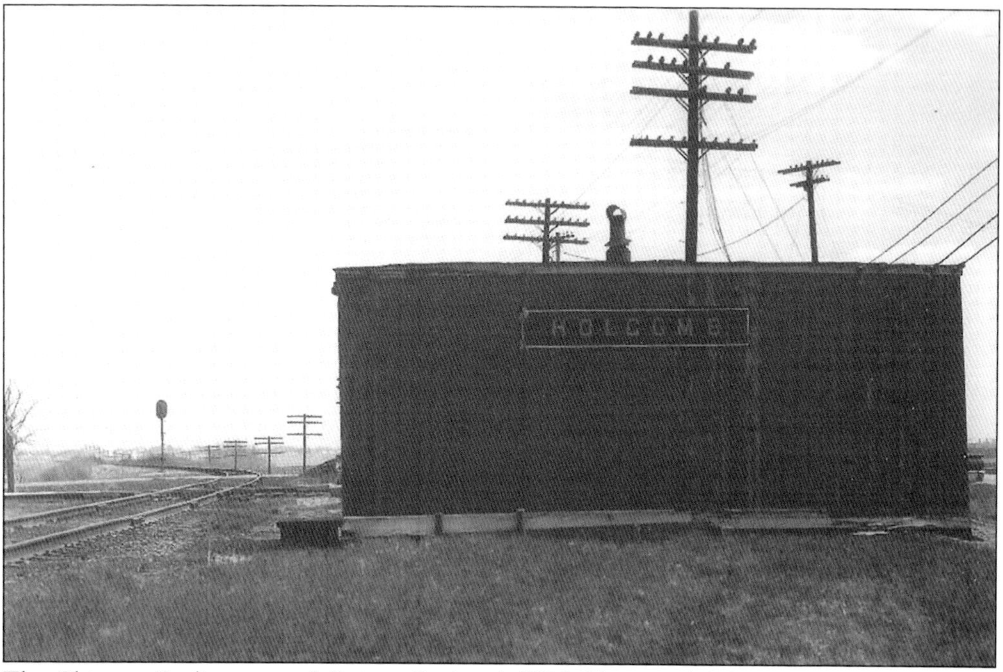

The Chicago, Burlington and Quincy Railroad (CB&Q) crossed CGW at grade at Holcomb station, three miles west of Lindenwood, and there was an interchange connection between the two railroads. Holcomb station was opened in 1887 and closed on March 20, 1950. (Joiner History Room, Sycamore, Illinois.)

Holcomb, Ill.			
Neidlinger Elevator	Grain-Fuel-Building Supplies	CGW-CB&Q	Yes
Ogle Service Co.	Feeds	Team Track	

A grain elevator was erected near the CGW main line in 1897, and it provided most of the business at Holcomb. A second industry, Custom Farm Service, also located a facility here in 1967. All shipping transactions were handled at Byron since Holcomb depot was closed by this time. (Author's collection.)

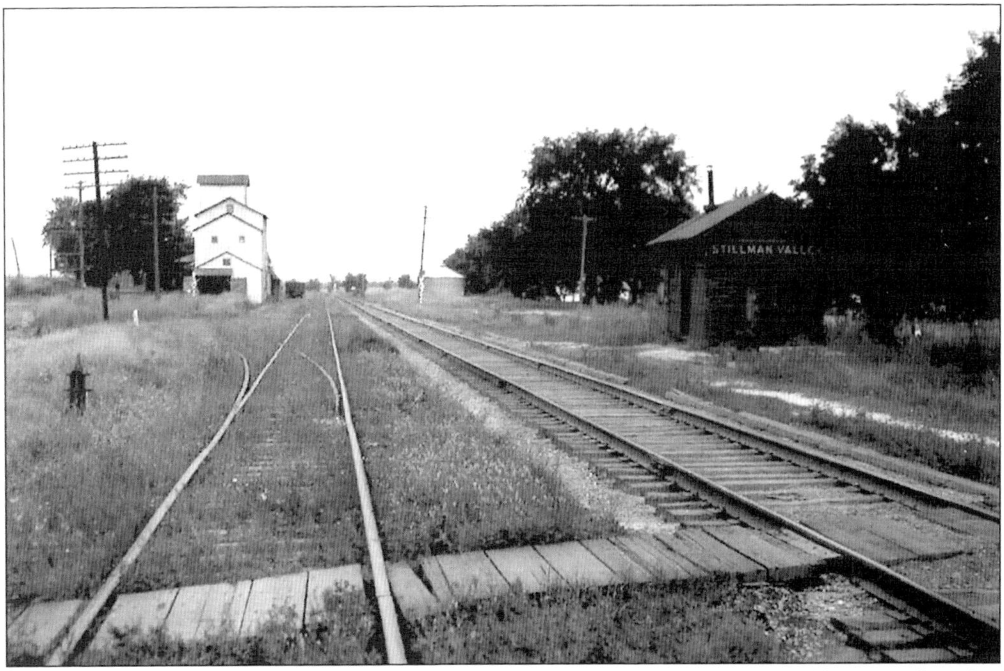

CGW must have handled a significant amount of livestock business at Stillman Valley, five miles west of Holcomb, because the company modernized its stockyard there in 1928 by adding a second pen with sheds and a stock scale. The station was opened by M&NW in 1887, and it included a depot and toolhouse. (Joiner History Room, Sycamore, Illinois.)

Stillman Valley, Ill.			
Clark, J. L., Mfg. Co.	Metal Products	Team Track	....
Rosensteil & Co.	Fuel-Grain-Feed	CGW	No
Stillman Valley Elevator	Grain	CMStP&P	No

The primary shipper at Stillman Valley was a grain elevator and feed dealer. The depot was closed July 22, 1931, and in 1943, it was dismantled and replaced by what CGW called a "frame shelter," as shown in the photograph. (Joiner History Room, Sycamore, Illinois.)

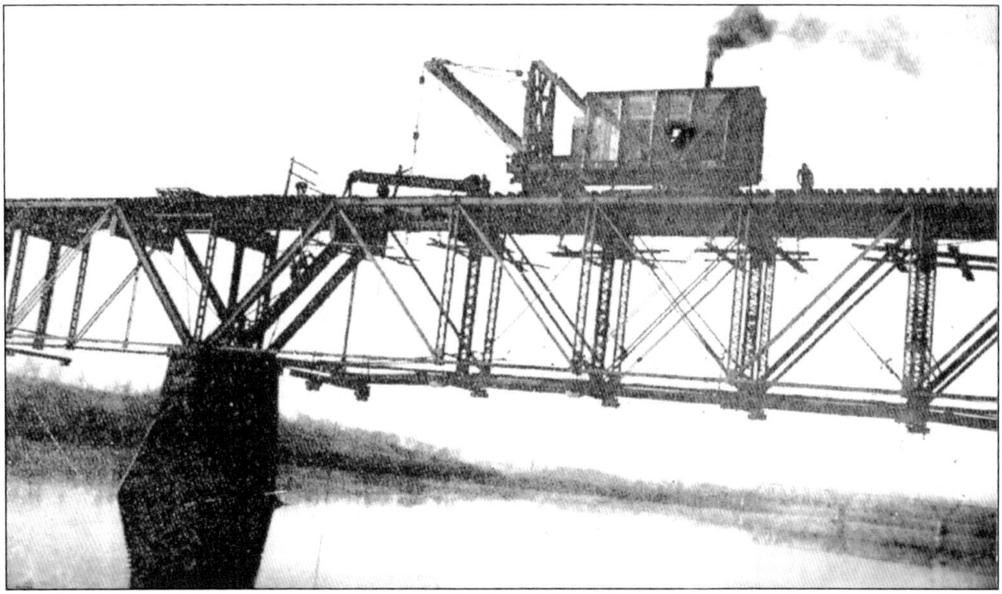

M&NW constructed this bridge across the Rock River in 1886. It consisted of five 143-foot deck truss spans and two 35-foot deck plate girder spans. This old photograph shows the bridge under repair during the early 1900s. (Author's collection.)

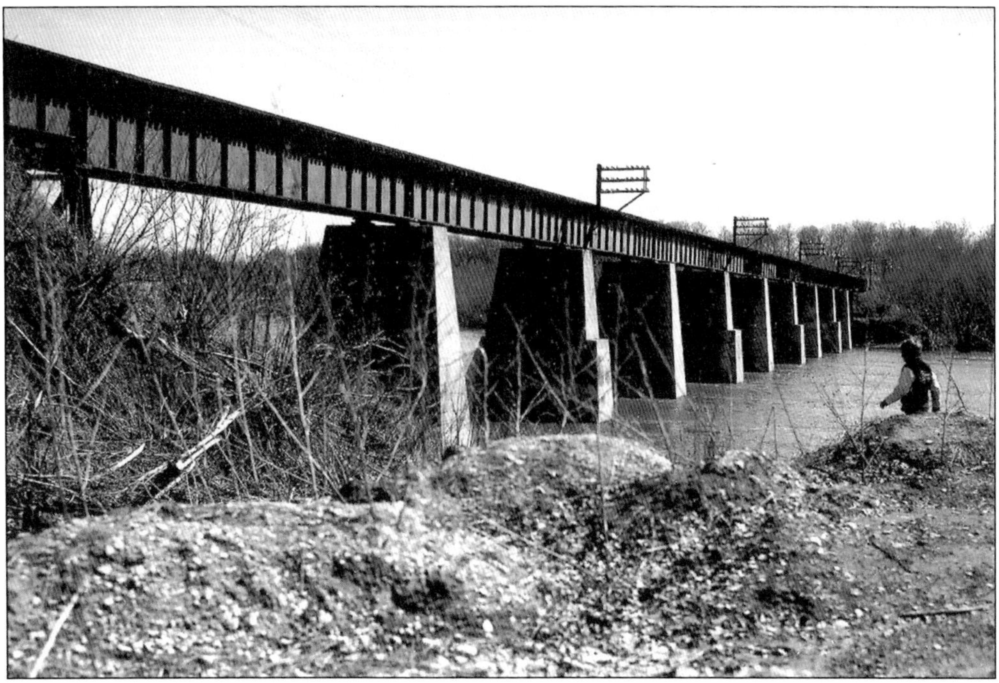

The first Rock River Bridge was replaced with this 12-span deck plate girder type in 1958. (Joiner History Room, Sycamore, Illinois.)

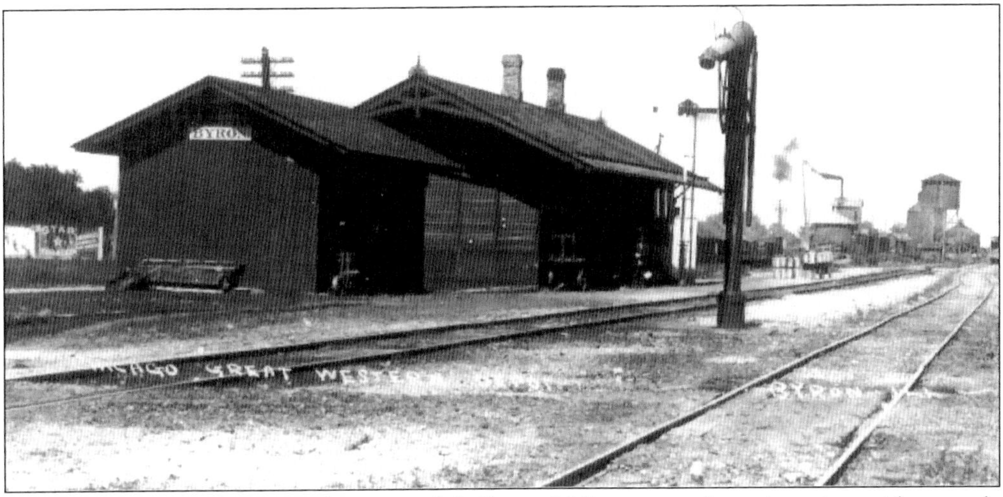

Byron, approximately four miles west of Stillman Valley, was a busy junction with a grade crossing and interchange connection with CMStP&P, sidings to several industries and a gravel pit, and locomotive servicing facilities. M&NW opened a station here in 1887, and Byron became a division point until CGW opened its East Stockton terminal in 1911. The station at Byron remained open after the 1968 merger and was not closed until May 1978. (Byron Museum of History.)

Byron, Ill.			
Auker Bros.	Livestock	Team Track	
Bainbridge Cattle Co.	Livestock	CGW	No
Barker Lumber Co.	Lumber-Fuel	CMStP&P	Yes
Blackhawk Builders Supply Co.	Building Supplies	Team Track	
Byron Cheese Co.	Cheese	Team Track	
Byron Elevator & Supply Co.	Feeds-Building Supplies	CGW	Yes
Byron Sand & Stone Co.	Gravel-Sand	CMStP&P	Yes
General Telephone Co. of Illinois	Poles	Team Track	
Illinois State Highway Dept.	Salt	Team Track	
Ogle County Marketing Assn.	Livestock	CMStP&P	No
Standard Oil Co.	Petroleum Products	CGW	Yes
Stevens Mfg. Co.	Metal Products	Team Track	
Walker Implement Co.	Implements	Team Track	

Milk and dairy products were an important source of business at Byron during the early years. CGW operated a milk train between Byron and Chicago that transported an average of 850 cans of milk a day by 1890. Also, an icehouse was constructed in 1891 to provide ice to keep the milk cold while in transit. The CGW 1914 annual report noted that a milk bottling plant with a capacity of 40,000 pounds of milk per day was in operation at Byron at this time. (Author's collection.)

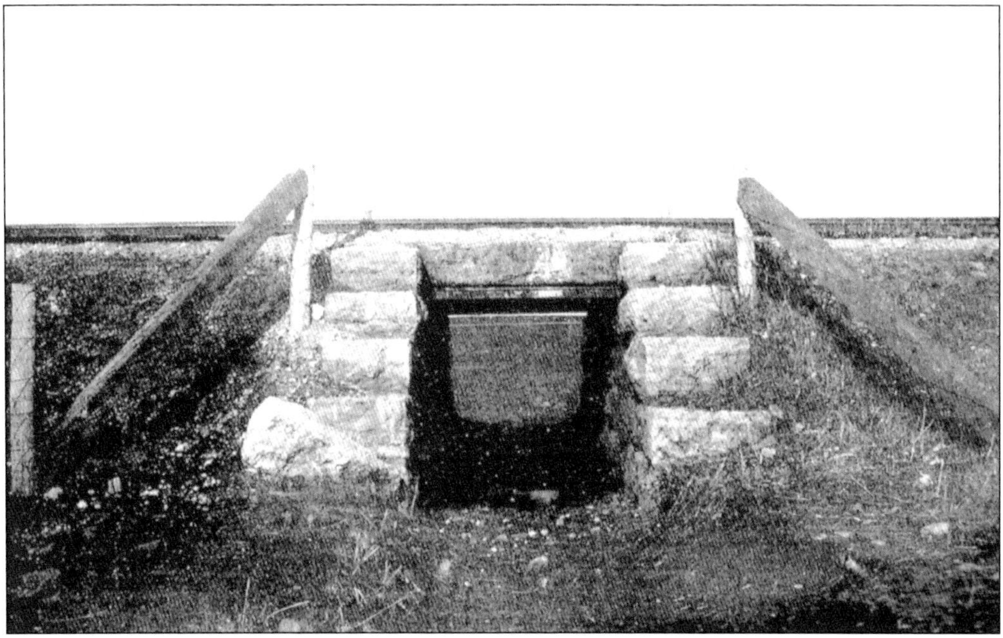

The main line across Illinois mostly traversed farmland, and CGW constructed stone rail-top cattle crossings at many locations. The standard crossing measured six feet by six feet. (Author's collection.)

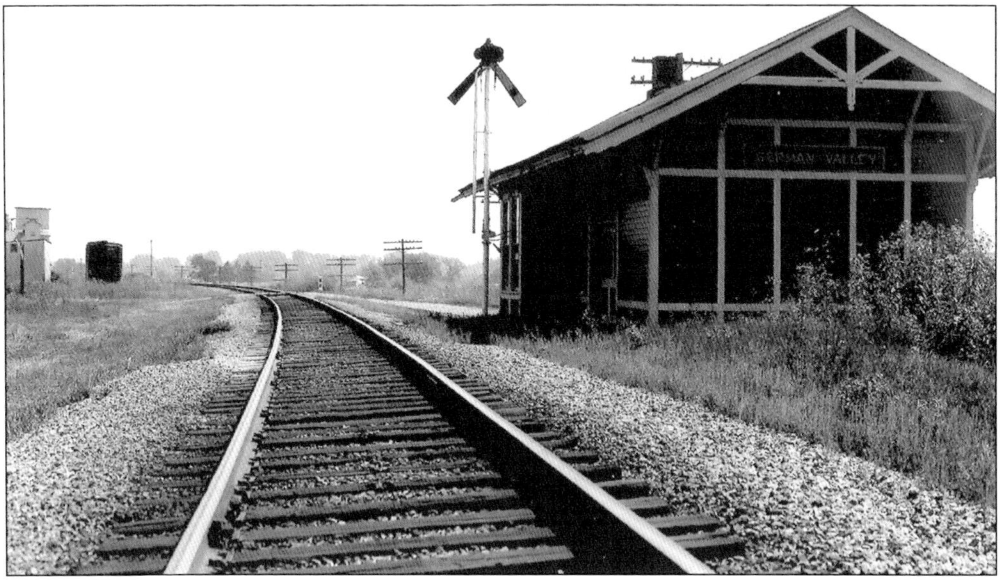

M&NW established a station at German Valley, 14 miles west of Byron, in 1887. At that time, there was a general store and one or two houses in the area. A village was platted in August 1887, and by 1910, the town had grown to include half a dozen stores, a creamery, a blacksmith shop, and the H. A. Hillmer Company grain elevator. German Valley was also the site of a terrible accident. A speeding westbound passenger train derailed in 1907, resulting in three fatalities. The accident was so severe that a mail car broke in two, and one section went through the lower floor of the grain elevator. German Valley was still open in 1969 but closed before the former CGW line was abandoned here in 1972. (Joiner History Room, Sycamore, Illinois.)

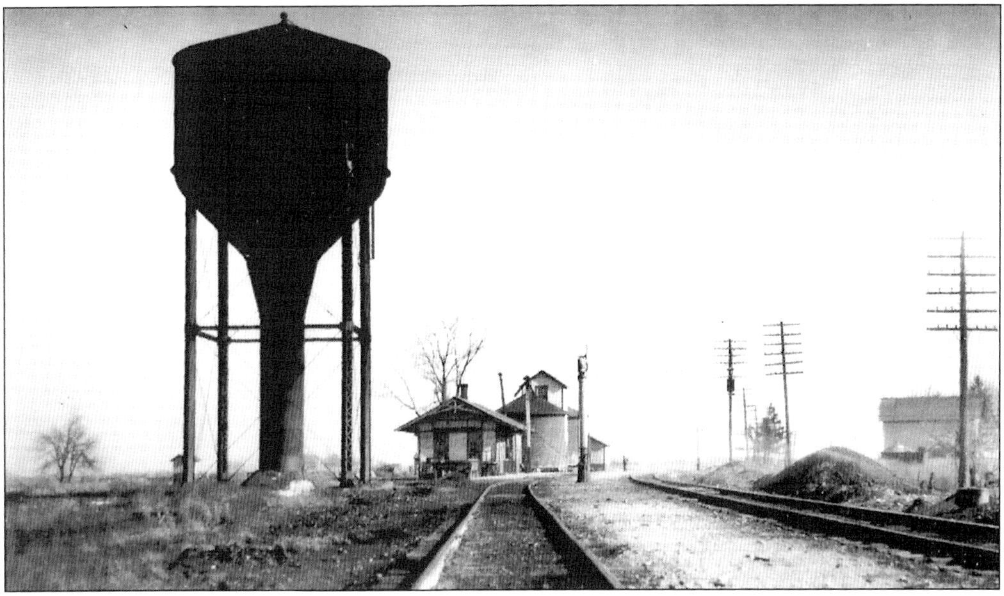

M&NW operated its trains over the IC between Dunbar, Illinois, and Dubuque from 1887 to 1888, when its own line in Illinois was completed. The station name was changed to South Freeport by 1891. The station, five miles west of German Valley, was an important interchange because IC delivered as many as 50 carloads of coal per day here from mines in southern Illinois for CGW steam locomotives. CGW owned coal mines and leased mining rights in Perry, Randolph, and Washington Counties through a subsidiary, Great Western Coal Company, which was incorporated on April 27, 1918. South Freeport depot closed on August 23, 1958, but the interchange remained open until it was abandoned in 1972. Great Western Coal Company was dissolved in 1960. (Joiner History Room, Sycamore, Illinois.)

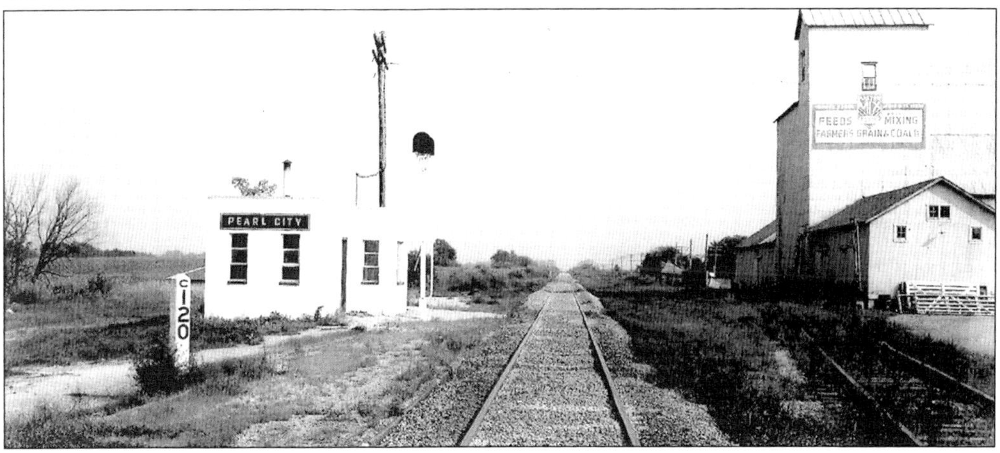

M&NW established a station 14 miles west of South Freeport in 1887 and named it Yellow Creek because it was a quarter of a mile south of a small village with that name. A new community developed around the station, and merchants relocated their businesses from Yellow Creek closer to the station. A number of progressive citizens, feeling that it was inappropriate to use the same name for their new town, changed it to Pearl City in 1895. CGW also changed the station name as well. The depot was partially destroyed by a derailment, and it was replaced with this small concrete structure in 1953. Pearl City was closed on September 1, 1962. (Joiner History Room, Sycamore, Illinois.)

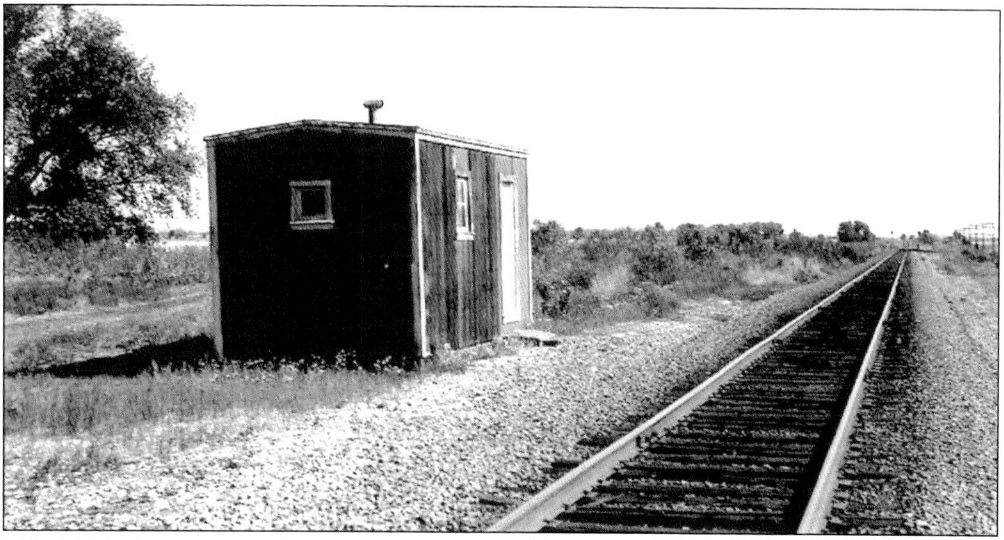

M&NW built a depot at Kent, five miles west of Pearl City, in December 1887, and a town with the same name was soon surveyed and platted near the station. Railroad facilities at Kent included a water tank, which was dismantled and removed by 1916. CGW double-tracked the main line from Kent to Galena Junction in 1910 and later removed the second set of tracks during the early 1950s. The depot at Kent was closed on July 9, 1951, and replaced with this shelter. (Joiner History Room, Sycamore, Illinois.)

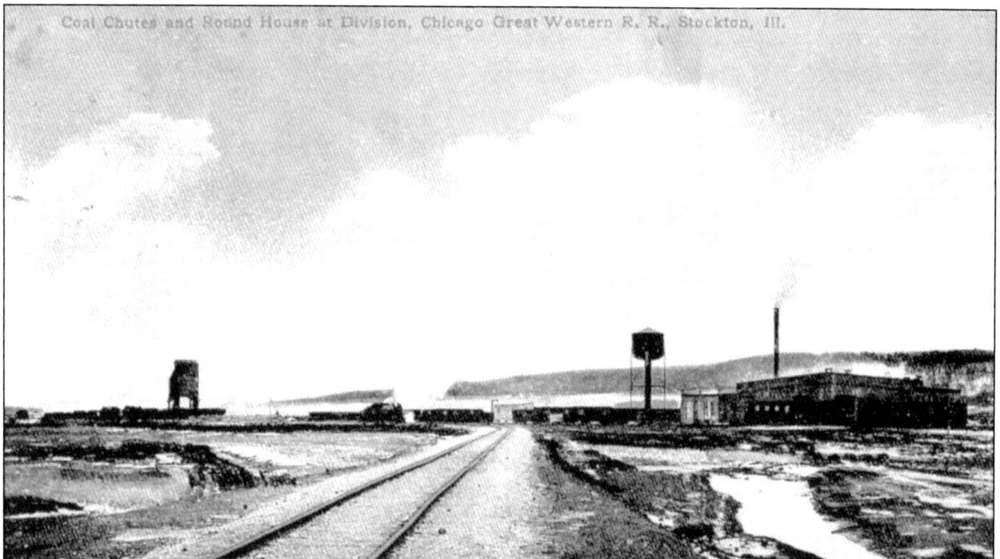

In 1910, CGW constructed a new division point and crew change point four miles west of Kent and a mile east of Stockton, which replaced Byron. The facility was named East Stockton, and it was placed in service on January 15, 1911. The terminal consisted of a rail yard, roundhouse, water tank, coal chute, car shop, and dispatcher's office that controlled train movements between Oelwein and Chicago. There were 65 steam locomotives assigned to East Stockton, which operated between the division point and Chicago and Oelwein. One hundred and fifty people were eventually employed there, and the annual payroll reached $300,000 in 1929. This scene is a 1920 postcard view of East Stockton. (Author's collection.)

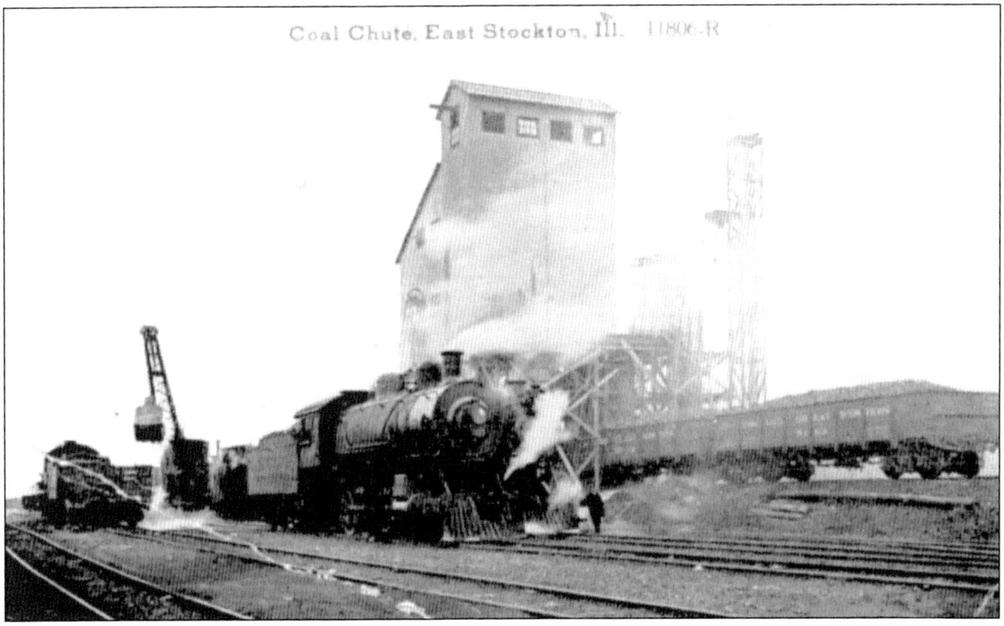

The fleet of Texas-type 2-10-4 steam locomotives acquired in 1930 were capable of operating between Chicago and Oelwein with only intermediate stops for fuel and water. The roundhouse and shops at East Stockton were no longer needed, and the terminal was phased out between 1930 and 1936. The vacated property was later sold to the City of Stockton. This is a postcard scene of East Stockton in 1911. (Author's collection.)

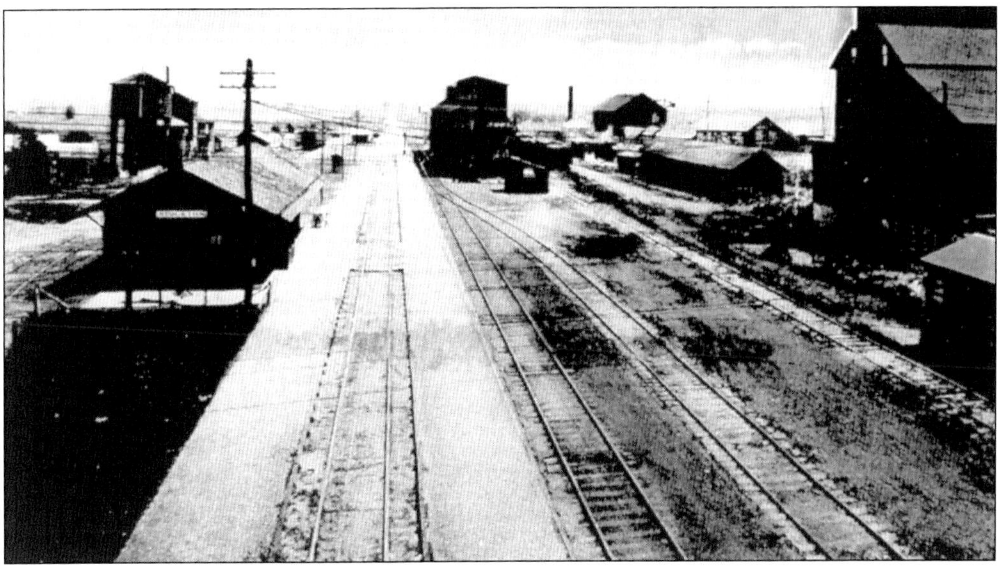

M&NW acquired property from several farmers in Stockton Township, Jo Daviess County, for a depot and station in 1887. One of the farmers was Marvin Freeman Carpenter, who platted a village near the station, which incorporated on April 17, 1890, as the village of Stockton. CGW began to expand its facilities at the station, which eventually included water tanks, coal chutes, and a rail yard. This postcard view faces east from the Main Street viaduct. The depot is to the left, the water plant is in the left background, and the coal chute is in the center background. These facilities were dismantled after East Stockton opened. (James L. Rueber.)

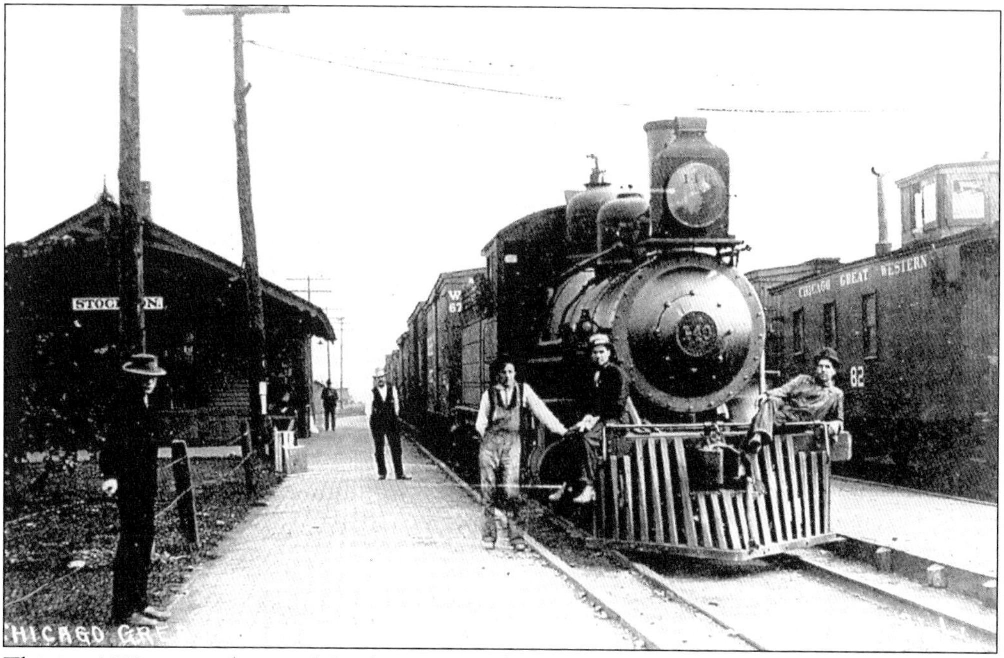

This is a 1910 postcard view of the depot at Stockton with the crew of a westbound freight train posing casually for the camera. (Author's collection.)

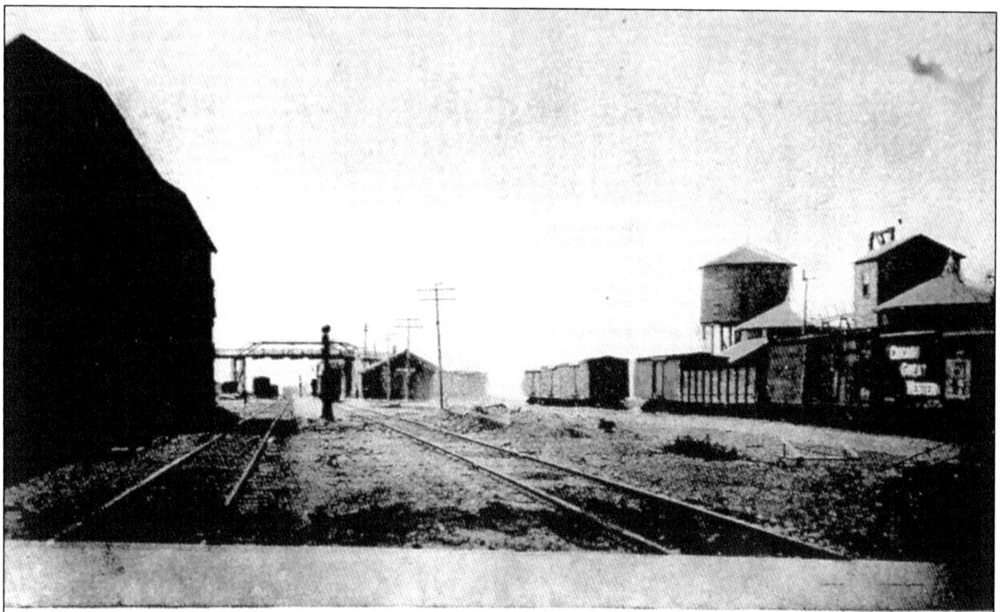

This 1909 postcard scene is from the Stockton rail yard facing west. The Main Street viaduct and depot are in the background. CGW replaced the water tanks at Stockton in 1935 and 1936. (James L. Rueber.)

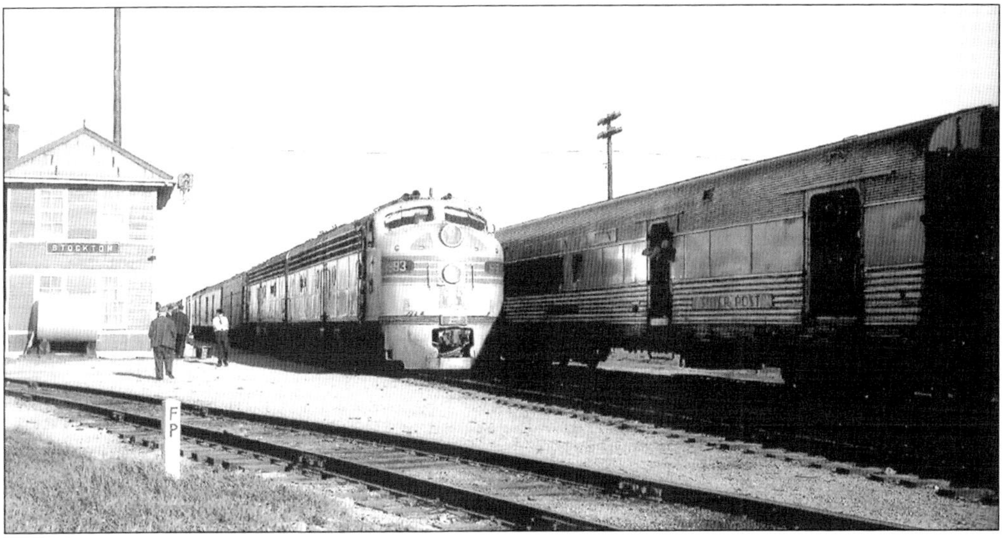

This photograph shows a westbound CB&Q passenger train on the CGW main line passing through Stockton. CGW allowed CB&Q to use its tracks as a detour when flooding along the Mississippi River placed the CB&Q main line out of service in April 1965. The two-story structure to the left is the old East Stockton dispatcher's office, which was relocated to Stockton in August 1931. It remained in use years later as a yard office after CGW consolidated all dispatching activity at Oelwein in 1949. The building was torn down and replaced with an office trailer in August 1971. C&NW closed Stockton station in March 1973. (Joiner History Room, Sycamore, Illinois.)

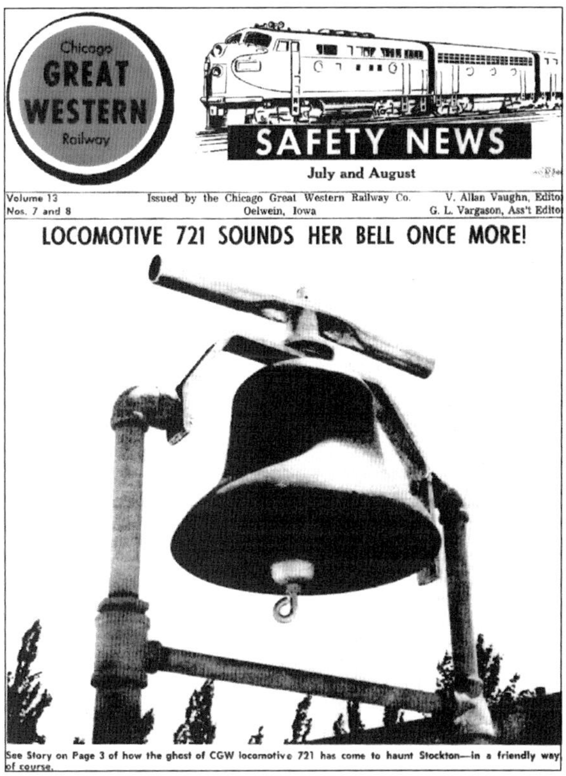

Chicago GREAT WESTERN Railway

SAFETY NEWS

July and August

Volume 13
Nos. 7 and 8

Issued by the Chicago Great Western Railway Co.
Oelwein, Iowa

V. Allan Vaughn, Edito
G. L. Vargason, Ass't Edito

LOCOMOTIVE 721 SOUNDS HER BELL ONCE MORE!

See Story on Page 3 of how the ghost of CGW locomotive 721 has come to haunt Stockton—in a friendly way of course.

CGW locomotive engineer Frank Mininni salvaged the bell from steam locomotive No. 721, which was scrapped in 1950. In 1967, he donated the bell to the Stockton Park Board, which placed it on display at the community swimming pool. CGW reported on the donation in an article published in *Safety News*. The company informed readers that the bell was heard hundreds of times as No. 721 hauled many countless tons of freight in and out of Stockton. (Author's collection.)

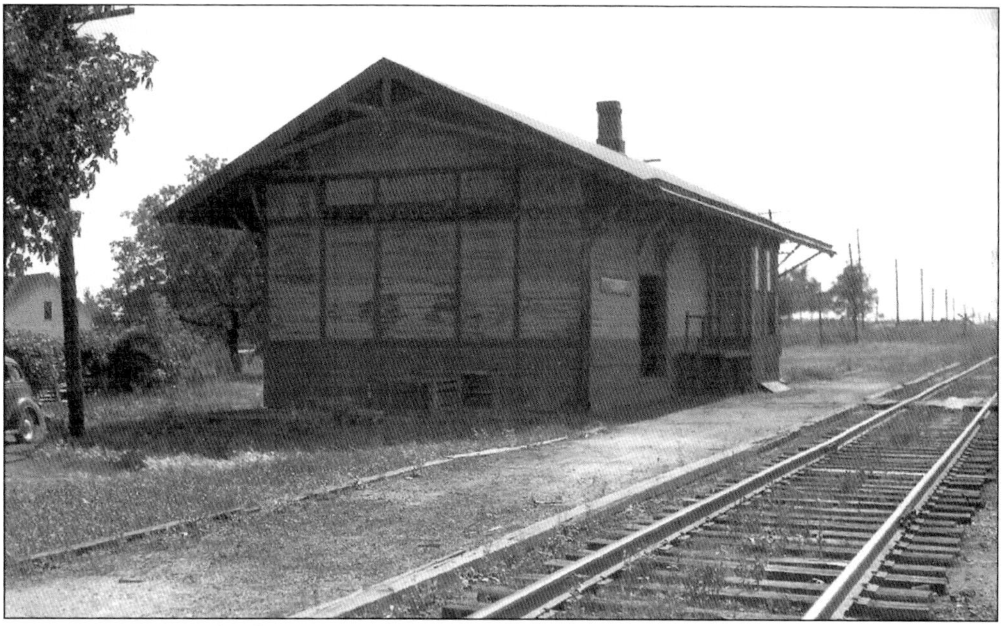

M&NW constructed a depot at Woodbine, seven miles west of Stockton, in 1887. The station included a depot, toolhouse, stockyard, and water tank. The tank was removed prior to 1916, and Woodbine closed on April 23, 1951. (Joiner History Room, Sycamore, Illinois.)

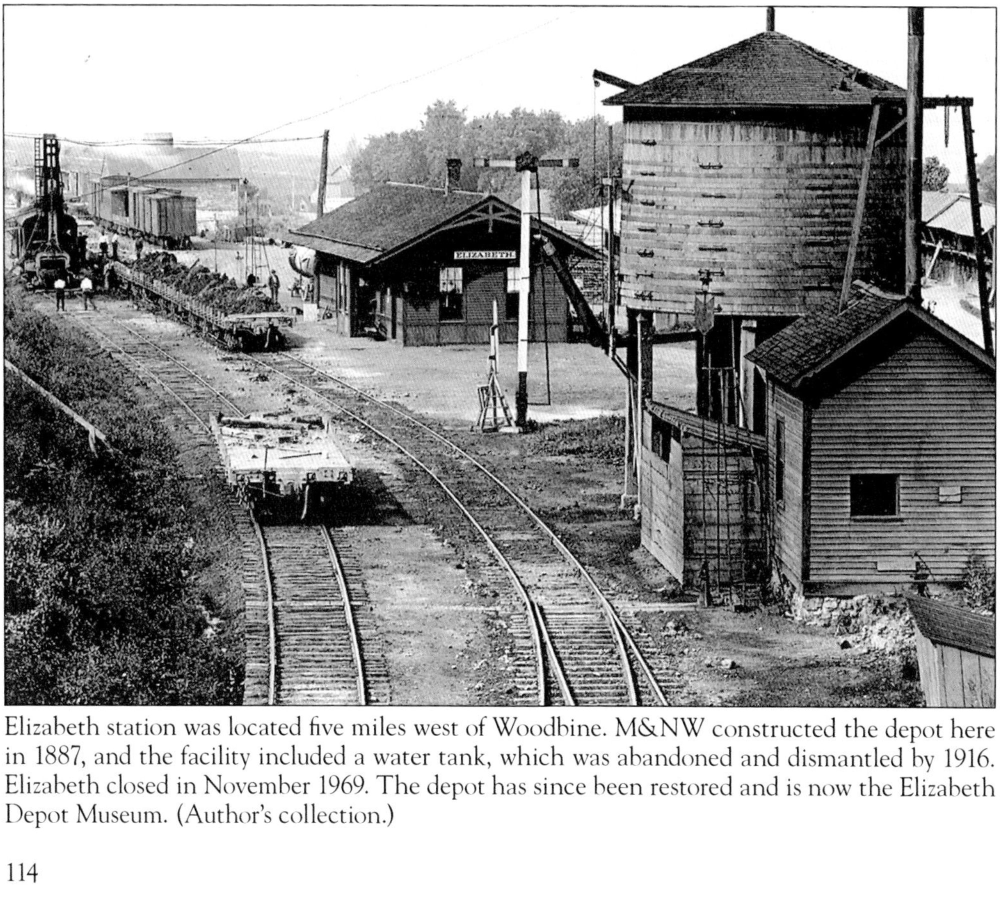

Elizabeth station was located five miles west of Woodbine. M&NW constructed the depot here in 1887, and the facility included a water tank, which was abandoned and dismantled by 1916. Elizabeth closed in November 1969. The depot has since been restored and is now the Elizabeth Depot Museum. (Author's collection.)

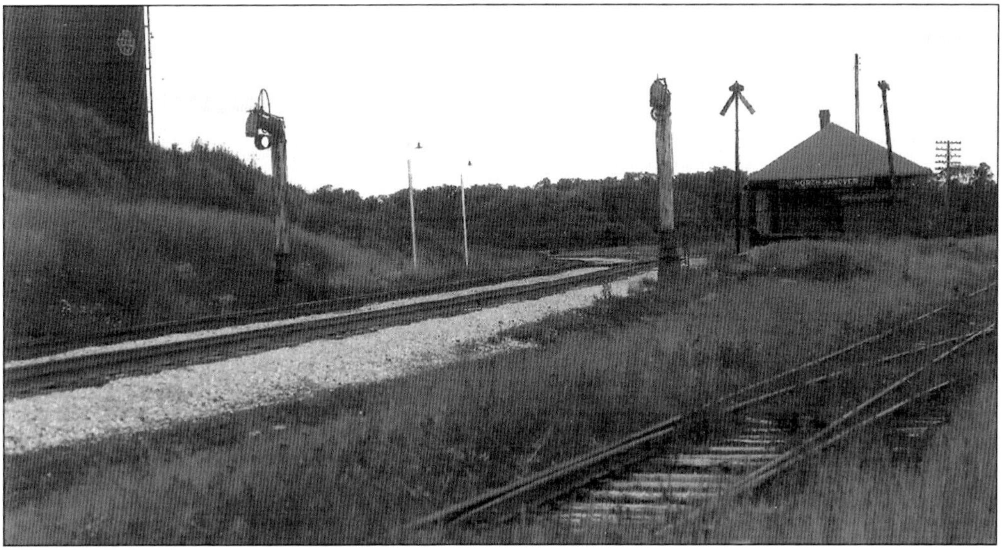

M&NW opened a station named Trousdale three miles west of Elizabeth in 1887. The name was changed to North Hanover during the 1890s. It was also the junction with the Hanover and Great Western Railway, incorporated in February 1898 for the purpose of building and operating a two-and-a-half-mile branch between the CGW at North Hanover and the Hanover Woolen Mills in the village of Hanover. CGW constructed an elaborate water station at North Hanover in 1912 that drew water from the Apple River and replaced water stations at Woodbine, Elizabeth, and Rodden. The depot was replaced in 1914. The Hanover railroad ceased operations in 1934. (Joiner History Room, Sycamore, Illinois.)

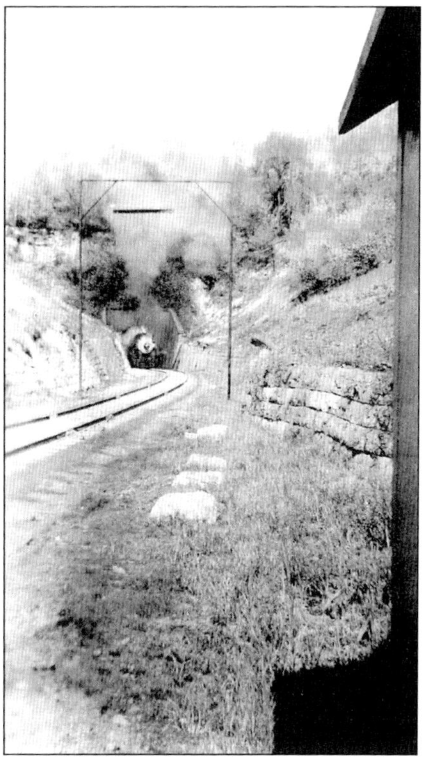

This is a 1940 view of the east portal of Winston Tunnel, about six miles west of Elizabeth. CStP&KC started construction of the tunnel at the west heading on May 12, 1887, and from the east in July 1887. The headings met on December 22 of that year. The first train to pass through the tunnel was a construction train on January 19, 1888. CGW had to install a forced draft system in 1913 to improve ventilation due to the operation of the 2-6-6-2 Mallet-type locomotives, which operated at slow speed and exhausted a tremendous amount of gas and soot. Winston Tunnel was 2,440 feet in length, and passage through this long, narrow bore in a creeping Mallet was unbearable and dangerous for the train crew. (James L. Rueber.)

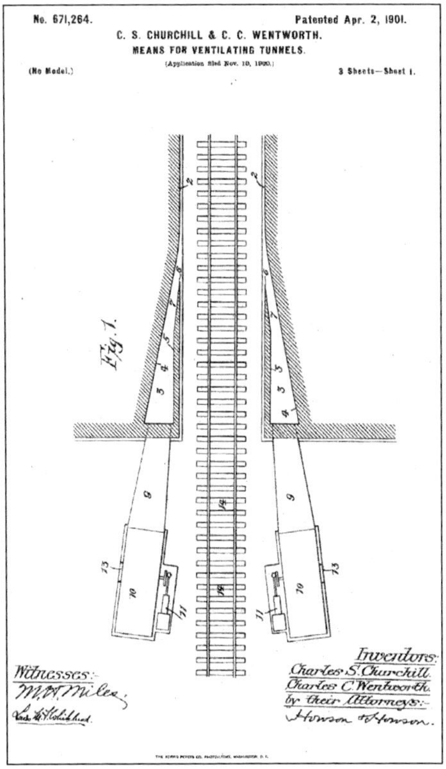

The company based the forced-draft system on the patented "Churchill method of ventilation." Patent sheet No. 1 of this device is shown. Two blowers or fans were situated on each side of the track with a ductwork system that directed forced air into a large chamber attached to the tunnel. An operator would start the blowers as a steam locomotive entered the chamber. Smoke and fumes would be directed ahead of the engine away from the cab. (Author's collection.)

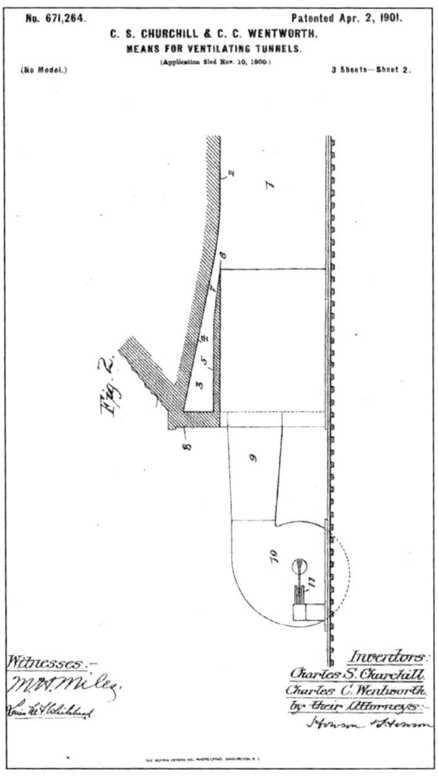

Sheet No. 2 shows the blower (left) with ductwork affixed to the tunnel (right). CGW used only one blower, a Sturtevant multivane fan, which delivered 280,000 cubic feet of fresh air per minute into the tunnel. (Author's collection.)

Sheet No. 3 shows how the chamber enclosed the portal. (Author's collection.)

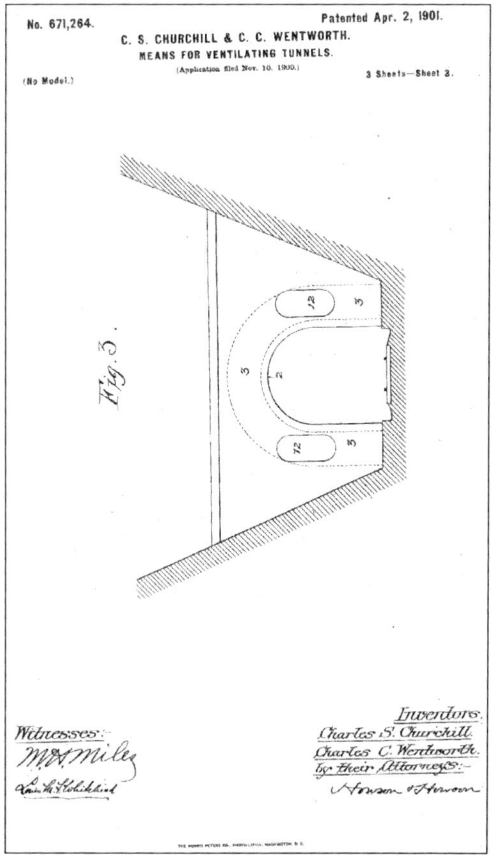

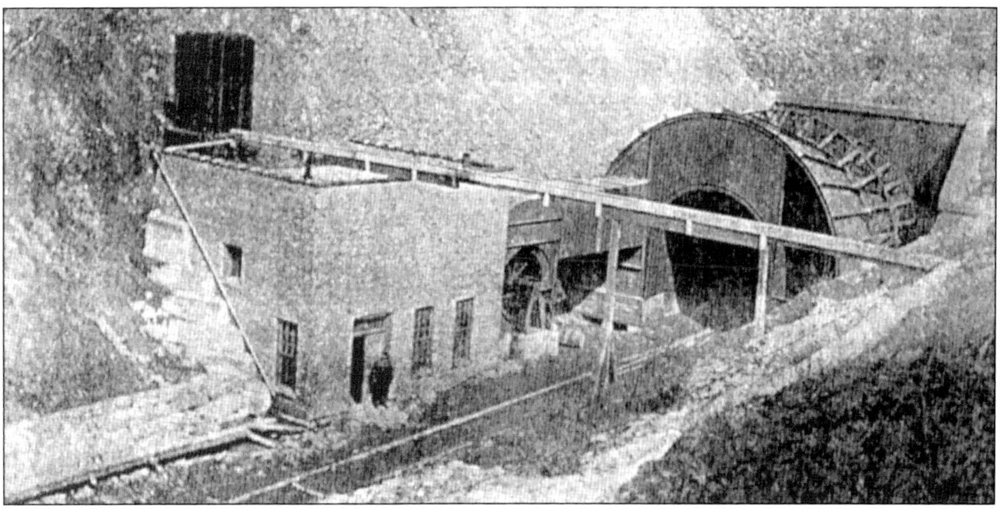

CGW powered the fan with a 180-horsepower diesel engine housed inside a two-story brick building (called a fanhouse), as shown in this old photograph. Note the blower and the duct and chamber, which the company called a "nozzle." It was a large steel and wood structure similar to an arched train shed roof, supported on concrete footings and positioned against the tunnel portal. The rectangular-shaped structure on the roof of the fanhouse was a cooling tower supplied from a well on the opposite side of the tracks. (James L. Rueber.)

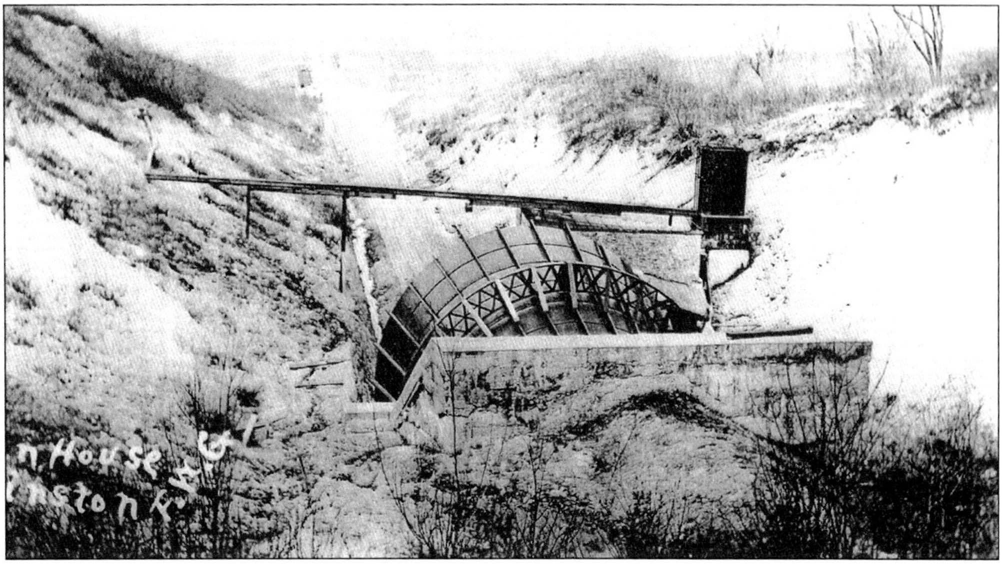

This photograph shows the nozzle and cooling tower before the fanhouse was constructed. Note the site of the fanhouse has been cleared and graded prior to construction. There was an ascending, eastbound grade inside the tunnel, which forced locomotives to work harder and produce more smoke and fumes while inside. Ventilation was not required for westbound trains, which could drift downgrade with throttle closed. Therefore, a ventilation plant was installed only at the west end of Winston Tunnel. (James L. Rueber.)

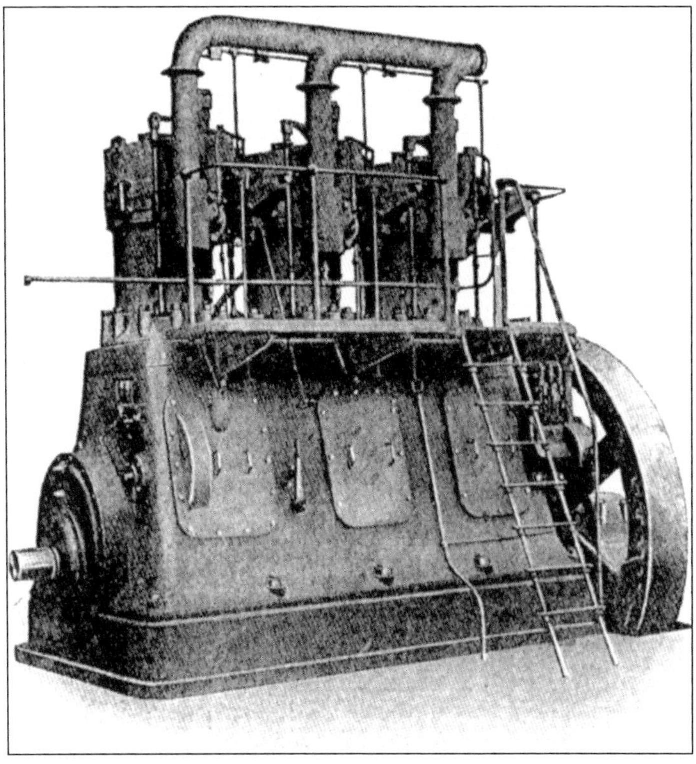

This illustration depicts the diesel engine used to power the blower. CGW did not identify the manufacturer in its records, but the engine was similar to the Fairbanks Morse Type Y power plant developed in 1912 for industrial and agricultural applications. (James L. Rueber.)

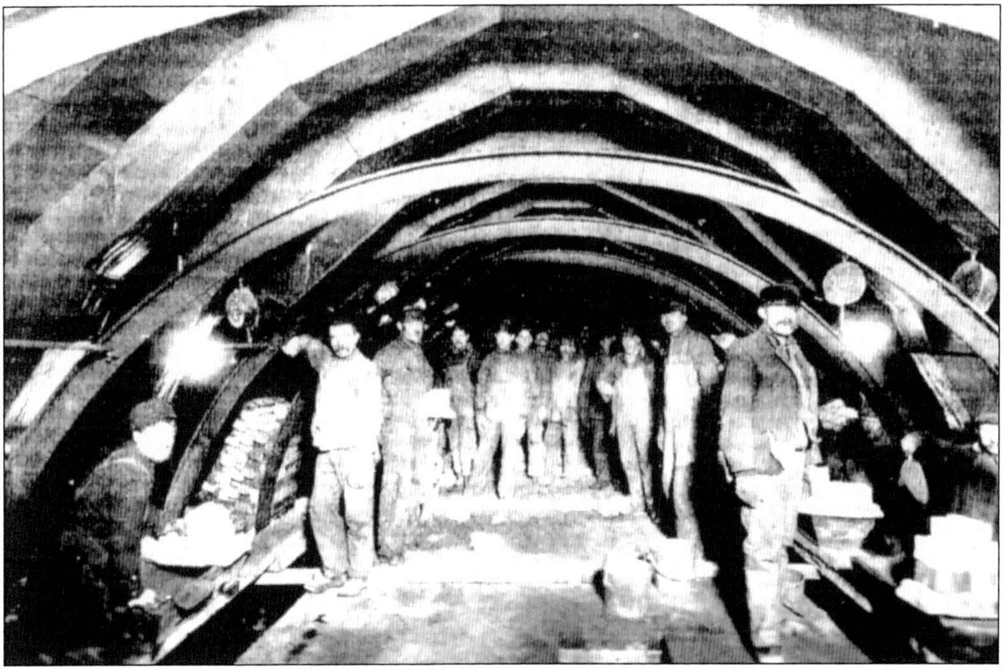

The tunnel builders found a layer of limestone above the site and supposed the tunnel would be bored through solid rock. They were mistaken and, as the tunnel was excavated, they realized that it would have to be built through hard blue shale. This material rapidly disintegrates on exposure to air and water, which made Winston Tunnel unstable and prone to cave in. CGW relined the bore with brick and concrete and made other improvements over a two-year period from 1902 to 1904. This photograph shows a mason gang repairing the tunnel ceiling. The workers stood on top of boxcars, and wet cement was passed up to them through the opened hatch. (Author's collection.)

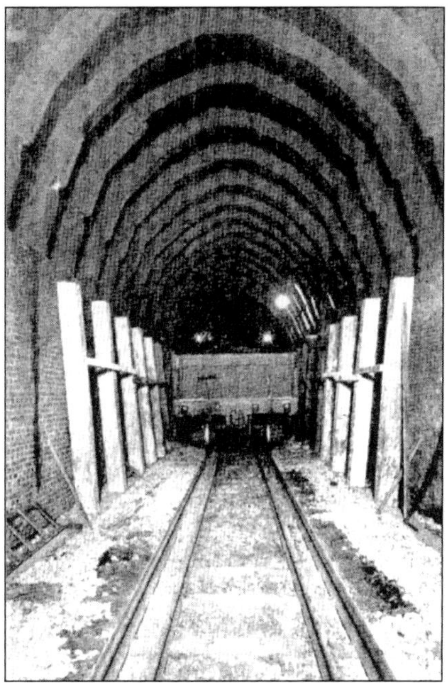

This is another view of the 1902 tunnel-relining project. (Author's collection.)

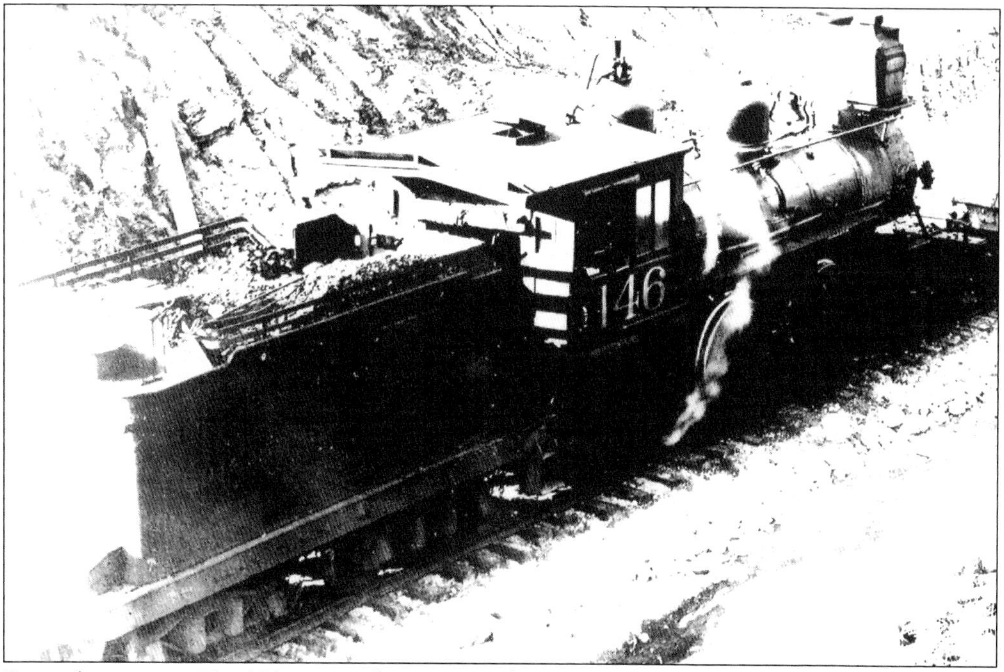

Steam locomotive No. 146 was used to position boxcars and other work cars inside the tunnel during repairs. (Joiner History Room, Sycamore, Illinois.)

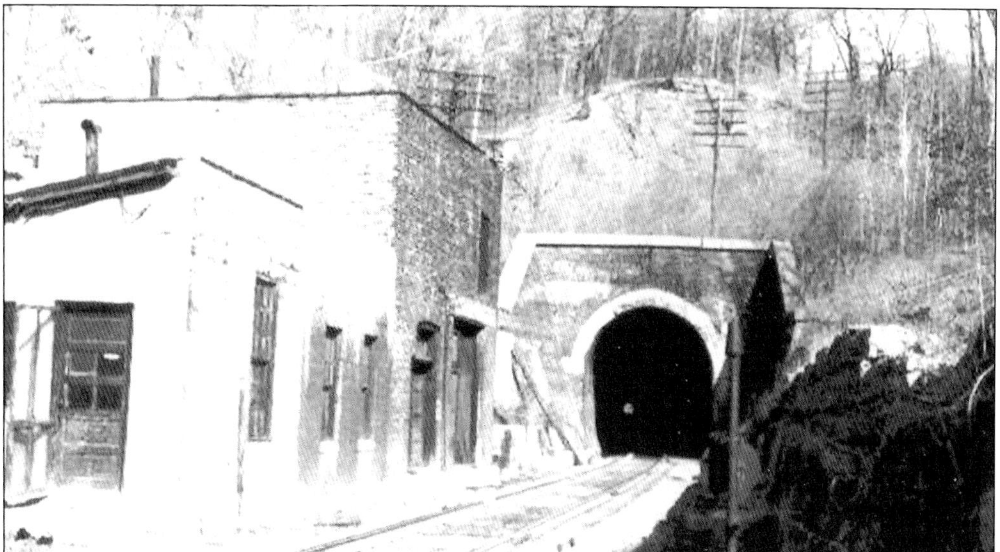

The tunnel cost $600,000 to build, and CGW continued to spend large sums of money in repair and maintenance over the years. This view shows the west portal with additional structures added to the fanhouse. CGW closed this facility in the early 1950s after CGW converted its motive power fleet to diesel-electric. Ventilation was not needed because the diesel locomotive cab is in front and ahead of the exhaust stacks. C&NW operated the last train through Winston Tunnel on October 31, 1971, and it was abandoned the following year. The site is now owned by the Illinois Department of Natural Resources (IDNR) and administered as a unit of Apple River Canyon State Park. (Donald Vaughn.)

BETWEEN STOCKTON AND GALENA JUNCTION.—45 miles per hour for passenger trains and 25 miles per hour for freight trains on descending grades and curves.

WINSTON TUNNEL.—Westbound trains twenty miles per hour. Eastbound trains, when fan is running, ten miles per hour. Fan out of service, twenty miles per hour.

GALENA JUNCTION.—25 miles per hour for passenger trains and 15 miles per hour for freight trains over Junction switches.

Trains crews operating through Winston Tunnel had to comply with speed limits as shown in Eastern Division employee timetable No. 22, effective June 4, 1922. Note that the railroad allowed a higher speed when the fan was out of service to permit crews to exit as quickly as possible. (Chicago and North Western Historical Society.)

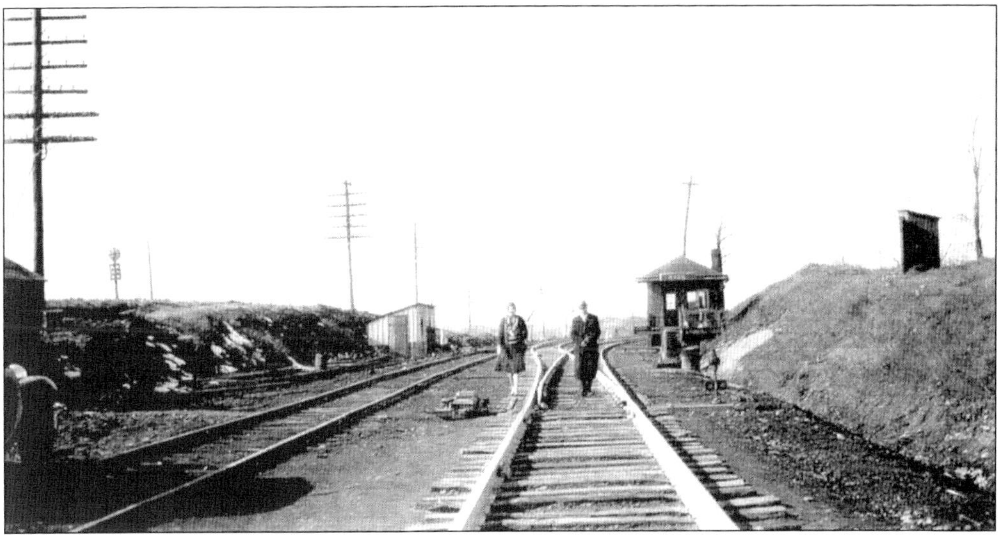

This photograph shows Rice station, February 3, 1931. CGW installed an electric staff system to control train movements through Winston Tunnel during the relining project in 1902. This train control system was retained after the project was completed, and it was later extended in 1905 between two new stations, Winston and Rice, east and west of the tunnel portals, respectively. The staff system remained in service for 26 years. CGW was one of the very few railroads in the United States that used this method of train control. It was replaced in 1931 with a centralized traffic control installation operated from a new addition to the fanhouse. The upgrade allowed CGW to close the staff stations at Winston and Rice on February 11, 1931. (James L. Rueber.)

DUBUQUE DISTRICT—Westward

Mile Posts	TIME TABLE NO. 24 Taking Effect October 25, 1959 STATIONS	FIRST CLASS			SECOND CLASS						
		11	13		79	75	61	71	77	73	
		The Hawkeye	The Land O' Corn		Dispatch CFS-3	Dispatch CAC-5	Freight	Dispatch C C 1	Dispatch C W 1	Dispatch	
114.4	----FREEPORT---- 2.4	L 12 50AM	L 7 13PM	----------	--------	----------	----------	----------	----------	----------	---
		Daily	Daily		Daily	Daily	Daily	Daily	Daily	Daily	Exc
116.8	C WEST JUNCTION 5.5	L 12 55AM	L 7 18PM	----------	L 12 05AM	L 1 45AM	L 4 25AM	L 7 40AM	L 9 00AM	L 3 00PM	---
122.3	------ELEROY------ 4.6	1 01	7 24	----------	12 14	1 52	4 35	7 47	9 07	3 07	---
126.9	C------LENA------ 4.1	f **1 06** 78	n 7 28	----------	12 21	1 58	4 41	7 53	9 13	3 13	---
131.0	--WADDAMS GROVE-- 4.0	1 10	7 32	----------	12 26	2 03	4 46	7 58	9 18	3 18	---
135.0	-------NORA------ 3.5	1 14	7 36	----------	12 31	2 07	4 51	8 03	9 23	3 23	---
138.5	D---WARREN----- 6.0	s 1 20	s 7 41	----------	**12 46** 78	2 11	5 08	8 07	**9 30** 14	3 27	---
144.5	D--APPLE RIVER--- 8.2	f 1 26	n **7 48** 72	----------	12 53	2 17	5 20	8 14	9 38	3 35	---
152.7	C-SCALES MOUND- 5.5	1 34	n 7 56	----------	1 02	2 27	**6 06** 76	8 23	9 47	**4 03** 74	---
158.2	---COUNCIL HILL-- 6.4	1 43	8 04	----------	1 19	2 37	6 24	8 35	9 57	4 15	---
164.6	------GRANT------ .9	1 53	8 13	----------	1 38	**3 07** 12	6 46	**8 59** 14	10 09	4 29	---
165.5	D----GALENA------ 3.3	s 2 02	s 8 16	----------	1 41	3 23	6 52	9 03	10 13	4 32	---
168.8	C----PORTAGE----- 12.7	2 08	8 22	----------	1 48	3 30	7 15	9 10	10 20	4 39	---
181.5	C---EAST CABIN---- .2	2 22	8 35	----------	2 05	3 46	7 40	9 26	10 40	4 52	---
181.7	--EAST DUBUQUE-- .6	2 25	f 8 37	----------	2 07	3 48	7 45	9 28	10 43	4 54	---
182.3	C-DUBUQUE JCT--- .9	2 29	8 41	----------	2 13	3 52	7 50	9 32	**11 01** 60	4 58	---
183.2	-----DUBUQUE----- 8	s {2 35 / 2 50 12	s 8 45	----------	2 15	3 58	**8 33** 14	9 38	11 06	5 03	---

CGW connected with CB&Q at Aiken and operated over that railroad along the Mississippi River north one mile to Portage and a connection with the IC. CGW trains ran on IC almost 13 miles to Dubuque and a connection with the company's own rails. The CB&Q connection was changed to Galena Junction in 1902. CGW train crews were governed by CB&Q and IC train orders, rules, and special instructions when operating on these lines. This image shows stations and sidings between Portage and Dubuque published in IC employee timetable No. 24, effective October 25, 1959. (Author's collection.)

This CGW illustration from the 1890s shows the IC main line between Portage and Dubuque. (Author's collection.)

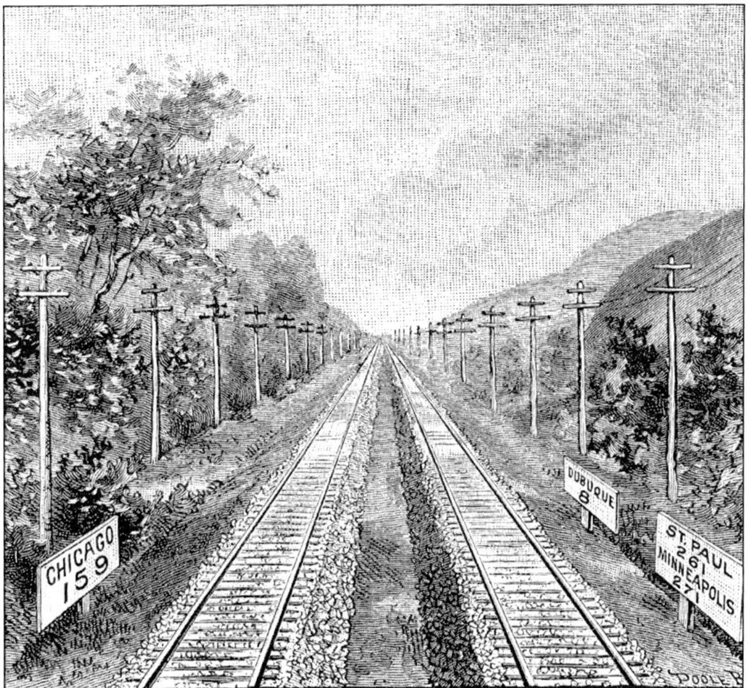

On Main Line of the Chicago Great Western Railway, approaching the city of Dubuque, on the bank of the Mississippi River.

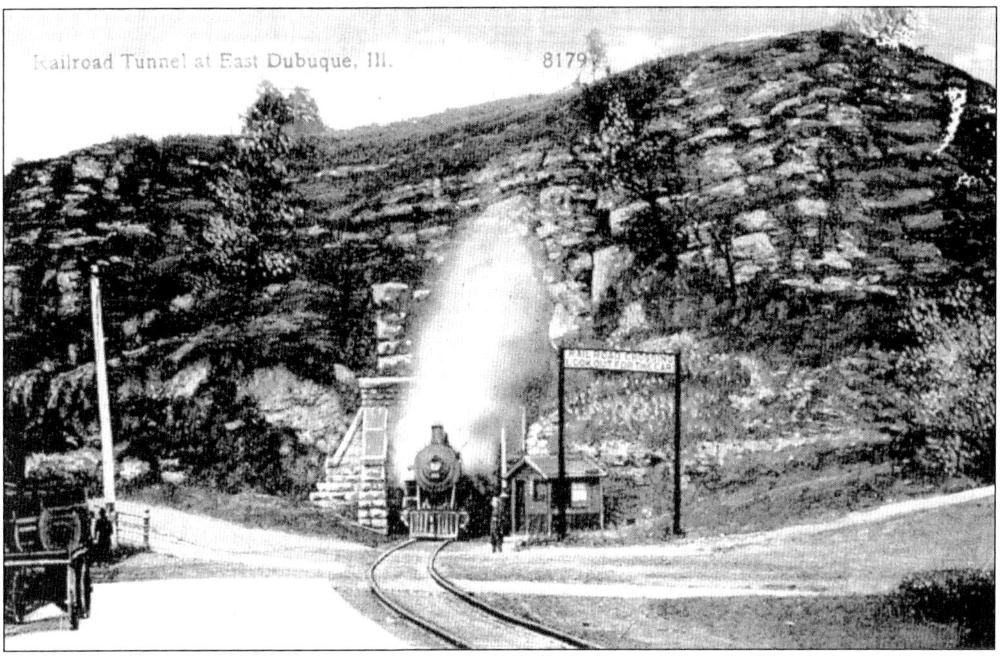

IC passed through a small tunnel at East Dubuque just before crossing the Mississippi River. This old postcard scene shows a westbound train exiting the tunnel headed toward Dubuque. (Author's collection.)

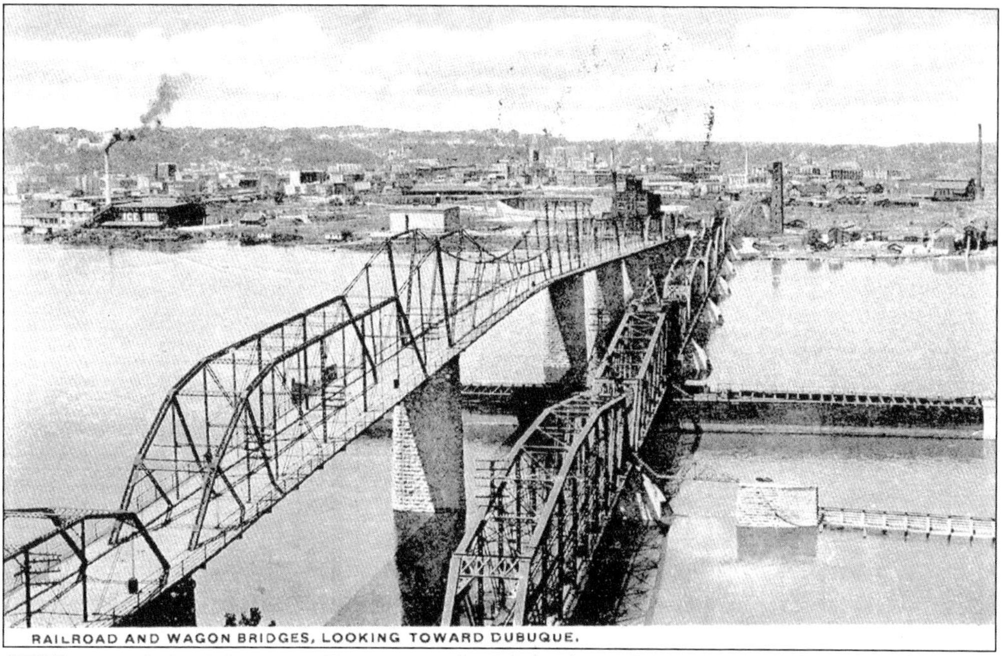

CGW crossed the Mississippi River over the IC bridge. This 1916 postcard view shows the railroad bridge (left) and Dubuque (background). (Author's collection.)

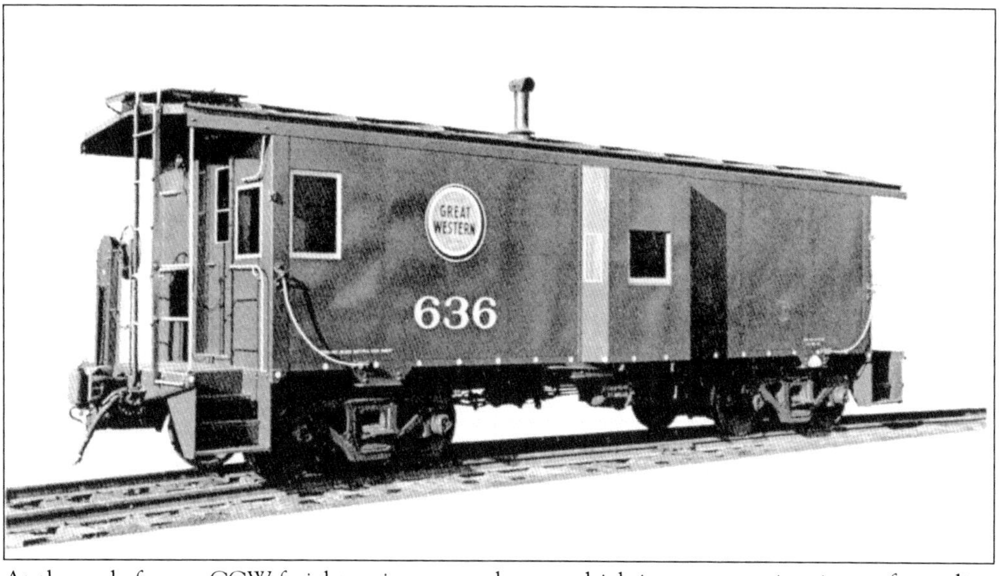

At the end of every CGW freight train was a caboose, which is an appropriate image for ending this chapter. This illustration of caboose No. 636 was published in the company's 1963 annual report. (Author's collection.)

Six

MERGER

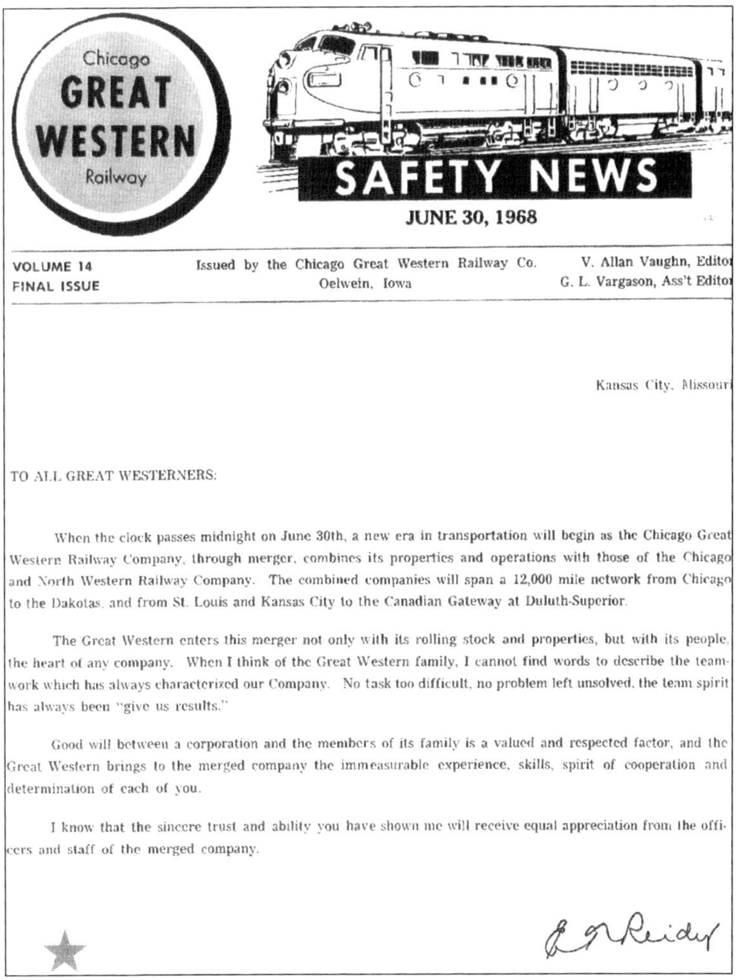

Chicago GREAT WESTERN Railway

SAFETY NEWS

JUNE 30, 1968

VOLUME 14
FINAL ISSUE

Issued by the Chicago Great Western Railway Co.
Oelwein, Iowa

V. Allan Vaughn, Edito
G. L. Vargason, Ass't Edito

Kansas City, Missouri

TO ALL GREAT WESTERNERS:

When the clock passes midnight on June 30th, a new era in transportation will begin as the Chicago Great Western Railway Company, through merger, combines its properties and operations with those of the Chicago and North Western Railway Company. The combined companies will span a 12,000 mile network from Chicago to the Dakotas, and from St. Louis and Kansas City to the Canadian Gateway at Duluth-Superior.

The Great Western enters this merger not only with its rolling stock and properties, but with its people, the heart of any company. When I think of the Great Western family, I cannot find words to describe the teamwork which has always characterized our Company. No task too difficult, no problem left unsolved, the team spirit has always been "give us results."

Good will between a corporation and the members of its family is a valued and respected factor, and the Great Western brings to the merged company the immeasurable experience, skills, spirit of cooperation and determination of each of you.

I know that the sincere trust and ability you have shown me will receive equal appreciation from the officers and staff of the merged company.

E T Reidy

On June 30, 1968, just before CGW ceased to exist, the company sent employees the last issue of *Safety News* with a farewell message from company president Edward T. Reidy. (Author's collection.)

CHICAGO & NORTH WESTERN RAILWAY

DES MOINES AND CENTRAL IOWA RAILWAY

MISSOURI DIVISION

TIMETABLE

No. 1

Effective January 1, 1969

AT 12:01 A. M.

CENTRAL STANDARD TIME

The entire CGW system became the C&NW Missouri Division on merger day, July 1, 1968. C&NW began to integrate train operations, close redundant facilities, and phase in CGW motive power into the C&NW fleet during the remainder of the year. The process was approaching completion when C&NW issued the first Missouri Division employee timetable No. 1, effective January 1, 1969. It contained schedules for all of the former CGW lines with special instructions that combined C&NW and CGW operating practices. (Author's collection.)

Westward—Stockton Subdivision—Eastward

SECOND CLASS 191 Tuesday Thursday Saturday	Mile Posts	Distance from Chicago		Timetable No. 1 January 1, 1969 STATIONS		Distance from Galena Jct.	Capacity of Sidings	SECOND CLASS 192 Monday Wednesday Friday
		0		CHICAGO		157.6		
A. M. 11.00		7.3		DQ CHICAGO TRANSFER Y	7.3	150.3		A. M. A 2.40
A. M. 11.20	10.3	10.3	D. T.	C FOREST PARK	3.0	147.3		A. M. A 2.20
11.30	13.1	13.1	D. T.	BELLWOOD	2.8	144.5		2.10
11.37	16.8	16.8	D. T.	ELMHURST	3.7	140.8	43	1.50
11.40	18.5	18.5	D. T.	VILLA PARK	1.7	139.1		1.45
11.45	20.9	20.9	D. T.	LOMBARD Y	2.4	136.7		1.40
11.55	25.6	25.6	D. T.	D CAROL STREAM	4.7	132.0		1.30
12.05	30.7	30.7	D. T.	DQ INGALTON	5.1	126.9	87	1.20
12.15	35.9	35.9	D. T.	D ST. CHARLES	5.2	121.7	96	1.10
12.20	37.3	37.3	D. T.	FOX RIVER	1.4	120.3	97	1.07
12.28	41.4	41.4	SINGLE TRACK	WASCO	4.1	116.2	65	12.59
12.36	45.6	45.6	SINGLE TRACK	LILY LAKE	4.2	112.0	52	12.51
12.42	48.6	48.6	SINGLE TRACK	VIRGIL	3.0	109.0		12.45
1.20	56.6	56.6	SINGLE TRACK	DQ SYCAMORE Y	8.0	101.0	222	12.30
1.25	59.3	59.3	SINGLE TRACK	FIVE POINTS	2.7	98.3		11.47
1.35	64.1	64.1	SINGLE TRACK	CLARE Y	4.8	93.5		11.37
1.45	69.8	69.8	SINGLE TRACK	D ESMOND Y	5.7	87.8	138	11.27
1.55	74.9	74.9	SINGLE TRACK	LINDENWOOD Y	5.1	82.7		11.17
2.05	78.4	78.4	SINGLE TRACK	HOLCOMB	3.5	79.2	55	11.10
2.15	83.4	83.4	SINGLE TRACK	STILLMAN VALLEY	5.0	74.2		11.01
2.25	87.8	87.8	SINGLE TRACK	DQ BYRON Y	4.4	69.8		10.53
2.40	96.7	96.7	SINGLE TRACK	EGAN	8.9	60.9		10.37
2.50	100.9	100.9	SINGLE TRACK	D GERMAN VALLEY	4.2	56.8		10.30
3.10	106.7	106.7	SINGLE TRACK	SOUTH FREEPORT Y	5.8	50.9	222	10.20
3.25	114.3	114.3	SINGLE TRACK	BOLTON	7.6	43.3		9.42
3.35	120.0	120.0	SINGLE TRACK	PEARL CITY	5.7	37.6		9.32
3.50	124.9	124.9	SINGLE TRACK	KENT	4.9	32.7		9.24
4.05	129.0	129.0	D. T.	EAST STOCKTON	4.1	28.6		9.16
4.15	131.1	131.1	D. T.	DQ STOCKTON Y	2.1	26.5		9.10
4.20	131.5	131.5	D. T.	GOLDEN	0.4	26.1		9.00
4.35	138.6	138.6	SINGLE TRACK	WOODBINE	7.1	19.0		8.46
4.48	143.3	143.3	SINGLE TRACK	D ELIZABETH	4.7	14.3		8.39
4.55	146.6	146.6	SINGLE TRACK	NORTH HANOVER	3.3	11.0	222	8.33
5.10	153.6	153.6	SINGLE TRACK	RICE	7.0	4.0		8.19
A 5.20 P. M.	157.6	157.6	SINGLE TRACK	GALENA JCT. Y	4.0	0		8.10 P. M.

Between Chicago (Grand Central Station) and Forest Park trains operate over track of B&OCT RR. B&OCT timetable and rules govern.

The former CGW main line in Illinois was designated the Stockton Subdivision of the Missouri Division, and it was changed to the Stockton Subdivision of the C&NW Galena Division by May 1969. C&NW terminated the trackage agreement with B&OCT and closed Chicago Transfer Yard in October 1969. The old CGW main line became a long spur track served by wayfreights dispatched from C&NW terminals over existing interchanges or new connections. Most of the former CGW main line in Illinois was abandoned during the next 30 years. As of early 2006, only two short sections of former CGW right-of-way remain in operation in Illinois between West Chicago and St. Charles and at Byron. (Author's collection.)

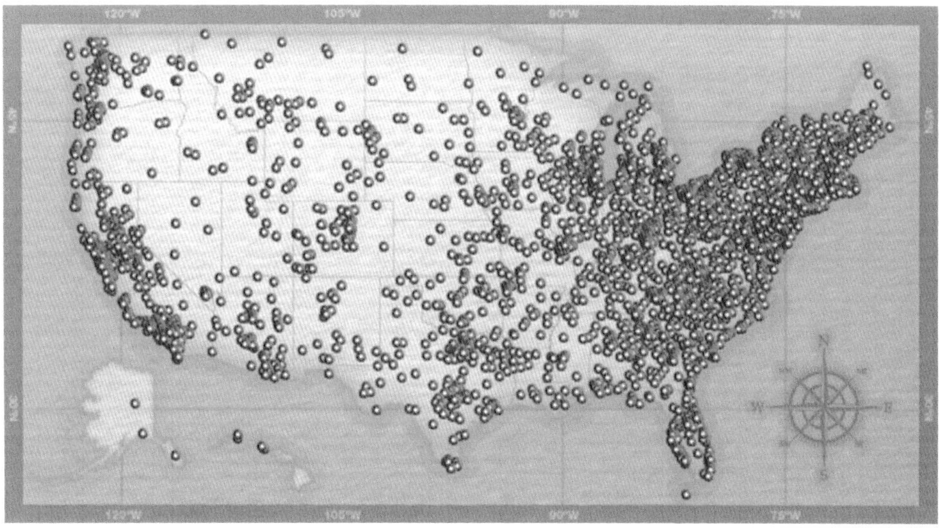